Gurkha Odyssey

Gurkha Odyssey

Campaigning for the Crown

Peter Duffell

With some illustrations
by
Ken Howard OBE, RA

Pen & Sword
MILITARY

AN IMPRINT OF PEN & SWORD BOOKS LTD.
YORKSHIRE – PHILADELPHIA

First published in Great Britain in 2019 by
Pen & Sword Military
An imprint of
Pen & Sword Books Ltd
Yorkshire – Philadelphia

A CIP catalogue record for this book is
available from the British Library.

Contains public sector information licensed under the
Open Government Licence v3.0.

Typeset in 11.5/15 Ehrhardt by Vman Infotech Pvt. Ltd.
Printed and bound in the UK by TJ International Ltd, Padstow, Cornwall.

Pen & Sword Books Limited incorporates the imprints of Atlas, Archaeology, Aviation,
Discovery, Family History, Fiction, History, Maritime, Military,
Military Classics, Politics, Select, Transport, True Crime, Air World,
Frontline Publishing, Leo Cooper, Remember When, Seaforth Publishing,
The Praetorian Press, Wharncliffe Local History, Wharncliffe Transport,
Wharncliffe True Crime and White Owl.

For a complete list of Pen & Sword titles please contact

PEN & SWORD BOOKS LIMITED
47 Church Street, Barnsley, South Yorkshire, S70 2AS, England
E-mail: enquiries@pen-and-sword.co.uk
Website: www.pen-and-sword.co.uk

Or

PEN AND SWORD BOOKS
1950 Lawrence Rd, Havertown, PA 19083, USA
E-mail: Uspen-and-sword@casematepublishers.com
Website: www.penandswordbooks.com

For all Goorkhas

Old men forget: yet all shall be forgot
But he'll remember with advantages
What feats he did that day.

　　　—Shakespeare, *King Henry V*

Contents

List of Maps

Acknowledgements

My old friend Ken Howard, now a distinguished Royal Academician, visited my Regiment and Nepal in 1979 and graphically recorded something of the Gurkha soldier, his character and background. Hopefully his drawings and paintings will help to illuminate the Gurkha story, and I am grateful to him for allowing me to publish them.

In putting this book together I must thank, firstly, Gavin Edgerley-Harris, Director of the Gurkha Museum at Winchester who, together with his staff, allowed me to dive deep into the Gurkha archive and library to fish, gannet-like, for facts and stories, for maps and photographs and to check that my accounts were accurate. Colonel James Robinson and his staff at Headquarters, the Brigade of Gurkhas, were ever helpful in ensuring that I understood some of the contemporary nuances of Gurkha politics and arranged for me to visit India and Nepal.

From my Regiment, Colonel Denis Wood, whose keen sense of Gurkha history knows no bounds was generous in sharing his encyclopaedic knowledge. The distinguished 2nd Goorkha officer, Captain Bhagtasing Pun, who sadly died aged 101 while I was writing this book, and his son, my good friend Major Bishnu Pun, both travelled and served with me at different times through part of my journey. They explained many things about their service and campaigning, and about their fellow countrymen and Nepal, that I might otherwise have only half known or understood. Another 2nd Goorkha, Major General Craig Lawrence, generously shared his collection of Gurkha images with me. I am grateful to them.

Lisa Choegyal, who has written extensively about Nepal and has lived in Kathmandu for over thirty years, gave me generous help and encouragement, as did her colleague Marcus Cotton at Tiger Mountain Pokhara Lodge. They explained to me something of the dynamics of Nepal. Richard Morris, our Ambassador in Kathmandu, and Colonel Ian Logan, the Defence Attaché, were also generous with their assistance and hospitality.

Dr Mark Watson from the Royal Botanic Gardens in Edinburgh, while searching for plants in Nepal, guided me round the British cemetery in Kathmandu and helped me discover its secrets. In Delhi, Brigadier Mark Goldsack, the British Defence Adviser, kindly looked after me and, together with Ben Stretton, Jonathan Green and the noted Indian military historian, Squadron Leader Rana Chhina, helped me retrace the dangerous and costly paths taken by Charles Reid and his Sirmoor Battalion of Goorkhas during the Mutiny in 1857. Rupert Litherland of the 10th Gurkha Rifles kindly allowed me to draw on his research into his Regiment's involvement on the Hong Kong border during Mao's Cultural Revolution in that hot summer of 1967.

Many of the Gurkhas with whom I happily served, and who are now scattered to all parts of the Gurkha diaspora, patiently recounted to me aspects of their lives and service that I had not appreciated before, including Captain Karnabahadur Thapa and Major Krishnabahadur Ale – whose father, Captain Manbahadur Ale, campaigned bravely with me alongside Captain Karnabahadur Roka and Lieutenant Kharaksing Pun. Major Hitman Gurung and Captains Ramkaji Gurung, Ganesh Gurung and Dudman Gurung were all fellow 2nd Goorkhas who met up with me at various places in Nepal. They reminded me of incidents in our service together that I had forgotten (or never knew!).

Major James Devall and Captain Mahendra Phagami of the Royal Gurkha Rifles allowed me to attend their recruitment and selection of today's Gurkha soldiers in Nepal. Major General Gez Strickland, Regimental Colonel of the Royal Gurkha Rifles, kindly shared his thoughts about the contemporary Regiment, and Lieutenant Colonel Christopher Conroy let me visit his 1st Battalion at Shorncliffe, wander round and talk to his soldiers at will, before they set off yet again for Afghanistan.

My Goorkha contemporary, Brigadier Christopher Bullock, was always helpful, and his brilliant book, *Britain's Gurkhas*, was a constant reference point. Christopher Lavender, a fellow 2nd Goorkha, and his wife Griselda looked after me in Hong Kong and helped me to rediscover some Gurkha military sites. David Scotson, also a Goorkha, provided some good-humoured Gurkha editorial support. Major General Bryan Dutton, the last Commander British Forces in Hong Kong before the handover to

China in 1997, told me of the arrangements he put in place for that event. My colleague, General Zhou Borong of the People's Liberation Army, provided some valuable input, as did Sir William Purves, former Chairman of HSBC, with whom I sat on Hong Kong's Executive Council. Field Marshals Sir John Chapple and Lord Bramall, both of whom feature in this book, gave me warm encouragement.

My daughter Rachel, an accomplished journalist and editor based in Hong Kong, was a constant source of professional advice and encouragement, as was my son Charlie with his sublime IT skills.

In thanking them all for their generous help I naturally accept that responsibility for the accuracy of historical facts and their interpretation, and for any stylistic faults and other horrors that may litter the text, lies entirely with me. I have diligently searched for owners of photographic copyright and if I have failed to acknowledge due ownership I can only apologise. It was my friend Henry Wilson, commissioning editor of my publishers, who persuaded me that I had a story worth telling and told me to commit it to paper. He patiently kept faith with this amateur historian and ever optimistically guided me through the publishing process. I am grateful to him and his colleagues and to my wise and eagle-eyed editor, George Chamier.

Lastly, my wife Annie, who travelled with me on part of my journey and who shares my enthusiasm for the character of the Gurkha soldier, has stoically tolerated my neglect of her needs while supporting me in every way as I laboured for many months to produce this book. As ever, I am grateful to her.

Unless otherwise stated, all photographs in this book are used by kind permission of Headquarters The Brigade of Gurkhas, the Gurkha Museum or the Gurkha Welfare Trust.

I am particularly grateful to the distinguished photographers, Richard Pohle, who gave me permission to use his distinctive photograph of the Colours parading at Buckingham Palace, and similarly Johnny Fenn, who allowed me to use his photograph at Barpak in the aftermath of the Nepal earthquake. My old friend Clovis Meath-Baker kindly allowed me to use his Delhi panorama that depicted the City in 1857. I have received similar permission from other owners of copyright to whom I am also grateful.

Unless otherwise stated, the maps in this book are used by kind permission of the Gurkha Museum and Third Millennium, the publishers of *Britain's Gurkhas* by Brigadier Christopher Bullock where the maps first appeared. I am indebted to them all.

Chapter 1

An Introduction

An honest tale speeds best being plainly told.
—Shakespeare, *Richard III*

This story is a fragment of history and a personal memoir; some footnotes from a military journey, with the Gurkha soldier at its heart. For the Gurkha riflemen it is a journey that started in Nepal over two hundred years ago. The early historical settings are the landscapes of Asia that were part of Britain's imperial past: India, Afghanistan and Burma; Malaya and Singapore, Borneo and Brunei and Hong Kong. There are further wartime episodes in Europe and North Africa, before Britain itself became a final destination. It was to these countries that the Gurkha soldier travelled; it was where he lived, where he fought his campaigns on behalf of the British Crown and sometimes died.

Joining my Regiment in 1960, I travelled with Gurkha soldiers in various guises for over fifty years. The genesis of this book was that early service of mine with the 2nd Goorkhas, as we who belonged to it called and spelled it.

After this lengthy association I thought I might be able to express a personal and distinctive view about the qualities and character of the Gurkha soldier and his service and constant fidelity to the British Crown; an historical snapshot seen through the prism of my own Regiment and my service. It will certainly be a fractured story – not definitive in any way – in some instances no more than a brief précis, but recorded in a style that I hope will mostly be reasonably objective and detached and might at least engage the general reader. It will certainly not be a work of historical scholarship.

My story includes personal experiences, some that are only tangential to the Gurkha history, and a certain prejudice and sentiment might also occasionally intrude. For the sake of the story's coherence I felt I needed to record some historical background to the Gurkha soldiers' campaigns, not least in India, Malaysia and Hong Kong and other theatres where the Gurkha soldier campaigned or where he and I had served together. Apart from Gurkha service, I have also spent part of my career in many of the more traditional stamping grounds of the British Army officer of my time – Northern Ireland and Germany, in Whitehall's Ministry of Defence and the Cabinet Office and elsewhere in UK. Those times play no part in my story.

Recounting something of the Gurkha story I saw this as one way of recognizing the generous people with whom I have so happily soldiered and led throughout a long military career. In so doing I will hopefully avoid at least some of the usual gallimaufry of hoary old Gurkha anecdotes and exaggerated tales of derring-do that occasionally litter books of this kind. I have campaigned modestly with Gurkha soldiers on operations; trekked through their hill villages in Nepal; met their families and helped to manage their future in the British Army. I have fought some rough battles on their behalf in the corridors of Whitehall before helping to set a new course for their history. In retirement I have, endlessly and happily, reminisced with them on regimental high days and holidays about our service together, and I have always been happy in their company.

This story is for the general reader, and I fear the military historian or those already steeped in the Gurkha story will find few new insights here. It involves very little of grand military strategy or the political imperatives that drive it, save where that shaped the campaigning of the Gurkha soldier. The problem with writing about Gurkha history is that after some two hundred years of existence, there is far too much of it. Every one of over a hundred Battle Honours has its own dramatic story to tell, as do the citations for their many Victoria Crosses. The general history of the Gurkha soldier and his homeland of Nepal, set in the daunting and magnificent Himalayas, have spawned a library of books, as has Nepal's turbulent history and politics.

So, this is just a small part of the history of the Gurkha soldier told in a selective and personal way. I have let part of my own Regiment's story mostly speak for the rest. The 2nd Goorkhas was the senior regiment of the Gurkha Brigade; it was there at the start and in some respects it led the way. I am familiar with its history; its Battalions have fought in almost every campaign in which Gurkhas have been involved; it has a pedigree that stretches back to the very beginning of Gurkha service to the Crown. We who belonged to it, proudly and probably arrogantly – although I hope not smugly – thought it was what every Gurkha regiment ought to be, only more so! But that was probably what every Gurkha regiment thought about themselves.

Of course, as my old regimental friend and former commanding officer Denis Wood used to remind me, every regiment has its ups and downs, and life is not all glory; the people of a regiment do not behave impeccably at all times and sometimes they make mistakes or let the institution down. Some officers and a few soldiers will always be misfits. Yet, in looking again at the history of the 2nd Goorkhas over two hundred years, I am impressed by the high standard of service that it has given and the high quality of so many of its officers, some of whom will be met in the later pages of this book. The Regiment's low points were relatively few and short lived; its fine military achievements were many and prolonged. Although it was never the custom for the Regiment to blaze its deeds abroad, well might one of its most distinguished Generals, Sir Francis Tuker, in extolling his Regiment's esprit de corps, call it 'One of the greatest fighting Corps that ever served the British Crown'. At its heart was the gallant and light-hearted Gurkha rifleman.

It was with the 2nd Goorkhas – otherwise known as the Sirmoor Rifles, from the province in northern India where it was raised – that I travelled throughout much of my own Gurkha journey. I grew to greatly admire what it stood for, and I believe my own experience might serve to illustrate something of the inimitable style and character of its redoubtable soldiers.

I hope that what I have written – selective and fragmentary though it may be – will be sufficient to convey the sense of it all.

Where I have felt it sensible to do so, I have briefly dipped into the archive of other Gurkha regiments to maintain the integrity of the story. In adopting this approach, I would not wish to imply that the other regiments that together constituted the Gurkha Brigade, in either the British or Indian Armies, have not made an equally important and distinguished contribution. There is ample evidence of this for those who are drawn to look elsewhere.

Much of the early history of the Gurkha soldier is set against the imperial backdrop of the British in India prior to the Indian Mutiny, as part of the Bengal Army of the Honourable East India Company. When that watershed event destroyed the Bengal Army's reputation – and the East India Company itself – the loyal Gurkha regiments became a hugely important element of the newly restructured Indian Army, when direct rule from London took the place of the Company.

In the post-colonial era that we now inhabit it seems to be academically fashionable in some quarters, indeed almost the popular orthodoxy, for historians, university student bodies and others to deplore Britain's imperial past, the Raj and the Empire. Anthropological discourse also attempts to chip away at the integrity of the Gurkha story. An unbalanced and skewed political agenda has arisen – an almost perpetual self-denigration that seeks to discredit 'the imperial narrative' in all its aspects. I suppose, as an aside, that the same criticism could be applied to every empire from the Romans onwards.

This general contemporary intolerance, together with much revisionist writing, maintains that British India was thoroughly malign in every respect and, not least, that it contributed nothing to the India of today. This is dangerous ground for a non-historian, but while there is much to criticise in our imperial past, this analysis seems, in part at least, to be deeply flawed; lazy unbalanced judgement of a complex past, using the mentality of today. It is against this climate of somewhat bellicose opprobrium that I must recount part of my story – a narrative that in its early years is not without imperial overtones. My experience and travels in India and elsewhere tell me that British rule, for all its manifest faults and iniquities, offered to India much that was positive and valuable. Of course, that comes from a British perspective not an Indian one, but it is a view that some Indians share. Much of the legal, educational and administrative systems of India today, together with its albeit fractured unity as a nation and the English language itself, remain, at least in part, a British legacy. The romance, grandeur, sheer bravado and swagger of Empire have been condemned, while the devotion of many who served in India to the welfare of their subject people is forgotten.

Similar disdain is also often displayed for the evocative and otherwise hugely popular prose and poetry of Rudyard Kipling, regarded by many of these same intolerant groups as unacceptably racist. This suggests an inability to recognize the magical way that Kipling captured the character and spirit of that particular imperial age in all its many shades and colours. I have had no inhibitions about using the occasional Kipling quotation where it seemed apt to do so.

These arguments are largely for another place. I am no outright apologist for Empire and I make no judgement. I would record, however, that some of the values lodged in the codes and doctrines, the standards, customs and practices of the pre-1947 Indian Army represented an ethos that was carried forward with pride into the regiments of the new post-independence Army. This is noticeable throughout the Indian Army, including their Gurkha regiments. The British historical provenance of each regiment is much treasured and respected today, and old British comrades, or their sons and daughters, are constantly beckoned back to India for memorial parades and reunions.

Part of this story carries us through times that are now long gone. It records the often heroic, always hazardous, occasionally painful and sometimes controversial military campaigns in which the Gurkha played his part – and the imperial policy that drove them. Campaigns that were all played out in the now vanished world of the Honourable East India Company, British India and the Raj. The violence on both sides was often savage, brutal and shocking. The record is tarnished by events such as the cruelty shown by both sides in the Indian Mutiny, in which my Regiment was to play a loyal and significant role. The grim and costly battlefields of the First and Second World Wars were central additions to an ever-burgeoning history. Those great wars have been catalogued in a vast historical library, so my coverage of them is very limited but still hopefully illustrative of the Gurkha soldier's gallant contribution. Through good times and bad and throughout our imperial history and beyond to the present day, the Gurkha soldier pitched his tent with the British and has remained true to his salt ever after.

With the independence and partition of India came a parting of the ways for the Gurkha Brigade. Four regiments including my own were apparently randomly selected to join the British Army, while six remained with the Indian Army. It was a fraught, painful and difficult separation and one that was singularly ill-managed at the top. For the British Gurkha regiments there then came an immediate commitment to operations in Malaya, then Brunei and Borneo that was to keep them campaigning for the Crown for the next twenty years.

At the end of the 1960s a significant period of the Gurkhas' post-war history drew to a close as British forces withdrew from most of the Far East. The Brigade's centre of gravity shifted from a largely rural and jungle environment in Malaysia to the more urban climate of Hong Kong. The style of soldiering changed; bemedalled chests grew fewer, and with the loss of a major operational impetus a certain cohesiveness and maturity was also lost. Perhaps a few high standards inevitably slipped.

The Brigade's strengths at that time lay first in the unselfish dedication of a long serving cadre of British officers; secondly, in the maturity and seasoned experience and positive leadership of its Queen's Gurkha Officers; and thirdly, in the traditional hardiness and individual skills of its non-commissioned officers (NCOs) and riflemen drawn from the hill villages of Nepal. High standards of routine and discipline were rigorously enforced by procedures and controls that were clearly understood. Recreational opportunities were limited and largely confined to activities in barracks or the surrounding rural areas.

The style of life that replaced it was rather different. In Hong Kong and in the UK there was increasing contact with western culture and greater affluence. Apart from a brief interlude in the Falklands, the Brigade was to see little active operational service for over twenty years. Uncertainty about the future prevailed. There were very occasional disciplinary lapses. As the Battalions became to some extent a Hong Kong gendarmerie – and performed their military duties there with much success – the recruitment of high-quality British officers became more difficult. Reliance on short-term seconded officers became too prevalent.

There emerged a dilemma for the Brigade. As it attempted to embrace modernization it lost some past practices; some were rigid and old-fashioned and would not be missed, but others of value were in danger of disappearing. As this new period of service continued, the challenge for Commanders was to recognize what was happening; to keep the best of the old while adapting to the new; to improve leadership and motivation and to deal effectively with those at all levels who failed to meet the traditional high standards that the Brigade of Gurkhas had always set itself. Gradually, as new operational and regimental challenges emerged, matters were put right, and with improved standards the historical trough was left behind. A recaptured élan and a new elite began to emerge.

The most recent chapters of the Gurkha story marked the final stages of our colonial withdrawal and a new set of military challenges for the British Army. With these challenges came also the redesign of Britain's place in the world, new threats, the restructuring of its defence policy and the resultant reshaping of the Army.

Surprisingly to many who did not know him, the Gurkha soldier, ever flexible and resourceful, translated his innate soldiering skills throughout all this historical change and into the present-day demands of the British Army with remarkable aptitude and intelligence. The numbers of Gurkhas in service hugely decreased as the British Army itself declined. But the Gurkha soldier continues to contribute as successfully to the Crown today as he has done over the last two hundred years, as new historians will record. He continues to demonstrate, once again, many of the same military and personal qualities of light-hearted courage and physical and mental fortitude that he showed in the past. If his background in Nepal has changed, new too are today's urban battlefield and the doctrines of counter-insurgency warfare; and to some extent these changes have complemented one another. Some doubted the Gurkha soldiers' place in that new landscape, but those of us who really know, admire and have served with the Gurkha are not surprised that he has now earned a rightful, respected and cost-effective place in the vanguard of the contemporary British Army. His numbers are expanding.

The Gurkha story has never required patronizing rhetoric or subjective regimental histories to record the quality of his service. Over the two hundred years of their history there have been occasional setbacks, the odd trough among the peaks, the occasional wobble. I experienced some of these myself. Not every Gurkha was brave all the time, not every battle was won. The Gurkha never was a *kukri*-wielding superman, as the tabloid press and military chroniclers would sometimes have him, psychologically useful as that picture occasionally might be. But a certain insouciance and light-hearted detachment from the fray seems to allow him to cope with some of the stresses of the battlefield. I recall the story on operations of a Gurkha rifleman waking his company commander at night with a gentle shake to the shoulder and stating softly, as if a family butler announcing an uninvited guest, 'Saheb, the enemy has arrived.'

Delightful as they are to serve with, not all are military paragons, and sometimes, as all soldiers do, a Gurkha lands himself in trouble. But these incidents are pretty rare, and the overall integrity of their record and the sustained quality of their military service certainly bear comparison with any other group of fighting men. Even those who may be keen to postulate pretentious academic theories or anthropological discourses to explain the Gurkha project, and who know little of what service with a Gurkha regiment really means, either for the Gurkha himself or for his British officers, should be able to accept that.

It is true that in more recent times some Gurkha pensioners have gradually become more politically aware and confident of their position as British Army veterans. Some have campaigned hard for the correction of perceived injustices in their past terms and conditions of service. This, too, is part of the overall story.

The fragmentary journey that I have attempted to record across two centuries is certainly unique. What is remarkable is that these men, born in a foreign land, whose homes are not threatened by invasion and for whom the cause for which they are fighting may often seem remote, should have served the British Crown with such fidelity. Their committed and carefully selected British officers are largely of a different faith, speak a different language and look physically different. Yet the British officer and his Gurkhas seem to bond with remarkable empathy and the deepest mutual respect and affection, serving together with great effectiveness. Perhaps we thought that bond went deeper than it did, but we certainly drew strength from it.

What is also certain is that wherever he has served, in whichever campaign he has fought, the presence of the Gurkha soldier seems more often than not to have made a significant difference. He certainly serves for pecuniary advantage. But his service is not a shabby matter of shifting allegiances, not a response to a military auction room bidding for his services; nor is it simply a casual hiring. His history represents two hundred years of sworn service to the British Crown. In terms of international conventions, he is certainly not a mercenary, and the British Government has agreed with Nepal that he will never be referred to as such. Men on occasions may flock to the Colours for pay – and the Gurkha soldier clearly does that – but it cannot simply be only for money that the Gurkha Rifle Regiments, with their sworn allegiance to the Crown, have earned such a remarkable military record. For that reason alone, a fragment of their story should be worth telling and celebrating.

Anyone who doubts the lasting strength and durability, the unique chemistry of Gurkha service and the magnetic power of the Regiment, should have witnessed the gathering in Nepal in 2015 to celebrate the 200th anniversary of the raising of the 2nd Goorkhas. Literally thousands of regimental pensioners and their families – young and old, British officers and Gurkha soldiers – travelled from across Nepal, from India and Hong Kong, from the UK and elsewhere, to gather at the Gurkha Depot in the western Nepali town of Pokhara. They had voluntarily answered the regimental call and they stayed together for two days to celebrate their service and fellowship. As I saw myself, everyone seemed genuinely proud, happy and grateful to be there to recapture again the spirit of their remarkable and distinguished livery; and none more so than I.

The etymology and spelling of the word 'Gurkha' as used by the British may require some explanation. The origin of the word is geographic, from the province of 'Gorkha' in the western hills of Nepal. Its use in Nepal is confined to that province and its modest but historically important capital town. Historically, the inhabitants of that Province were known as 'Gorkhas' or 'Gorkhalis', although this term has now fallen into disuse within Nepal.

The title 'Gurkha' is now used primarily outside Nepal and generically to describe the hillmen of Nepal who served in the past in the old Indian Army or serve today in the Gurkha regiments of the British Army. The name does not imply a particular Nepali clan or caste, although traditionally these men came from the pastoral martial tribes that live in the country's middle hills. The name was transcribed from a Nagri script, so it is not surprising that different spellings pertain. To complicate matters further, the British initially used the spelling 'Goorkha' to describe their soldiers, and in my Regiment, unofficially, that usage remained. The Indian Army now uses the original spelling 'Gorkha' to describe the men and titles of its own regiments. The Nepalis themselves tend to use the term *lahure* when talking of the Gurkha soldier. This word stems from the city of Lahore, where men from the Nepal hills went to enlist in the armies of the Sikh ruler, Ranjit Singh, long before the British ever thought of recruiting them. There are other variations, and all sorts of misspellings litter the records, but I think that is enough. The rationale for the alternatives that I use in different places in the text will I hope be plain enough.

Finally, I am conscious that as in any story with a biographical element the use of the personal pronoun cannot be avoided. This may be repetitious but I hope it is used with due humility. If it leads to misplaced accusations of excessive vanity, well, there we go.

Chapter 2

Starting Out

We few, we happy few, we band of brothers.
—Shakespeare, King Henry V

RIFLEMAN

The Queen's Coronation – 2 June, 1953. If I didn't know it at the time, it was this last great imperial flourish that started me off on my Gurkha journey. As a thirteen-year old schoolboy I watched the procession with my father from a window in Whitehall. As the various marching contingents from all over the Empire and Commonwealth came by in the rain, I noticed a company of soldiers who looked rather different. They were dressed in dark green, they were short and stocky in stature, they carried their rifles at the trail and not at the shoulder, and they seemed to raise a special cheer from the crowd. My father told me they were British Army Gurkhas, they came from Nepal and they were formidable soldiers.

Coinciding with that parade, and demonstrating almost exquisite imperial timing – or at least timing as decreed by the editor of *The Times* – had come news from James Morris, its correspondent on the mountain, that a Sherpa guide and climber, Tenzing Norgay, and a New Zealand beekeeper, Edmund Hillary, had reached the summit of unclimbed Everest in the Nepal Himalaya. They were part of a British expedition led by Colonel John Hunt – a last great amateur adventure to crack the mountain. There seemed to be a clear connection between these two events, and I was much taken with what I had seen and heard. I lodged it all away.

I was not set upon a military career, but National Service at least gave me a push in that direction. In December 1959 I was one of the last young men to be called up. Fortuitously, the letter from the Ministry of Labour instructed me to report to the Rifle Depot at Winchester. That first order was my introduction to the 2nd Battalion, the Royal Green Jackets, formerly the 60th Rifles, and the very particular Rifle ethos that they represented. It was to this Battalion that I had been badged.

That Rifle ethos was a product of the 60th's early days, when it was raised in North America in 1755. The ponderous movement and formal tactics of the British redcoats had failed disastrously against the French. The 60th adopted light and inconspicuous clothing and equipment, together with a simple drill, open formations and rapid movement. Personal initiative was encouraged, together with a more tolerant discipline based on a relationship of trust and respect between officers and men. These characteristics made the 60th a distinctive and distinguished part of the eighteenth century British Army, one that was to prove itself in Wellington's Peninsular War. The tradition of speed was reflected in a marching pace of 140 to the minute, twenty paces faster than other infantry of the Line, together with a march past in double time on ceremonial parades.

The Rifles excelled particularly at fighting in small groups, scouting and skirmishing ahead. Quickness and initiative, sharp-shooting and the development of new ideas were the watchwords of the Regiment. *Celer et Audax* – Swift and Bold – was its motto. Some sensed that riflemen were beginning to be the thinking part of the Army.

All this gradually found its way into my mind as I set out, with the rest of my many reluctant fellow conscripts, to qualify as riflemen. We sweated hard on weapon training and marksmanship, judging distance, the naming of the parts and the endless stripping and assembling of the light machine gun, until we could do it blindfold; to this was added the fast and sharp rifle drill and the gruelling fitness demands of the assault course and the route march. We were eventually fashioned into a more than passable Rifle Platoon. This had been achieved under the eagle eye of Sergeant Squirrel with his red chevrons, black buttons and highly polished boots. I can still recall his final words as he gave us a short parting lecture behind the NAAFI.

'Don't try to fight the Army, gentlemen – it's too frapping big!'

With Sergeant Squirrel's euphemistic exhortation still ringing in my ears, I set off for an Officer Cadet Training Unit in Aldershot, to be turned into an infantry officer. The Green Jackets and the War Office Selection Board had decided, in their wisdom, that I had sufficient soldierly promise to warrant attendance on the six-month commissioning course. I was to draw gratefully on my Winchester experience as a rifleman throughout that early training, and for the whole of my military career and beyond.

There were lectures on the principles of war – offensive action, maintenance of morale and surprise were the ones I particularly remember from that time. There were exercises and manoeuvres, attack, defence and withdrawal; staff duties and the composition and delivery of orders; the manual of military law and charge sheets for miscreants; drill parades and the seemingly endless polishing and pressing of kit. We strained to prove ourselves worthy of the Queen's commission and more importantly, to avoid being back-termed or, even worse, suffer RTU – Returned to Unit – the final ignominy.

Aside from successfully passing out, the major issue for cadets was to choose the regiment they wanted to join. You then needed to persuade that regiment's representative – an officer on the training staff – that you were just the man they needed and that you ought to be placed in front of the Regimental Colonel so that he might hopefully ratify your decision.

Following my experiences at Winchester, I was keen to remain a rifleman, and the 60th indicated that they might be prepared to have me. The trouble was that the Regiment was stationed in Ballykinlar in Northern Ireland. It was to remain there for the rest of my National Service. Much as I liked and admired the 60th, sixteen months of service in an isolated barracks in County Down, with little prospect of any excitement or travel, did not appeal.

The regimental representative could not believe that anyone could possibly turn down a commission in the 60th Rifles. But generously he suggested that I might try their affiliated regiment. That regiment was in Malaya, they were Gurkhas and maybe they would offer the excitement I was looking for. Cautiously, I took up the suggestion.

The Gurkha regiments were thought to be extremely choosy about who they took on. They were apparently reluctant to take too many National Service officers like me; officers that were here today and gone tomorrow, with little time to absorb the language and culture before they were on their way. It represented a bad investment. Nervously in various interviews I persuaded the assorted grandees of the Gurkha Brigade that all I cared about was a commission in one of their regiments. I was sure I had something to offer them, even if I could not quite articulate what it was. I told them that their soldiers had made the strongest impression on me at the Coronation. I was lucky.

Before long, Field Marshal Montgomery had taken the salute at our passing out parade, and I was commissioned as a Second Lieutenant in the richly titled 1st Battalion 2nd King Edward VII's Own Gurkha Rifles (The Sirmoor Rifles). I wrote suitable letters to the Colonel of the Regiment and the Commandant of the 1st Battalion, saying how pleased and grateful I was to be accepted. Somewhat proudly, excitedly and rather nervously, I set off to join my Regiment in tropical Malaya.

SINGAPORE

It was about four o'clock on the morning of 14 September 1960. My trooping flight from England had just landed at Royal Air Force Changi on the tropical island of Singapore, delivering me to join my Regiment. Already at that early hour the place seemed hot and humid. I had arrived in a very Chinese city – and the scene of one of the most disastrous defeats in the history of British arms. It was here that our 2nd Battalion had been forced to surrender to the Japanese after nobly fighting its way down the spine of Malaya. I had also not realized until I was briefed by Julian Noakes, a charming, laid-back National Service subaltern from the 1st Battalion who had kindly met me and who I was to replace, that I had arrived on a very auspicious regimental day.

All regiments of the British Army have a special day, one that has resonance for all ranks. It is usually a Battle Honour with primacy above all others, one that serves as a marker for everyone in the regiment, not least for its old and bold pensioners. Ours was 'Delhi'.

The Land Rover, with a diminutive Gurkha at the wheel, wove its way through the darkened streets pungent with the putrid and memorable aroma that used to rise from the drains and *nullahs* of the East, and in some places still does. As we drove, Julian told me that although the 1st Battalion was based in Malaya, the two Battalions of the Regiment were on a ceremonial parade together at the 2nd Battalion's Slim Barracks in Singapore some four hours or so later. We would be watching, and it would be a suitable introduction into the Regiment for me.

The parade was to mark 'Delhi' – the Regiment's most important Battle Honour, won during the Indian Mutiny in 1857 at the Siege of Delhi, the ancient Mughal city that had been invested by the rebels. The Sirmoor Battalion, as the Regiment was then titled, had played a particularly gallant and significant part in the defeat of the mutineers. On 14 September the Delhi Field Force – to which the Regiment and its friends the British 60th Rifles belonged – had blown the Cashmere Gate and entered Delhi to assault the mutineers' stronghold.

I would study the detail of those terrible days in due course, but that much I had learned before we entered the drive of Slim Barracks, home to the 1st or 2nd Battalion of my Regiment until the British Army withdrew from the Far East in the early 1970s.

Slim Barracks were fine regimental lines built especially for a Gurkha Battalion and its families in the immediate post-war years. Following Partition and the British withdrawal from India, mine had been one of four Gurkha regiments transferred to the British Army. The regiments had two battalions – eventually, each of some 750 men. On arrival, one Gurkha Battalion was to be based in Singapore, another in Hong Kong and the remaining six in Malaya. The barracks had high ceilings and broad and airy verandas, surrounded by playing fields and gardens. Together with their white stuccoed married quarters covered in purple bougainvillaea, they had almost the air of a tropical Tunbridge Wells with palm trees.

I have now only a hazy recollection of that first parade – but I remember smart, serried ranks of Gurkha riflemen. They were turned out in highly pressed and starched short-sleeved olive-green shirts and those broad, uniquely Gurkha shorts. These were set off by dark green hose tops and puttees above highly polished black boots. Distinctive Kilmarnock pillbox hats, with red and black dice board ribbon around the rim, completed the outfit. Red and black chevrons adorned the shirts of the NCOs, and everyone marched at the same Rifle pace that I had first experienced and tried to master on the drill square at Winchester. There seemed to be huge clusters of medals on the chests of many on parade. To my inexperienced eye, the Regiment looked pretty good. It paraded with a certain confident élan that I found impressive and rather admirable.

There were three further features of that first parade that I also clearly recall. First was the arrival of the Queen's Truncheon, received with a Royal Salute – a unique Colour, about six feet in height, its bronze staff was surmounted by a silver crown supported by three Gurkha soldiers, also in bronze. It had been awarded to the Regiment to mark its gallant service at Delhi. It was carried by the Truncheon Jemadar – a Gurkha Lieutenant – flanked by a Colour escort of two Sergeants and two Corporals. I soon learned that it was held in great reverence by the Gurkhas.

Second was the reading in Gurkhali, to all present, by the 1st Battalion's senior Gurkha officer – the Gurkha Major – of an account of the Regiment's part in the Siege of Delhi. This was clearly designed to impress on all ranks the example of loyal and valorous service set by their regimental predecessors. It was a moving testament to the Regiment's historic past. Lastly, I noted the executive word of command to call the parade to attention. It was not the rather brutish 'ATTEN-SHUN!' but 'SIRMOOR-RIFLES!' I liked the sound of that.

The parade over, the British officers moved with everyone else to the Regimental Quarter Guard, and one by one we saluted the Truncheon, held in front of the guardroom by the Jemadar. Then, led by the Commandants, as the Commanding Officers were titled, one by one and in strict seniority, we placed a tropical red hibiscus or some other appropriate petal at the foot of the Colour. This was in remembrance of those men of the Regiment who had perished during the siege at Delhi.

Next came a splendid breakfast in the officers' mess. On highly polished dining tables, groaning with gleaming silver and regimental artefacts, we were served by white-uniformed Gurkha waiters with hotly seasoned mulligatawny soup. Kedgeree followed, then copious amounts of what everyone else called 'rumble-tumble' but which, up to that innocent point, I had known simply as scrambled eggs. Black Velvet was enjoyed from inscribed silver goblets.

A leisurely move was then made to the football field. Sheltering from a tropical sun under canvas awnings, and to much enthusiasm from the spectators, we watched the two Battalions compete against each other at athletics. Finally, after a modest pause for rest and showers, we changed into evening dress and celebrated Delhi Day with a grand dinner in the mess.

Everyone except me was clad in black overalls and white tropical mess jackets, whose high collars were decorated with the silver collar dogs of the Prince of Wales's plumes, the motif that was the regimental cap badge. The collar itself was trimmed with red piping, called *lali*. Julian told me this had been adopted from the red facings worn on their tunics by our English friends on Delhi Ridge, the formidable 60th Rifles. Mess dress – in Rifle tradition – carried no badges of rank. Uncomfortable in my heavy English dinner jacket, I envied mess dress like this and mentally vowed I would soon possess it. The 60th Rifles was of course the regiment in which I had fortuitously started my National Service some nine months earlier. It was where I had learned something of a Rifle Regiment's ethos.

The Queen's Truncheon now reappeared. It had been brought to the Mess by the Truncheon Jemadar and handed over to the 2nd Battalion's Adjutant. Unscrewing and removing part of the supporting staff, the Adjutant inserted the top half into the First World War commemorative centrepiece on the table, placed opposite the two Battalion Commandants – Monty Ormsby of the 1st Battalion and Peter Kemmis Betty of the 2nd Battalion. I would learn more about them in due course. While we enjoyed our anniversary dinner we were entertained by the regimental band. The bugle platoon joined them for rousing regimental quick marches, 'Lutzow's Wild Hunt' and 'What's A' the Steer, Kimmer?' – tunes that I recognized from the morning parade.

The evening eventually over, I drifted off to the large airy bedroom I had been allocated in the upper reaches of the mess. Under a high ceiling and below a softly whirring fan, for the first of many times I pulled open a mosquito net and climbed thankfully into bed. As I did so, the evocative, muffled sound of riflemen clapping and singing in unison to the rhythmic beat of the *madals* (hand drums) floated up towards the mess verandas as celebrations continued elsewhere in the Lines. These were age-old Nepali hill songs, soon to become very familiar to me. For a newly joined Subaltern fatigued with jet lag it was a memorable initiation into the Regiment that was to become my home and family.

MALAYA AND THE 1ST BATTALION

The following morning, feeling somewhat the worse for wear, I set off with Julian to drive to the 1st Battalion's home at Burma Lines, in south Malaya. We travelled through Singapore to the causeway that joined the island to Malaya, passing as we did so the notorious Ford Motor Factory. It was here, in 1942, that General Percival had signed the fatal document surrendering British forces to the Japanese – an act that had disgracefully condemned the remnants of our 2nd Battalion to Japanese captivity.

The 1st Battalion's Lines were about twelve miles north of the causeway. The attractions of the island with all their heady promise would, if needed, remain in striking distance. Once through the coastal town of Johore Bahru, I began to experience the flavour of the Malayan countryside. Dark green, heavy and seemingly impenetrable secondary jungle guarded either side of the road, interspersed with lines of rubber trees. Tied to the thin trunks of each tree I could make out the clay cups that collected the latex, bled and harvested daily from its bark. Dark-skinned Tamil people from southern India were very much in evidence, encouraged by the British to migrate from Madras (Chennai) to work on the rubber plantations – a staple source of wealth for the Malayan economy. It was still hot and humid, but not without a particular tropical allure.

Before long we reached the small nondescript Malay village of Ulu Tiram and Burma Lines. The Battalion's Lines had none of the architectural style of Slim Barracks. But as a hutted camp, spread out across some low hills on the fringes of the jungle, it was not without a certain charm. There was room to breathe and plenty of space to train; ample playing fields and rifle ranges were close at hand. Across the valley to the south, a few hundred yards away, were the administrative buildings and classrooms of the British Jungle Warfare School. The School had been established years earlier by a formidable Gurkha officer called Walter Walker. Another influential commander of the school had been John Cross from the 7th Gurkhas. He was one of the most experienced jungle operators in the Gurkha Brigade and this, coupled with his marvellous facility with Asian languages – he spoke eleven of them fluently – made him something of a legendary military figure in South-East Asia. It was there at this centre for jungle warfare that a succession of British (and foreign) officers and NCOs had been trained in the arcane arts of living and fighting in the jungle. Skills formulated and taught here had played a decisive role in the defeat of the Communist insurgency that gripped Malaya for twelve years from 1947. No doubt I would become familiar with these skills in due course.

After the celebrations and regimental excesses of Delhi Day, it was now time to sort out my uniform and equipment and begin to get to know my Regiment. The 2nd Goorkhas was the senior and oldest of the four Gurkha regiments that had joined the British Army on 1 January 1948. My Regiment was apparently regarded by everyone else as rather smart, somewhat idle, but militarily very effective. Some called us the *Lali Paltan* – the Red Regiment – because of our sartorial distinctions. I was told that the other regiments were the 6th Gurkhas, who were thought to be rather straight-laced and heavy, the 7th, who were unshaven, whatever that might imply, and the 10th Gurkha Rifles, who were regarded as decidedly alcoholic. Naturally, I soon discovered that most of this was rubbish; while each of the regiments had its own characteristics, they all had fine fighting records.

I quickly learned that my 1st Battalion of 750 men was very experienced. As I had seen on the Delhi parade, many of those with long service had several medals, and most of the Gurkha officers and senior NCOs were veterans of the Battles of El Alamein and Monte Cassino. Others who had transferred to us from the Regiment's wartime Battalions had fought in Burma, or had survived as prisoners of war of the Japanese. For the last twelve years the men of the Battalion had campaigned, continuously and vigorously, in the Malayan jungle, against Chinese communist terrorists. They had shared this experience with the other Gurkha Battalions, as well as many British, Malay and Commonwealth units. The end of that campaign had been celebrated, only weeks before I arrived, with a grand victory parade in Kuala Lumpur. The Regiment had been continuously on operations for over twenty years, and it all made me feel rather humble and inadequate, not least because I was the only man in the whole Battalion without a medal.

I was introduced to my fellow British officers. There were about twelve of us – a rich and diverse group of personalities. Half were bachelors and lived in the British officers' mess, while the married officers, like those Gurkhas accompanied by their families, had quarters in another barracks about ten miles away and commuted by car and bus into the lines every day. There were of course other regimental officers on our books who were temporarily away; on long leave in the UK, on specialist courses or serving in staff or training appointments elsewhere in the Army. They would periodically reappear in the Battalion, while others would be temporarily posted away.

The British officers tended to command the Battalion's four Rifle Companies or hold certain Battalion appointments such as Adjutant or Signals Officer. They would provide the technical leadership for the specialist platoons: Mortars, Anti-tank Weapons, Reconnaissance and Assault Pioneer Platoons, all grouped together in Support Company. New, rather useless arrivals such as I, the so-called *sano sahebs* – small officers – would start off in the nebulous role of Company Officer, a general dogsbody and gofer for their Company Commander. We would remain in this position perhaps for six months or so, until we had mastered something of the language and generally understood how things worked in a Gurkha Battalion.

Colonel Monty Ormsby, generous with his welcome to me, commanded us all with great vivacity and charm. He had joined the Regiment in early 1939 on the North-West Frontier and had been with the 1st Battalion throughout most of his service. In North Africa, in the aftermath of El Alamein, he had taken an energetic part in the Battalion's brilliant battle at Wadi Akarit, where Subedar Lalbahadur Thapa had won his Victoria Cross. Then, moving with the Battalion to Italy, he had commanded A Company with much gallantry at the battle of Monte Cassino – twice wounded in that grim affair, where he had earned the first of his two Military Crosses. He had been similarly courageous during the Malayan Emergency, during which he was awarded a bar to his Cross for a very dangerous and successful operation against the Communist terrorists. He was a great countryman and a natural soldier, a brave and resourceful leader. We much loved and admired him.

Colonel Monty was at his most captivating as a raconteur. He had a magical turn of phrase and possessed a fund of improbable stories, often told in a self-deprecating style. There was constant laughter as he regaled his captive audience of Battalion officers at breakfast every morning with his stories. There were innumerable and improbable fishing and shooting escapades: how a giant fish, a *mahseer*, had been landed on a huge marlin-sized hook, or how he had bought his shotgun from a Persian dentist. Then there was the call on the field telephone in North Africa that he took from the Commander of the Eighth Army, General Montgomery, after the Battle of Wadi Akarit:

'Hallo – Monty here!'

'No, this is Monty here – now about this Gurkha officer that has been put in for an immediate award.'

'Yes, sir.'

'That's worth a VC!'

Later he told us how he had personally delivered an Italian woman's baby as he passed through her village on his way to the Monte Cassino battle.

'No problem really. Pretty normal stuff!'

Only once did I hear of a Monty story being outclassed. A senior Gurkha officer, Bharti Gurung, perhaps familiar with his Commanding Officer's extravagant claims, came up with a tale of how he had damned a jungle stream with mosquito nets. He then planned to chuck in a grenade to stun the fish and collect them in the nets – but as the grenade was about to hit the water, a turtle surfaced, caught it and swallowed it whole, with dramatic results. Monty couldn't cap that, but he soon added it to his repertoire of stories, together with the odd additional twist!

If the Colonel had a weak spot, it was staff work and responding to the administrative needs of his Battalion. Ammunition and ration issues were for the Quartermaster, and difficult letters from Brigade Headquarters would often mysteriously disappear. Here, luckily, he was blessed with a brilliant Adjutant, John Chapple. A Cambridge history graduate from Trinity, John was not only a most efficient and imaginative staff officer, but a polymath of some note. He was steeped in military history and the culture of Rifle regiments and a particular expert on the Indian Army. He collected its medals, badges and insignia. His hinterland was in ornithology and zoology, in which areas his knowledge was unsurpassed. A walk in the jungle with him was a revelation of botanical and zoological scholarship. Further, he ensured that the junior officers were always correctly turned out on parade, that we knew how to carry our swords properly and were well versed in regimental history. He knew the works of Kipling backwards, and he and his wife Annabel were very hospitable to all of us. Thirty years later, he would be Chief of the General Staff, a Field Marshal and President of the Zoological Society.

Memories of two other officers from those early days remain with me. Firstly, there was Digby Willoughby, a romantic gallant if ever there was one. With him I was to share a good deal of my regimental life. He was a loyal and fearless officer, pompous and autocratic at times and, just occasionally, completely and utterly over the top. A man out of his time, he had an Edwardian, almost Wodehousian style that seemed to spring straight out of Blandings Castle. His early life had been shaped by the Raj and India, where he had spent his childhood and where his family had served for several generations. It had seemed natural for him to graduate to a Gurkha regiment, and perhaps we recognized that there was an element in him of 'Staying On'.

Digby was a powerful influence among the bachelor officers, a stickler for high standards and regimental excellence in all that we did. He did most things with dash and flair. As I was to learn, he was at his best in an operational crisis – decisive in action, firm with his orders, and brave in their execution. Digby's major problem took the form of a series of tangled and tortuous relationships with a succession of delightful girls that inevitably seemed to founder with much emotional heartache. In this personal agony we were all forced to share. Later on, after he had left the Army, he was to run the St Moritz Tobogganing Club – the Cresta Run – with equal vigour and courage. I was to be his Best Man at one of his impossible marriages, and I was also persuaded by him, against my better judgement, to hurl myself down the Cresta Run.

Lastly there was David Stephens. Nearest to me in age and a fellow subaltern, he had strong family links with the Regiment. His father had commanded the 1st Battalion after suffering as a Japanese prisoner of war in Singapore's notorious Changi jail. He took me under his wing, briefing me about Gurkha officers and soldiers – what to do and what not to do. During drink-fuelled tutorials in the mess he told me how the Regiment had been raised by Frederick Young of the Bengal Army in 1815; how we were older than any other Gurkha regiment and thus by implication very much better. He spoke very good Gurkhali and translated some of the curiosities of the language – the *kura*, he called it – that seemed to have slipped into the daily English conversation in the officers' mess. Four useful words that entered my lexicon included:

> *Bandobast*: organization or arrangement. This could be used to describe any event or programme and how it was run. Thus, 'Chapple runs a very good *bandobast*', or 'Brigade Headquarters has no *bandobast*' or perhaps, referring to girls, 'Digby has a new *bandobast*.'

> *Kaida*: method or rule. It was applied to how you did things regimentally: 'Don't do that Peter, it's just not the *kaida*.' Digby would use this word interminably.

> *Shyabash:* well done, congratulations. I used this word all the time as a form of encouragement with the Gurkha soldiers, before I knew any other words.

> *Dukha*: pain, trouble, sorrow. This was used to complain about any disagreeable activity, such as a particularly difficult jungle patrol: 'God, that was *dukha!*'

David's enthusiasm for imparting knowledge extended to attempts, at the weekends, to introduce me to some of the shadier dens of Singapore's nightlife. He seemed to possess an encyclopaedic knowledge of these dives and was keen to impart it to me. I fear I did not always share his unbridled enthusiasms. But in all other regards he was a valuable mentor.

There were also officers of the Regiment who were not present in that first year of my service but who were the subject of a steady stream of affectionate anecdotes during dinner in the mess I was to meet all them in various stages of my regimental life. Peter Richardson was one of a group of diehard 2nd Goorkha bachelor officers whose ambitions lay no further than commanding a Rifle Company, preferably B Company, and doing it as far away from Battalion Headquarters as possible. 'Lugubrious' should have been his middle name – either that or 'Whisky *pani*' (and water), to which he was much addicted. During the Malayan Emergency he and his Company performed with great courage and effect, year after year, including the two most successful engagements with the communist terrorists in the whole history of the campaign.

There were also two former officers of the Regiment both of whom had left the Army before I joined but had clearly left a lasting impression.

Colonel Jimmy Roberts was a distinguished Himalayan mountaineer, the conqueror of Annapurna II and a formidable soldier with a Gurkha Parachute Battalion in Burma. He was also the founder of modern-day tourism in Nepal. He had an independent and lugubrious nature, not dissimilar to Peter Richardson's, and like him he was a somewhat eccentric and confirmed bachelor. Occasionally he would let off his shotgun in the mess. I was to meet and get to know him during my various visits to Nepal, where he had settled after retirement, managing the tourism and trekking business that was eventually to achieve worldwide renown as Mountain Travel, and rearing rare breeds of Himalayan pheasant.

John Nott had been a regular officer with the 1st Battalion for about four years during the Malayan Emergency. His great-great-great-grandfather, Sir William Nott, had been a distinguished General in the Indian Army. In 1842 he had rescued that Army's reputation, and become a Victorian hero, in the aftermath of the disastrous retreat from Kabul in the first Afghan War, when he had exacted retribution from the Afghans. I think it was that connection that had brought John himself into the Regiment – slightly awkward and maverick, in some ways an unlikely soldier, distant to many and easily bored, a hugely talented and cerebral man, direct and honest. He was to have a distinguished career after his regimental service in Malaya that took him, in the wake of John Chapple (who I think put in a good word for him) to Trinity College Cambridge, then into banking, where he became a big wheel in the City.

John was then elected Conservative MP for St Ives and eventually became a member of Mrs Thatcher's cabinet, first in Trade and then as Defence Secretary during the Falklands War. After bailing out of politics he was chairman of the merchant bank, Lazards. He also wrote several amusing, self-deprecatory and occasionally racy biographies. Throughout all of this, he retained a deep and affectionate loyalty for his Regiment, to which he was kind and generous throughout his successful career. Our paths crossed many times, and we became quite friendly and occasionally lunched together. As a raconteur he could be wonderfully indiscreet, and later on, he was particularly helpful to me when I was battling with Whitehall over the future of the Gurkha soldier.

At the heart of the Battalion were the Queen's Gurkha Officers – the QGOs – a rank that was junior to all British officers but crucial to the

Battalion's leadership. This rank was similar to that of the VCOs, Viceroy Commissioned Officers – the Jemadars and Subedars of the old Indian Army – and in the British Army unique to Gurkha regiments. The QGOs were experienced Gurkha soldiers with exemplary service throughout the ranks. They would be competitively selected for a commission from the Battalion's warrant officers and sergeants at around eighteen to twenty years of service. As lieutenants they would command all the Rifle platoons, while those promoted to captain would fill the post of company second-in-command and some specialist appointments. They had their own mess, where they threw very good parties, to which we were often invited. We addressed each other as *Saheb*, and the soldiers called us all *Saheb* as well. Newly arrived young officers such as I, recognizing and respecting the deep experience of the Gurkha officers, moved with considerable tact in early dealings with them, in spite of our seniority. I longed to be accepted by them.

There were other classes of Gurkha officers as well. One or two outstanding and well educated Queen's Gurkha Officers had been given full British commissions. These men were titled Gurkha Commissioned Officers (GCOs) and were on a par with their British counterparts and members of the British officers' mess. Major Bhimbahadur Thapa was a fine example; a former Gurkha parachutist from the Burma campaign, he commanded A Company.

Finally, we were shortly expecting the arrival of Second Lieutenant Lalbahadur Pun, who had recently passed out of Sandhurst as the first Gurkha to do so. He was the son of a distinguished wartime and much decorated Gurkha officer who had served with the 3rd Battalion's Chindit column in Burma – Major Tikajit Pun. LB, as he was known, became a good friend of mine and, like his father, was to have a distinguished career in the Regiment.

Presiding over all the Queen's Gurkha Officers, and indeed all ranks, was the singular Gurkha Major, responsible to the Commanding Officer for all matters Gurkha. Major (QGO) Pirthilal Pun was a stern disciplinarian, an unbending and much respected figure, who held great sway over the whole Battalion, including its British officers. He had been an outstanding operational soldier and possessed an authoritative, steely and somewhat austere personality. Enlisted in the Regiment in 1933, he possessed vast fighting experience through early service on the North-West Frontier and, during the war, in the Middle East, North Africa, Italy and Greece. Promoted Jemadar in the field in 1943, he had won a Military Cross at the battle of Monte Cassino during the attack on the Monastery. All ranks, myself included, were somewhat in awe of Pirthilal.

Another Gurkha officer that I particularly remember from those early days was Captain Bhagtasing Pun. He, too, had joined the Regiment before the war, in 1937, and had initially gained active service experience on the North-West Frontier. He would recount how he had come under fire from tribesmen while manning a forward picquet in Waziristan. He then had the misfortune to be sent, with a reinforcement party, to our 2nd Battalion in Singapore. He arrived just two weeks before the Battalion was forced to surrender, having fought the Japanese invaders all the way down the spine of Malaya before arriving on the Island.

I remember his graphic descriptions of life as a prisoner of war in terrible conditions, working as a coolie unloading Japanese ships, moving their ammunition around the island and cleaning toilets, all coupled with the most awful diet. Bhagtasing and his fellow Gurkhas were forced to endure this for three and a half years.

He was a gentle and intelligent man who, two years after his return from captivity, would be back in Singapore with the 1st Battalion in happier circumstances. He had won a Military Medal for bravery in the Malayan Emergency and, although I did not initially realize it, I had seen him once before, since he had been a member of the Coronation contingent that I had watched parading in London in 1953. I often went to him for advice about Gurkhas. Twenty years or so later, his son, the light-hearted Bishnu Pun, enlisted in the 1st Battalion and was also to have a distinguished career in the Regiment.

Then there were the NCOs and riflemen. They were short, mostly about five feet four inches, thickset and sturdy hillmen of Mongolian appearance. Many possessed fine features with high cheekbones, slanting eyes, strong clean limbs and wheaten complexions. Initially they were very polite, shook my hand, grinned and saluted – but that was about it, for few had much English, and all Battalion business was conducted in Gurkhali. While they appeared to be very open and generally straightforward in character, they were difficult to get to know at first. I was impressed by the easy way my fellow British officers communicated with their soldiers in their own language. There seemed to be a close fraternity amongst all ranks and endless banter – it was a large family in which I had not yet earned my place. Everyone except me seemed to know exactly what to do, and no one appeared to shout. After all the tales of Gurkha derring-do that I had heard, the riflemen, while obviously tough, seemed surprisingly non-belligerent and possessed of much mild-mannered charm.

The men the Regiment recruited came largely from the traditionally martial Gurung and Magar tribes in the middle hills of western Nepal. The Magar tribe broke down into several clans that included Pun, Thapa, Ale, Rana and Roka, amongst others. Some Gurungs were from a sub-clan called Ghale, who considered themselves rather special. The tribe or clan to which a soldier belonged was tacked on as a kind of surname to his first given name. The soldiers were mostly of yeoman farming stock, inured to hard work in challenging conditions. They were largely recruited at the age of seventeen, and generally served in the Regiment for fifteen years before retiring back to their villages with a military pension. Those men promoted to sergeant and above could extend their service for several years.

There was thus a high level of experience in the Battalion, and by the time you made sergeant you certainly knew your business. Although the officers always used a soldier's given name in conversation or on parade, amongst themselves the riflemen commonly used the last two numerals of their Army numbers to address each other. Nicknames also abounded.

Within a couple of days of my arrival I set about learning the language. Every morning before parade, an English-speaking Gurkha clerk would come to my room to teach me the rudiments, preparing me for attendance at a language course at the Gurkha Training Depot in northern Malaya. I honed up on the vocabulary. Although the language was generally written in Nagri script, a Romanized version had been produced for the Army, and this certainly made it easier to learn. The language we learned was the language of the soldiers, and that was helpful, for in some respects it did not place us apart.

On arrival I had been posted as a Company Officer to Support Company, commanded by a dynamic and delightful Captain called Brian Skinner, who was the senior bachelor and who I much admired. I began to learn what was expected of me, and Brian was an excellent tutor. I got to know the Gurkhas in his Company, their characteristics and their customs. I was struck by the number of brothers and cousins in the Battalion; most soldiers seemed to have had fathers and grandfathers in a Gurkha regiment, many of them in the 2nd Goorkhas. Some came from the same hill village, and this all made for a pretty tight family unit.

I soon recognized that I needed to use my right hand to receive something from a Gurkha, and then raise it gently upwards in receipt to thank him. I sampled the cookhouse curries – the twice daily meal for the soldiers – and I experienced the extreme dangers of Gurkha rum, issued on a weekly basis to the riflemen. I got to grips with the intricacies of dress and turnout – not least, discovering that I should not sit down in highly starched Gurkha shorts during early morning parades. That must wait until breakfast, lest an ugly crease mar their sharp precision. Breakfast was normally taken after the early morning parades were over at around 9 o'clock.

I inspected the Gurkha knife – the curved, sharp, beautifully weighted *kukri* – and acquired an example for myself. All the soldiers wore this traditional knife on their belts both on parade and in the jungle. They owned two versions: a smart highly polished blade in its bulled black scabbard, carried when on ceremonial guard or other parade duties; and a working knife in a camouflaged sheath for use on operations in the jungle. This was essentially a very useful working tool as well as an operational weapon of last resort. Over the years I heard more nonsense talked about the *kukri* than any other element of Gurkha mythology.

With a few experienced men from my Company, I made my first tentative entry into the jungle, where the Gurkha soldier had made his name in Burma and Malaya. I slithered and slid and tripped over vines and creepers in the rotting vegetation, while the riflemen, ever tolerant of the poverty of my performance, seemed to dance lightly from log to log avoiding every hazard. Eventually I began to feel more comfortable in the jungle environment and began to use its character to advantage. I learnt how to move relatively quietly, to manage the business of living and make myself reasonably comfortable without cutting down the whole jungle in the process. I began to notice my surroundings and have confidence in my compass bearings. I mastered the art of carefully removing the leeches that seemed to be so attracted to me. I understood the need for water discipline, and for pausing and listening and looking. I watched the riflemen seeming to take all this in their stride and I tried my best to copy them.

That first year of service was a steep but enjoyable learning curve for me. I began to appreciate the qualities of the Gurkha officers and riflemen: their keenness to learn; their professional standards; the excellence of their basic skills in weapon handling and fieldcraft; the natural feel they had for using ground and their eagle eyes that spotted threats and hazards long before I had noticed anything. I saw only the occasional flash of truculence, irritation or disappointment in otherwise light-hearted soldiers. As I started to master the simpler elements of the language so I began to feel that I was becoming accepted and that just maybe I might have something to offer. Then I would make some hideous mistake, show my ignorance or fail to express myself in Gurkhali, and I would be momentarily consumed with self-doubt.

The culture of the Regiment, its style if you like, was known as the 'Sirmoor system'. It had been codified by the Regiment's most accomplished General, Sir Francis Tuker, when he commanded the Regiment on the North-West Frontier, before the war. He was later to be a highly successful and distinguished Commander of 4th Indian Division in North Africa. The Sirmoor system codified the same 60th Rifles principles of initiative and speed of reaction, of thinking outside the box, of trust and respect between officers and men, that there was no need to shout or threaten. There is an old Nepali proverb: 'I can't hear what you are saying for the thunder with which you say it.'

People seemed to know where they stood and what was expected of them. They took individual responsibility for their duties, however mundane, and strove not to let themselves down or the Regiment, in which all ranks took much pride. Confident in ourselves, I sensed we were a happy band. This mood pervaded the general harmony of the British officers' mess where, save for Monty Ormsby, always addressed as 'Colonel', we used only Christian names. We all knew everyone's seniority and did not need to recognize it with formality. A suggestion from a senior officer that something might be done was understood to be an order.

We had an agreeable mess. When not on exercise, the five or six bachelor officers would dine together most evenings. We would dress every night in 'penguin order' – evening dress trousers, black cummerbunds, a white shirt and black tie. The Regiment possessed fine silver, china and glass that always looked pristine, and there were good historical pictures in the ante-room and elsewhere. Books in the mess library were all bound in red or black vellum and inscribed with the Regimental cypher that had all been organized by John Chapple. It served to create a collegiate and convivial atmosphere in which conversation knew no bounds, among a set of intelligent officers with much to say and well-stocked hinterlands. Once a week we wore regimental mess dress, and the Band would play for us. Brian Skinner, the senior bachelor, ensured that we all behaved reasonably well – with only a few wild excesses.

My first year passed quickly. There were several Battalion and Brigade exercises. I attended my six-week Gurkhali course and started to use the language with more confidence. I left Support Company and was appointed Intelligence Officer. I took my place in Battalion Headquarters, with a small team of Gurkha riflemen and NCOs to command and train.

Much has changed since those early days of Gurkha service well over fifty years ago. We then felt very much part and parcel of the British Army, but in spite of sterling service in the Malayan Emergency, there was no doubt that some outsiders still regarded us as some form of colonial relic – a sort of fag-end of the Raj. We were certainly very different from a British Battalion in our dress and culture, if no less effective. We had our separate British and Gurkha commissions inherited from the old Indian Army, and the Gurkhas' terms and conditions of service were very different from their British counterparts.

Firstly, Gurkha pay and therefore the pension that it earned, was lower than that of the British soldier. It was based initially on a tripartite agreement with India and Nepal. These levels of pay, on a par with that of the Indian Army Gurkhas, were enhanced by some local allowances, but the difference remained. The Treasury argument ran that Gurkha pay and pensions reflected the cost of living in Nepal. The British Government had entertained the idea of recruiting and retaining the Gurkha soldier in part because he was cheaper, and thus more cost effective than maintaining British soldiers in the Far East. Further, these rates of pay seemed hugely attractive in the Gurkha market place, where the potential supply of volunteer recruits greatly exceeded demand. The Gurkha pension was in fact very generous, for it was paid after fifteen years of service, perhaps at the age of thirty-two. In general, most soldiers were keen savers and sent large remittances back to the family home.

The morality of such arrangements was not then questioned, and there was always the fear that pressing too hard for any sort of increase would spell the end of Gurkha service, since the Gurkha could easily price himself out of a job. In comparison with his compatriots at home in Nepal, the argument further ran, the Gurkha soldier was still a rich man.

There were two other issues that in retrospect might have appeared militarily antediluvian to some. The first was the issue of much prized accompanied family permission. The Gurkha soldier and his British officers were granted six months leave at the end of each three-year tour in the Far East. Normally on his first or second leave a Gurkha would get married – often as arranged by his parents – but he was only allowed one tour back in the Battalion accompanied by his family. This would normally be his third tour. For the rest of his service, unless promotion to sergeant and beyond arrived, he was unaccompanied. This ensured that there were sufficient numbers of senior men living in barracks and readily available for operations. The arrangement also reduced costs and enabled many Gurkha wives to play a vital part in maintaining the homestead back in the hills. But it was not popular, and I don't think, at first, that some of us really appreciated the tribulations and pressures of separation that this policy wrought. It also played havoc with the education of Gurkha children, split as it was between an Army school and one in a hill village.

Finally, there was the question of civilian dress for all junior ranks. Here the rules were very strict and there was a firm code for regimental mufti: white shirt with smartly pressed black shorts and black stockings with red and black dice board tops, knitted by Gurkha wives, together with 'shoes highland' and a green side hat with the Regimental cap badge – the black Prince of Wales's feathers, displayed on a red cloth background. This was the acceptable attire on regimental occasions in barracks. In the evenings, grey long trousers, white shirts and a regimental tie were permitted inside and outside the barracks. Smart as it all looked, and much as it enhanced the reputation for smartness of the Gurkha soldier in the eyes of many, it allowed no freedom of sartorial expression. It was several years before these rules were relaxed. I did recognize in my early days, however, that without crushing his initiative, the Gurkha soldier seemed to perform best within a broad framework of fairly tight, laid down standards.

I had not initially paid much attention to the religious customs of the Gurkha, and they did not at first seem to intrude greatly, individually or collectively, into the day-to-day life of the Battalion. As far as I could discover, the soldiers were nominally Hindu – the official religion of Nepal. But Buddhism and animism also played their part in a diverse mosaic of beliefs. I never quite disentangled the threads of Gurkha religious thought, but there seemed to be very few constraints on soldiers' activities, beyond a rejection of beef in the diet. This was an area, in those early days, into which I tended not to delve too deeply, for fear of saying the wrong thing. There was a small temple behind the Quarter Guard, and a high caste Brahmin priest – the *Pandit* or *Bahun* as he was known – was employed to look after the religious wellbeing of the Gurkhas. He was very much under command of the Gurkha Major, and his duties were entirely religious. Unlike a British Army chaplain, he had no pastoral or welfare duties. At least twice a year, however, he came into his own.

The first occasion was the great Hindu autumn festival of *Dashera*. This was and remains an important feature of regimental life. It was a ten-day celebration of the goddess of war, Durga. For the British officers, the two central days were those of *Kalratri* followed by *Mar*, when we were invited to participate as guests. The Gurkha Major was the leading producer, director and stage manager of these events. *Kalratri* was a grand party for the whole Battalion and given over to singing, dancing, eating and drinking – important ingredients of any good party. The whole affair was brilliantly organized in every detail by Major Pirthilal and his assistants in a large set of marquees, complete with a complex stage, lighting and decorations. The officers all wore mess kit, and the soldiers wore their regimental evening mufti. There was an excellent curry, and rum flowed. A programme of entertainment was the central feature of the evening.

There would be several dances, with young soldiers dressed as women – the so-called *marunis* – as the stars of the show. Although their appearance was greeted with many ribald cheers, no one seemed to think the performance unnatural in any way. It was regarded much more as a social accomplishment. In those days the soldiers' wives would never dance. The *marunis* would dance on their own, or with young male dancers called *pursinges*, all accompanied by *madals* and tambourines and possibly an accordion. Later, as the evening wore on, the *marunis* would drag the officers on to the stage by a gnarled hand, and semi-reluctantly one would gyrate and wave arms about for a bit, before thankfully regaining one's seat. Digby was a particularly noisy participant in these dances and he performed them very well. My favourite dance was the *thal nautch* – the plate dance. A single *pursinge*, clad in attractive and colourful dress, would gyrate and whirl at an increasing pace and fervour to a pulsating drumbeat from the *madals*. All the while he would be grasping two dinner plates by their backs, seemingly stuck to his hands as if by glue. This dance was always well received. There would also be comic sketches, with regimental and British customs and foibles lampooned. The party went on to the early hours before one staggered back to the mess. It was much enjoyed by everyone.

The climax to *Dashera* was *Mar*. This took place the morning following *Kalratri*, when in an elaborate display in front of the regimental weapons, blessed by the *Pandit*, a male buffalo, several goats and assorted poultry were sacrificed by losing their heads. They were all beheaded by a specially selected NCO, using a large *kukri* called a *khanra*. The NCO would have been chosen by the Gurkha Major for his strength and skill, to ensure that the cuts were clean. The Battalion's luck depended upon it and, his successful work accomplished, he was rewarded with great cheers from the assembled Battalion, a purse of money from Colonel Monty and a white scarf tied around his head by Gurkha Major Pirthilal. I'm not sure that I enjoyed this ritual very much.

Gradually over time, the custom of *Dashera* in the Regiment changed. With Battalions serving in Hong Kong and England, and an ever-intrusive press, animal sacrifices were confined to Nepal on behalf of the whole Brigade. Fearful of misinterpretation in England, *marunis* also disappeared from the *Kalratri* agenda. In due course they were to be replaced by more contemporary forms of entertainment. The Gurkha wives and daughters began to dance. The soldiers, together with their fashions for music and dances, had moved on.

In 2017 I was a guest for *Dashera* with an Indian Gorkha Battalion. It was the 5th Battalion of the 8th Gorkhas based in Hyderabad. This Battalion had originally been the 4th Battalion of my own Regiment raised during the Second World War, and they still titled themselves 'Sirmoor Rifles'. At Partition, the Battalion had been transferred en bloc to the Indian Army. Their *Kalratri* and *Mar* were exactly as I remembered Pirthilal's party in

1960, albeit *Kalratri* was enhanced by some modern technology on stage. The *maruni* dances were as captivating as always, and the officers were as reluctant as ever to participate but invariably did so. At *Mar* the sacrifice of buffalo and goats was cleanly executed, and general good luck prevailed.

Some three weeks after *Dashera* came *Diwali* – the three-day festival of illumination. It celebrates Lakshmi, goddess of wealth and prosperity. Gambling was the Gurkha soldier's worst vice and, except during *Diwali*, was forbidden both in the Army and in Nepal. *Diwali* allowed it, and stalls appeared in the Company lines with crown and anchor and other games of chance and skill. All these were played with huge enthusiasm, excited cries and much triumphant banging of fists on tables at a winning fall of dice or card. From time to time the British officers, encouraged by the entreaties of their company's riflemen, joined in. Inevitably we beat a hasty retreat, generally the poorer.

After about a year with the Regiment I began to think about the possibility of trying to convert from National Service to a three-year Short Service Commission. I was enjoying regimental life, but National Service rates of pay were just about covering my mess bill and not much more. Additional service might provide a rather better salary, while allowing me more time to decide my future and explore possible career opportunities in the Far East, to which I was increasingly attracted.

While l had no clear idea what I might do when I left the Army, another year in the 2nd Goorkhas seemed an attractive option if the Regiment would have me. I talked to John Chapple. He supported a modest extension and having discussed it with Colonel Monty would set the paperwork in motion. Meanwhile, he suggested that if I extended my service, I might like to go to Nepal to assist with recruiting and learn something about the Gurkha homeland. I would then help to train the recruits for nine months at the Gurkha Training Depot in northern Malaya, before returning to the Battalion. When I got back, John suggested, I could then think about trying to convert to a full Regular commission. These seemed to be generous and exciting options, and I would pursue them. But first to Nepal.

Chapter 3

Nepal – Travels and War

And the wildest dreams of Kew are the facts of Kathmandu.
—Rudyard Kipling

CALCUTTA

Nothing prepares the western traveller for his first visit to Calcutta (Kolkata). Winston Churchill, writing to his mother, remarked that having once seen the city there was fortunately no need for him to ever visit the place again! I think I might have written in similar vein to my mother. The assault on the senses, the affront to the dignity of mankind, the pervading quality of hopelessness that hit me on that first and last acquaintance with the city in 1961 are still with me.

I had arrived there on a trooping flight from Singapore, along with a hundred Gurkha soldiers all moving in the same direction as me – to the hill villages of Nepal. They were heading for six months home leave after three years in the Malayan jungle, or they were travelling this route for the last time, having left the service and earned their Army pensions. As John Chapple had suggested, I was planning to get to know the country of my soldiers and assist with the enlistment of new recruits. Meanwhile, I was to have a few days lodging at our transit camp at Barrackpore, part of the old military cantonment, twenty miles north of the city. Here I would familiarize myself with local Gurkha issues, including the predatory habits of Indian customs officers who made an habitual beeline for the well paid Gurkha soldier. The illicit smuggling of gold acquired in the emporia of Singapore was a perpetual problem, and the hollowed-out heel of a soldier's shoe was, as the Gurkha quickly discovered to his cost, a well known hiding place. I was then going to head off, courtesy of Indian railways, across Bengal and the fertile plains of northern India to the border of Nepal. Today there is no reason for the Gurkha soldier to transit through India, for international airlines deposit him on the tarmac of Tribhuvan International Airport in Kathmandu. There he can tangle with the equally predatory Nepalese customs officers before heading home, but that option did not then exist. Before I set off by train there was a chance to experience what Kipling had described as 'the Big Calcutta Stink'.

It was in Calcutta, spreading north and south along the unhealthy mudbanks of the broad Hooghly River, that the East India Company had established its first trading post in the late seventeenth century. It was where Robert Clive, privateer and fortune hunter, had set off to win the day at Plassey against the Nawab of Bengal and his French allies, a victory that consolidated the Company's presence in Bengal. The battle had set in train the Company's expansion that a hundred years later, having subjugated much of India, was to end disastrously in the rebellion and mutiny of the Company's Bengal Army in 1857.

Under Company rule, and later under direct rule from London, Calcutta was the richest, largest and most elegant city in India. In 1911, however, its steamy climate, political turbulence and geographical disadvantages combined to lose it its status as the British capital of India to Delhi. There a new city would rise, designed by Edwin Lutyens, to replace both Calcutta and the historic Mughal city of Old Delhi. At the Partition of India, Calcutta witnessed a tragic episode of political unrest and communal horror. Fury and mayhem engulfed the city, with at least 3,500 dead and 45,000 troops deployed to stem the tide of violence.

I visited the city's grand central thoroughfare of Chowringhee and wandered across the vast piece of parkland set alongside it – the *Maidan*. There stood the anachronistic Victoria Memorial, in an architectural style that suggested 'Renaissance with traces of Saracenic influence' according to my guidebook, but with the virtue of housing some interesting pictures by Zoffany, William Daniell and others. Close by were the vast Eden Gardens cricket ground and the Raj Bhavan, the former Government House, once home to the Company's Governor Generals and after 1857 to the Viceroys of India, built at vast expense by the Iron Duke's brother, the 1st Marquess Wellesley. There also, in solitary splendour, stood the column that memorialized General Sir David Ochterlony, about whom more later.

I also remember the scale of the beggary and poverty. I could not move within the city itself without my charity being invoked; there were endless cries of '*Paisa saheb*' and outstretched and often mutilated limbs; when you relented with a rupee or two, the pathetic eyes would continue to plead or press for more. There was the sight of a dead child's body lying in the street, or a whole wretched family living within half an oil drum on the seedy banks of the Hooghly River. Then came the rickshaw cyclists, always at your shoulder with their harsh ever-tinkling bells, as they plied endlessly for trade; and everywhere the slowly meandering sacred cows with a bovine indifference to their squalid surroundings. Dangling on sagging wires above the entrance to Chowringhee, a sad but surely over-optimistic banner caught my eye proclaiming, 'Keep Calcutta Clean Week'.

Swelled by many hundreds of Bengali immigrants, I was told that there were 400,000 unemployed in the city, although how anyone counted them was beyond me. It certainly seemed that half were camped out on the platforms of Howrah railway station. When I arrived at the terminal after a white-knuckle ride in a Calcutta taxi, a legion of licensed porters fought tooth and nail for the doubtful privilege of carrying my baggage and bedroll. Together we manoeuvred our way around a thousand recumbent forms, each shrouded in dirty white linen, to reach my reserved compartment on the '54 Up' night train to Benares (now Varanasi). Here the passage of rupees produced from the porters' pockets a key to unlock the compartment and an electric bulb to light its interior. It was with some relief that I set off on my 700 miles of railway travel. As I journeyed, it was to be a further salutary introduction to the harshness and deprivations of life on that vast subcontinent.

Two days later, having spent a few hours in Benares exploring the banks of the Ganges, the burning ghats and that extraordinary religious hub of a city, I crossed the great river and caught a new night train. On this I continued to trundle across northern India, and at Gorakpur I changed trains yet again on to the narrow-gauge line that took me the last 50 miles to the railhead of Nautanwa. I was by now very familiar with that most dangerous of dishes – railway curry! Seven miles further, having been met by a pensioned Gurkha driver and his Land Rover, I crossed the border into Nepal.

TRAVELS AND SOME HISTORY

In the flat Terai region of Nepal, close to the border and its Indian railways, sat the modest but immaculate British Gurkha Recruiting Centre of Paklihawa, a tranquil oasis that was to be my base for the next three months. To this Centre, once a year, came boys from western Nepal hoping to be selected for British Army service. The veteran 2nd Goorkha officer, Alistair Langlands, a sage and seemingly ageless bachelor, was in command and he showed me to my tent on the mess lawn with its tidy and colourful gardens. Alistair knew the country better than anyone else, for he was reputed to have walked to every village in western Nepal that either owned an enlisted soldier or possessed a potential recruit.

There was a heavy requirement for those recruits in 1961, since many of the junior ranks who had come across to the British Army in 1947 were now at the end of their fifteen years of service. Nearly 1,600 Gurkha soldiers were due to be enlisted for that reason. Half of these would be drawn from eastern Nepal and its Limbu and Rai communities, and half mainly from the Magar and Gurung villages of the west. The eastern boys would be enlisted in the Gurkha Depot in Dharan, close to eastern Nepal's Indian border, while the Paklihawa Centre focussed on the west.

A month after my arrival and following four weeks of walking in the hills, my work with Alistair began. I discovered that there were two ways for boys to be considered for enlistment. Firstly, a number of retired senior NCOs had been appointed as hill recruiters. They were trusted pensioners known as *gallawallas* – literally, responsible for recruiting. These men were each allocated a modest district in the hills in which to recruit and were required, against a set of laid down criteria, to bring in twenty boys around seventeen years of age for assessment. For a year they would tour their domain seeking suitable candidates. On top of a basic salary, they were paid according to the numbers from their *galla* that were selected, and for boys considered to possess outstanding potential there was an extra bonus. Service as a *gallawalla* was a much sought-after appointment, but a recruiter doing his rounds would often come under intense pressure, and no doubt on some occasions given inducements, to select favoured sons. In general, however, the system seemed to work satisfactorily. These boys would be the first to be considered by Alistair and his team, and on average perhaps fifteen or sixteen boys might be selected from each *galla*.

Once the official *gallas* had been considered, then, depending on the numbers that were still required, there was the huge pool of possible talent that had arrived under their own steam from their villages. Many thousands of these boys were encamped outside the Centre. Each morning, we moved into the dusty local bazaars and inspected these hopefuls, drawn up by the Gurkha Assistant Recruiting Officers in a hundred yards of ragged ranks, chests thrust out and all desperately hoping to catch the eye of the recruiting officer. Boys from the bazaar and boys from the hills, boys from anywhere, some clearly far too old and others far too young. Alistair's experienced eye soon picked out those with the potential to make up the numbers. These would be invited inside the Centre to submit to a more formal assessment, with physical, medical and intelligence tests, gratefully accepting a tented bed space and two meals a day. Gradually over a period of several weeks, 800 candidates came through this selection process and were enlisted and attested for British Army service. Those who failed might consider joining the Indian Army and would travel down to their recruiting centre at Gorakpur; others would face the ignominy of walking back to their villages and returning to labour in their fields.

The successful boys were issued with a modicum of military clothing and instructed in basic drill and the behaviour expected of soldiers of the British Crown. Then, escorted by NCOs drawn from regiments in Malaya and with Second Lieutenant Duffell in command, we set off for Malaya. Together with the 800 new Gurkha soldiers we travelled by train back to Calcutta before boarding a British India Line steamer. We sailed, via Chittagong and Rangoon for the loading and unloading of cargoes, and docked two weeks later in the harbour of the island of Penang, close to the north Malayan mainland. Only when I commanded my Battalion twenty years later would I have more Gurkha soldiers under command. Ten months in the Gurkha Training Depot, close to the Malay town of Sungei Patani, would turn these young men into fighting fit Gurkha soldiers.

I should record, very briefly, some history and geography of the Gurkha homeland and say something of my early travels in it. Landlocked Nepal lies sandwiched between the geographical and political heavyweights of China and India. This independent country stretches some 500 miles from east to west, while from north to south it covers 100 miles, through great ridge lines, from the Himalayan mountains to the Indian border. Along that southern border, just above sea level, runs the Terai – a flat area of cultivation and modest townships, now increasingly developed and averaging some twenty miles in depth before the foothills are reached. It was here that Paklihawa was situated. Here, too, away from swelling urban areas and a few rough roads, was Sal Forest and elephant grass, in many places swampy and malarial in the summer months and inhabited by people more Indian than Mongolian in caste and character. Rising on the Tibetan plateau, over many centuries great rivers have gouged deep gorges through the Himalayas, before surging down through the middle hills and slicing their way across the Terai.

It was in the Terai, too, long before I visited, that the great tiger shoots of old had taken place, mostly involving monarchs, viceroys and assorted nobility from East and West. These were grand regal affairs full of theatre, set in huge tented camps, perhaps involving 600 elephants and a vast paraphernalia of beaters, servants and followers. Then highly successful conservation took hold, and cameras replaced rifles. On one of my later visits to Nepal I stayed with a regimental party in one of the magical tourist lodges located in the Terai's Chitwan National Park, just east of Paklihawa. This was Tiger Tops, the lodge established by Mountain Travel, founded by my regimental colleague, the soldier and climber Jimmy Roberts. This attractive lodge, sadly no more, offered elephant safaris and observation of all the varied wildlife of Nepal.

It was in Chitwan that I first saw that prehistoric curiosity of nature, the leathery behemoth and herbivore *Rhinocerus Unicornis*, the greater one-horned rhinoceros, as it ambled through the forest, occasionally stopping to gaze at me with enquiring gravity. I would always wonder what, in the great sum of things, this animal's purpose was. Excellent conservation in Nepal has brought *Rhinocerus Unicornis* back from the brink of extinction, as it has with the Bengal tiger.

For it was on that visit to Tiger Tops, on the edge of the Sal Forest one late afternoon, that news reached us that there was a tiger about. We immediately clambered precariously into our *howdahs* atop those wonderfully steady and patient elephants and moved slowly into the long pampas grass, hoping to get a rare sighting. Our elephants, led by a large tusker and guided by the bare feet of the *mahouts* digging their coded instructions into the back of the animals' ears, swayed and steadied themselves on the uneven and often swampy surface. Ahead, only the lead elephants could be seen, rhythmically rocking above the height of the grass. Everywhere was a wonderful silence that you could almost hear. Above us Bulbuls and Hoopoes, Kites and Bee-eaters darted, circled, swooped and dived. We passed kapok trees rich with their red blossoms. There was tension and excitement in the air as we swayed forward and back some 15ft above the ground, all eyes scanning the landscape ahead for our quarry.

Suddenly there was urgent gesticulation and suppressed shouts from the *mahouts* ahead, and we closed up. There in the grass was the carcass of a wild Indian bison killed the night before by our tiger. It lay still, eyes open in death and staring fixedly heavenwards. The elephants started to trumpet, ears flapping and trunks swaying, as they sensed the presence of a tiger resting close to its prey. Collectively the *mahouts* urged their charges forward, and we moved into close formation, line ahead. Now instinct seemed to take us in the right direction, and within a few minutes we were in a half circle, three yards from a golden and black striped tiger. The *mahouts* were now fighting to control their charges, digging their feet in ever more urgently and shouting orders in traditional Assamese, sticks thrashing on their mounts' solid craniums. The elephants trumpeted more loudly, rearing and jostling, ears and trunks alive with the excitement or fear of it all, in the presence of this king of beasts. Some ambitious animals tried to move yet closer to the tiger, while other more nervous elephants backed away. Expectancy and noise filled the air.

The tiger seemed thoroughly unperturbed by our arrival. Slowly that magnificent solitary creature rose from its resting place, growling and purring as it padded round in a grassy circle no larger than its body length and lay down again to continue its digestion. Proud, arrogant and fearless, contemptuous of our presence and total master of its environment. From atop my elephant I looked the tiger straight in the eye. Bright burning eyes stared back at me. Was I for a moment the Viceroy, with rifle at his shoulder back in the days of the Nepal Ranas and the great Edwardian tiger shoots? I took a shot with my cumbersome camera, but the constant heaving of my mount made it difficult. Then gradually and almost reluctantly, the *mahouts* turned the elephants away from our quarry and we began the slow but elated journey back to our camp as the evening darkness closed in. I had seen my first tiger.

In Paklihawa, before recruiting began, Alistair Langlands had given me instructions for my first trek. There was a long gap to be filled before my work as Alistair's modest assistant was to start. Until then there was nothing for me to do, and I was to set off for a walk in the hills and come back in four weeks! There were some welfare issues that Alistair would like me to check on as I travelled, but the real aim was to get a feel for life in the hill villages of the Gurkha soldier and pensioner and begin to understand Nepal. Alistair gave me a list of villages to visit, some sound advice on routes and the suggestion that if I made good progress I might even get as far as Kathmandu. That capital city lay in a large valley, centrally placed in the country and about 150 miles to the east of Paklihawa as the crow flies, although it was obviously a good deal further on foot. I should also visit the small township of Gorkha, where our soldiers' story had its beginnings.

Over the course of my service and beyond I have paid many visits to Nepal. I became familiar with certain parts of the countryside as well as with Kathmandu, and visiting every four or five years or so, I was able observe what changed and what remained the same. I became reasonably familiar with the country but I never possessed the intimate knowledge gained by men such as Alastair, with a succession of postings to Nepal in various guises. There were other officers, too, who had walked the length and breadth of Nepal. They had, through their service in various administrative posts there, garnered a detailed understanding of the country's culture and politics that an infrequent visitor such as I could not easily obtain. My visits were

invariably short and limited in scope, dictated by the demands of my service
and the time it took to move about.

On that first walk I had set off lightly clad, with one civilian porter,
Manbahadur Gurung, provided by Alistair, to help me with my kit. I was
planning to travel simply, with a sleeping bag, a few spare clothes, a trekking
medical kit to do what I could for any sick people, and some washing kit.
In addition, I carried Nepali rupees, a trekking permit, maps, my Nepali
dictionary, some whisky for sustenance, modest gifts to distribute in return
for hospitality, a water bottle and cooking utensils, a walking stick and not
much else. I quickly realized that I was something of an innocent abroad.
I was utterly dependent on my feet, for in 1961, outside of the Terai, there
were no roads in Nepal west of Kathmandu, or indeed in the east. Only a
single road link existed to the outside world – a recently completed highway
that ran directly south from Kathmandu to India. Further, after only a year
in the Battalion, I knew few soldiers who would be on leave at home while
I was walking and who might have shown me around.

I therefore planned to depend on simple hostelries for food and lodging.
These inns were generally presided over with ribald good humour by
women who came from the district of Thak, high up near the slopes of
Annapurna – western Nepal's most distinguished and distinctive mountain.
These ladies were particularly adept at running what might be described
as extremely simple B & Bs for travellers on the road. Their wayside inns
were essentially temporary and basic, often no more than modest lean-tos,
set up in the walking season outside of the monsoon, and stationed on the
major routes. They were known as *bhattis*. This was long before tourism got
under way and smart lodges began to appear, designed for the international
trekker.

On later visits to Nepal and as I became more senior I abandoned the
bhatti as a resting place except for the occasional meal. Instead, I travelled
in greater comfort with two or three porters, tents, and a modicum of
rations, all of which provided a degree of independence. It allowed me to
camp just outside a village that I wanted to visit but without having to rely
on the innate hospitality of the always generous hill people. On those later
walks I would probably be accompanied by one of my Gurkha officers or a
soldier on leave from the Regiment, someone who seemed happy to act as
my guide and mentor for a couple of weeks or so. By then I knew people in

the Battalion well enough and could plan my walks, or treks as they were christened by Jimmy Roberts, to meet up with regimental soldiers on leave or our pensioners, and check on their welfare.

On that first journey of mine into the hills of Nepal, the country was slowly emerging from 200 years of isolation from the outside world. It was only in 1951 that Nepal had come out of an era that had been, socially and economically, medieval in character. Until then, the whole country had been closed to the outside world and split in two: the ruling class, in the valley of Kathmandu, and the peoples of the hills, of a different caste and about whom the elite of the capital appeared to care little. For most intents and purposes, 'the Valley' and 'the Hills' were two different countries. Furthermore, Europeans, outside the main centres in the hills, were a rare commodity and provoked much inquisitive, although not unfriendly interest.

The development of India under British authority had made little direct impact on Nepal, and in spite of the recruitment of hillmen for service in Gurkha regiments, entry to foreigners was almost totally forbidden. Then in 1951, King Tribhuvan, the hereditary Shah monarch, had with Indian support, overthrown the ruling Rana family, re-established royal authority, formed a new coalition government and gently opened his country's doors to the outside world. For me, a suitable starting point for exploring further the complex and convoluted history of Nepal would be the administrative headquarters of the district that took its name from the small town of Gorkha, sat high in the middle hills of Nepal about fifty miles due west of Kathmandu.

Over the years I visited the town of Gorkha several times – one of my personal iconic places in Nepal. It is close to one of the most notable Gurkha villages of the hills, Barpak, home of the Gurungs' Ghale clan and the birthplace of Gaje Ghale, a distinguished Gurkha soldier and the holder of a Victoria Cross won in Burma. Several soldiers from my Battalion also hailed from this large village that was sadly, cruelly damaged in the earthquake of 2015 – for Gorkha was the epicentre of that awful convulsion. On my first visit, reaching Gorkha represented an extremely exhausting walk, climbing and descending at least 4,000ft before reaching the historic site. Today, a Land Rover will carry you relatively easily up and down the hill road to this famous town. In the town itself there is now a fine Welfare Centre, one of many throughout Nepal established by our Gurkha

Welfare Trust that looks after the interests of all our ex-servicemen and their families in the area, as well as providing community aid within their villages. Former Gurkha officers or warrant officers are employed to run these centres, where ex-servicemen can go to collect their pensions. Medical assistance is also available in all the centres. Fifteen hundred feet above the town, and requiring a further exhausting climb up several hundred steps, is the sanctuary of Gorakhnath.

There, one's exertions are rewarded by a wonderful and unchanging view, east and west, of the magnificent Himalayas as well as the site of what was, in the middle of the eighteenth century, the Prince of Gorkha's fort, palace and temple. The name of this Rajput boy chieftain was Prithwi Narayan Shah, and in 1742 at the age of twenty, and possessed of a ruthless ambition, he began to expand his power. He raised an army from amongst his hill people, including Magar and Gurung hillmen from his province, and by 1765, with most of Nepal's many scattered and divided states already in his thrall, he laid siege to the valley of Kathmandu and its Newar people. As he advanced, he exacted terrible retribution on those he had conquered. By the time of his death in 1775, Prithwi Narayan was the paramount ruler of much of his almost unified country. He had further established a Shah dynasty in Kathmandu that in various forms was to last two hundred years.

In the wake of Prythwi Narayan's death came a plethora of ineffective rulers, internecine struggles, intrigues and conspiracies. It is sufficient to record that Prithwi Narayan's grandson, Rana Bahadur Shah, although showing signs of insanity, in 1804 appointed a Gorkha noble, Bhim Sen Thapa, to be his Prime Minister. Bhim Sen was to become the effective ruler of Nepal for thirty years, and under his rule the Gorkha army continued to expand the kingdom. Following Bhim Sen's suicide in 1839 there followed another period of instability. In the wake of a power struggle, the Kot massacre of 1846, engineered by General Jang Bahadur, killed many of the Nepali aristocracy and heralded the foundation of a Rana regime of hereditary Prime Ministers. Until 1951 they reduced the Shah dynasty and its Kings to puppet status, with successors held as virtual prisoners in their own palaces, until King Tribhuvan rose against them and restored the authority of the monarchy.

My first walk had introduced me to the middle hills – that area of the country that lies between the Terai and the start of the Himalayas themselves.

In some areas there is a gentle preamble as you leave the Terai, but before long the steep ascents begin as you cross the intermediate terrain that leads you into the heart of Nepal's middle hills. The countryside and the people change quickly, and after two or three days of hard walking I was reaching the villages of the Gurkha soldier, situated at levels between 4,000 and 8,000ft. The grain of the country is from north to south, so that a journey across Nepal tends to be one of constant and arduous ascent and descent, with high hills followed by the deep valleys that lie between. Simple steep paved tracks connect these villages, and everywhere terraced fields cover the landscape. I found myself constantly travelling up or down, and only rarely would movement along a ridge line offer some respite. I soon discovered that when I was climbing I longed to arrive at the start of an easy descent, only to find little relief as a jarring on the knees going down replaced the panting struggle uphill. It was energetic walking, but soon enough I settled into a rhythm. I recognized that hillmen were inured to this constant rise and fall of the countryside, even if it left the average outsider somewhat fatigued. But the landscapes and views were constantly beguiling and exhilarating, and I relished the gentle pace of life.

As I crossed the hills I could only admire the strength and stamina of the strings of porters that passed me by on those rough and well-worn tracks. They were carrying loads of back-breaking size and weight, the only way to transport materials such as kerosene, timber and other household goods across the country. All loads, many carried in a traditional cone-shaped wicker basket, were supported by a headband across the forehead. While we walked, for all of us there was one, essentially Nepali, welcome resting place – the *chautaro*. Constructed by the local communities, these are two-tier platforms of rough paving stone slabs and earth, with perhaps a *pipal* tree of spreading branches centrally placed above to provide shade. The platform allows the wicker basket to be rested on the lower tier and gently eased off the back, before one climbs to the upper tier to sit and recover one's breath. It is then an easy matter to lift the basket on to the back once more, at the right level for loading.

In those early days of my service I usually trekked in the spring and autumn, when the weather was at its kindest. In these seasons it could be balmy during the day, but at night the hills were enveloped by a Himalayan shadow of cold coming down from the mountains. The closely clustered houses of the Magar and Gurung villages, higher up in the hills, are solid and rectangular and mostly built of local stone, with strong beams and roofs of slate. Lower down, the houses are constructed of bricks and mud and many have thatched roofs and a circular shape. The aesthetically displeasing but efficient corrugated iron has now become prevalent. The villages themselves are agricultural and pastoral, occasionally falling victim to life-shattering landslides and hail storms and demanding constant hard labour. The life cycle of these farmers is similar to that of farmers the world over – ploughing, the sowing of rice, millet or maize, depending on altitude, tending and harvesting – but the terrain and the lack of mechanical aids make it especially challenging. Hill paths and steps linking the villages are maintained collectively by those who use them. It was to these villages that I was constantly drawn to meet up with my soldiers and gossip about Nepal and families and the doings of the Regiment, sometimes to investigate a welfare case. I was always humbled by the generous way in which I was received. In spite of the harsh regime of village life in those early days of my travel I found the village communities strong, closely-knit and undemanding, independent, lively and cheerful – many of the same characteristics that marked our soldiers.

Many retired Gurkha soldiers returned with their pensions to subsistence farming in their hill villages. Some, such as my friend Captain Bhagtasing Pun, returned in retirement to one of a cluster of strong Pun communities in the Baglung hills – in Bhagtasing's case to a village called Ramche. Here he devoted his energies to improving the educational opportunities in the local area and to the health and hygiene of his village. He steered well clear of local village politics. His son, Bishnu Pun, would have his initial primary education in nearby village schools, to which he walked over the hills every day.

Recognizing the opportunities that education might offer his children, Bhagtasing eventually moved from his village and purchased a house in Pokhara close to the British Gurkha Camp that had replaced the early Centre at Paklihawa. Living there he was able to secure a place for his son at Pokhara High School, where Bishnu prospered. At the age of seventeen, and in spite of fear that he was too slight of build to be enlisted, the local *gallawalla* took him to Paklihawa. He was accepted and eventually joined his father's old Battalion; no doubt his paternal credentials had impressed the Recruiting Officer. Bishnu was to have a hugely successful career of soldiering with both the 2nd Goorkhas and the Royal Gurkha Rifles. In addition, he spent some time on the Prince of Wales's personal staff and as a Captain secured the appointment for a year as Gurkha Orderly Officer to the Queen. He retired as a Major and now works for the Gurkha Welfare Trust in Salisbury, where he has bought a house. He has embraced England but he remains at heart both a Goorkha and a Nepali.

Captain Bhagtasing Pun had, earlier than most, recognized the opportunities that existed within Nepal's major cities for better education and employment, as well as the existence of medical and other facilities such as electricity and running water. He had been at the forefront of a movement that was to take many ex-service Gurkha families away from their hill villages to the urban areas of Nepal. In so doing, Bhaktasing's son Bishnu had been able to develop the not inconsiderable talents that, confined to his hill village, might not have flourished so readily.

Today, of course, the development of internal communications and a strong network of roads has further changed the lifestyle of the hill villages. The exodus from the hills to the valleys by those that can afford to move and a drift to the towns have continued; additionally, supplies can now move by truck to many of the remote communities. Where roads have not yet forged their way across this demanding countryside motorcycle trails reach all but the highest communities. For the sentimental of yesterday it is sad to see the hill communities of ex-soldiers withering on the vine, but so far as one can judge their qualities of hardiness and endeavour remain.

If a visit to Gorkha represented a pilgrimage for those associated with its background, and the hill villages were where I most wished to travel, there were two other locations that certainly exerted a strong pull on my imagination. The first of these was the remote kingdom of Mustang.

Two of the giant mountains of the Himalayan range in western Nepal, both over 26,000ft and possessed of great scenic grandeur, are the neighbouring peaks of Dhaulagiri and Annapurna. These peaks are only 22 miles apart and between them runs the generally wide valley of the Kali Gandaki – a great breach in the Himalayas. The bed of this river lies at some 18,500ft below the summits, and the great flow of water has produced a gorge between the mountains of some magnificence, with banks at times gentle and in other places precipitous. Follow the river line through the mountains and eventually you reach a Nepali salient of the Tibetan plateau. Here you come to the ancient kingdom of Mustang, lying on the river's upper course and something of a fabled Shangri La. Totally closed to the outside world, its small capital of Lo Manthang lies on an important trade route with Tibet. From pictures I had seen it appeared to be a lost Tibetan kingdom, and its very remoteness and inaccessibility exerted, on me at least, a magnetic quality. Assuming you had permission to visit, it demanded at least a two-week journey with a yak or mule train accompanying you to what appeared to be the roof of the world. It was not directly part of the Gurkha story, but I longed to go there.

In my early walks in Nepal in the 1960s I had trekked in the lower reaches of the Kali Gandaki river, visiting Gurkha villages. Occasionally on the main routes I would meet colourful mule trains driven by peoples from the high Himalayas – men of Tibetan character who came from settlements on the mountain passes, including Mustang. But because of political problems, with Tibet and China close by, Mustang was closed to visitors. At the time of my first visit it had become a centre and cross-border refuge for Tibetan Khampa guerrillas engaged in operations against the Chinese army and its occupation of Tibet. I had noticed that some of the men accompanying the mule trains were wearing shirts fashioned out of parachute silk and rubber-soled army boots. As I soon learned, this was evidence for the guerrillas being supplied by CIA airdrops. Later, and clearly in the face of possible political embarrassment, these guerrillas were cleared out of Mustang by the Nepali army, but the area remained closed and I doubted that I would ever have a chance to reach it.

In 1991 my luck changed. I was paying an official visit to Kathmandu in my capacity as the Major General, Brigade of Gurkhas and I called on my friend, Nepal's Chief of Army Staff, who had been my guest in Hong Kong. He generously offered to fly me in an army helicopter anywhere in Nepal. Where might that be? I immediately opted for the remote city of Lo Mantang and a few days later was flying up the Kali Gandaki gorge to the rarefied Tibetan plateau. We were far to the north of Annapurna, Dhaulagiri and the main Himalayas, and I looked down on a yellow and ochre desert. There seemed no sign of life. Yet in a land preserved by the dry air and sculpted by the wind a fragile society of scattered villages and monasteries continued to exist, although still largely closed to the outside world.

Here the people were Tibetan yet under Nepal's jurisdiction, retaining a feudal and almost independent way of life largely unchanged for centuries. Landing on the edge of the white-walled city close to the Tibetan border, and at an altitude of 13,500ft, I was struck by the barren quality of the countryside that surrounded it. Yet the fields of the Loba people yield barley and millet in the spring, and the surrounding hills provide summer grazing. Within the city itself there were few amenities and no sign that the west had touched it. I saw not a scrap of paper anywhere, but there appeared to be calm, happiness and bustle. The eight hundred inhabitants were dressed mostly in traditional red Tibetean *chubas*, monks and monasteries abounded, the children stared and smiled and the Tibetan mastiffs looked particularly fierce. Having flown fairly rapidly from 3,000 to 13,500ft without the benefit of oxygen or pressurisation, I found at first I was having difficulty in walking, my leaden legs moving very slowly. But I soon recovered.

This unique society is now facing the dilemma of intrusion. Sensibly, the Nepalese authorities continue to control access, but the poverty of the people demands change. The lure of an untouched culture will prove irresistible to tourism, and the fragile ecology must bend as the Loba people seek to improve the quality of their lives. Whether this delicate society will survive such pressure remains to be seen. But its remoteness and beauty provided a memorable visit, and I was glad to have briefly seen it and its noble Loba people before change arrives.

Finally, of course, there is the fabled city of Kathmandu. I had paid my first visit to the capital in 1961 on that initial early walk through western Nepal. Subsequently, I had passed through on many occasions, but I had never loitered there very long. I had witnessed, at a distance, the somewhat bizarre invasion of hippies and the drug-ridden 'Freak Street' they established in the swinging 1960s. But usually I was simply on my way elsewhere in Nepal to trek or attend regimental reunions in the west of the country. Sometimes, particularly when having senior responsibilities for the Gurkha soldier, I would call on the British Defence Attaché, who also commanded the British Gurkha organization in Nepal. As the Brigade's Major General I would also often stay with the British Ambassador to discuss Gurkha affairs and be briefed on the latest political developments. I would then personally give an annual verbal report on British Gurkhas to the Prime Minister.

Otherwise I always seemed to be in transit and unable to fully appreciate the extraordinary variety of this unique city.

But when there I would wander around the three original cities that together make up the Kathmandu. I would take in the temples and shrines and sample something of its amazing history: 'More temples than houses, more idols than people!' Like all tourists, I would enjoy the city's medieval streets and bazaars, its Durbar squares, the old Rana palaces and the complex mosaic of its shrines. Everywhere there are heritage sites. I would admire the artistry and craftsmanship of the Newar people, the original inhabitants of Kathmandu, who created their unique style of pagoda architecture, and examine the skill of their intricate wood carvings which feature on so many of Kathmandu's buildings. At the same time, I would despair of the chaos at the international airport, the gridlock on the streets, the tangle of electricity wires that stretch above you, the dust and pollution and the burgeoning population. That population now includes many of the latest generation of Gurkha pensioners who have left the hills for the perceived benefits of city living and want to talk to you about yesterday and generously entertain one of their old officers.

A particular historical curiosity that always enthralled me in Kathmandu was a site that recalled some of the varied reasons that had brought the English, and others, to Nepal. It was the British Cemetery, lying almost hidden down a small side street close to our Embassy. Here the graves of a hundred people collectively present a picture of expatriate life in Nepal that stretches back over two hundred years. Here a gravestone announces: 'Robert Stuart, Esq, Assistant to the first British Resident at the court of the Raja of Nipaul, who died at this Capital on 14th of March, 1820'. Another Assistant Resident, Hastings Young, is recorded as dying at twenty years of age in 1840, so this appointment was clearly not without its dangers. Here is John Moore, who died in post as 'Band Master to H.H. the Maharajah' in 1876. Many young infants' graves illustrate the hazards of childbirth and local diseases in the nineteenth century. Here are mountaineers who fell in tragic circumstances or succumbed to altitude sickness. There are soldiers and surgeons and waiters and barmen and air crash victims and people whose history is unknown, save that they fetched up and died in this most singular of cities. Maria Richardson was the wife of Brigadier Gordon Richardson, who had commanded my Regiment at the Battle of

Monte Cassino. She was killed by a landslide and lies here, as do two men that I had met.

First there was Boris Lissanevitch, an unlikely name to find a place on a gravestone in a British cemetery. I had very briefly met Boris when I arrived in Kathmandu, footsore and weary after walking there from Paklihawa in 1961. At that time Kathmandu had a certain serenity and calm, with few cars and a general sense of order that over the years it has increasingly lost. After many days travelling over high hill and dale, I wanted to spend a day or two in the capital to clean up and recover before trying to catch a lumbering DC3 aircraft back to the Terai and my duties in Paklihawa. There was one hotel of any standing in the city and that was the Royal; it was housed in a grand old Rana Palace and had been founded by Boris

Boris had become an institution in Kathmandu. He sprang from a wealthy Tsarist family amid the hardships of the Russian revolution and had become a celebrated dancer with Diaghilev's Ballet Russe, before finding himself in Calcutta during the Raj. Here he started an exclusive night club – Club 300 – where he met King Tribhuvan and participated in the scheming that restored the monarchy to power. He moved to Kathmandu in 1951 and opened the Royal Hotel – the first hotel of any distinction in Kathmandu. Here, and knowing nothing of his background, I had a brief conversation with him in the capacious bar. He was much in demand to organize State banquets for the King, including that for the visit of Queen Elizabeth and the Duke of Edinburgh in 1961, and later he ran other hotels and restaurants in Kathmandu. He died in 1985 and near his grave are those of his two grandmothers and his Danish wife, who all died in Kathmandu. Today the old Royal Hotel houses Nepal's Electoral Commission and has, I fear, lost its former glory.

Secondly there was Jim Edwards, cavalier and buccaneer, who built on the work of Jimmy Roberts, expanded Mountain Travel, developed Tiger Tops and along with Jimmy was the founder of commercial tourism in Nepal. He was always generous to the Gurkha Brigade, and many a happy day did I have with him. He was full of wise advice.

'Peter', he would say, apropos of nothing, 'bad swimmers make the best boatmen!'

He died in 2009.

THE NEPAL WAR

By 1814, sixty years on from Prithwi Narayan's bloody arrival in Kathmandu and nearly forty years after his death, Gorkha power in Nepal was at its zenith. Under the effective rule of the Prime Minister, the Gorkha noble Bhim Sen Thapa, its aggressive army had, with some brutality, spread its authority east and west beyond the kingdom's original, ill-defined boundaries, even occupying lands that lay within the purview of the East India Company. To the north-east the Gorkha army occupied Sikkim, and in the west, the provinces of Garhwal, Kumaon and Sirmoor, voraciously imposing taxes as it went. There had even been an unsuccessful foray into Tibet, but the Chinese saw them off. Attempting to spread further west, the Gorkhas' ambitious advance was halted in the Punjab. There, at the battle of Kangra in 1809, amidst much suffering, the Gorkhas had met their match in the numerically superior forces of the one-eyed Sikh leader, Ranjit Singh. Impressed by their martial skills, however, Ranjit Singh subsequently enticed some of the Gorkha hillmen into his own army.

Hemmed in by the Sikhs in the west and by the Himalayas and China to the north-east, the aggressive Bhim Sen turned his attention to the Indian plains to the south – territory under the protection of the East India Company. Customs posts were seized and policemen killed. After a succession of skirmishes and attempts at a diplomatic démarche, there was a general collision of interests. The Gorkhas had become dangerous neighbours, and in the wake of an ignored ultimatum, the patience of the East India Company, who had long monitored the incursions and activities of the Nepalese, was exhausted. On 1 November 1814 the Company declared war on Nepal.

The armies of the Company's three Presidencies had grown from the seed corn provided by the doorkeepers and watchmen who had first guarded its factories in Calcutta, Bombay and Madras in the seventeenth and eighteenth centuries. In due course these three expanded armies were to include both Native Indian Regiments and British Regiments of the Line and Artillery. The Bengal Army also maintained irregular battalions with local security responsibilities, less formal drills and fewer British officers. Prior to the

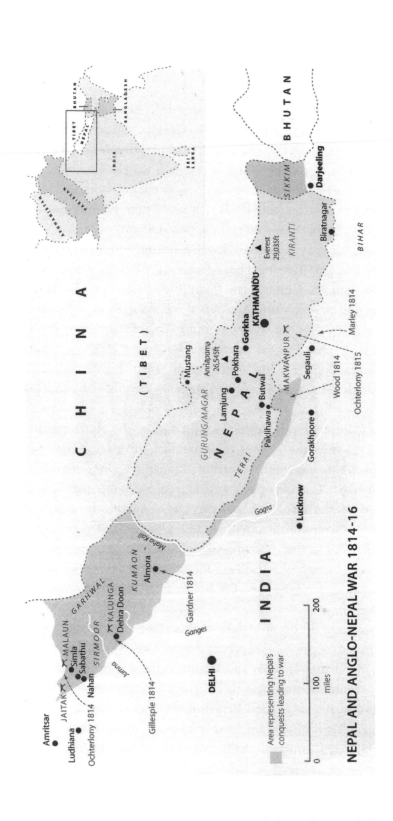

NEPAL AND ANGLO-NEPAL WAR 1814-16

rebellion of 1857, the Bengal Army largely recruited high-caste Brahmins and Rajputs from Bihar and Oudh and was the most experienced and largest of the Company armies.

In recounting this part of the Gorkha story, three important servants of the East India Company should be briefly introduced, for they were all to play an important role in eventually enlisting Gorkha soldiers into the Bengal Army.

David Ochterlony, born in Boston, Massachusetts but of Scottish ancestry, was commissioned into the Bengal Native Infantry in 1777 at the age of seventeen. By the outbreak of the Nepal wars he was an experienced and canny commander and diplomat, albeit with a somewhat chequered career behind him. Briefly serving as Resident of Delhi, he had somewhat eccentrically embraced Mughal culture. *Nautch* girls and *hookahs* were his style, and he was reputed to have thirteen Indian wives, every evening taking them all on a promenade around the walls of the Red Fort, each on the back of her own elephant. But he was familiar with the northern hills that were now part of the Gurkha land grab; he had also become acquainted with his eventual adversary, the Gorkha General, Amar Singh Thapa. His initial impression of Amar Singh's soldiery was not favourable. He regarded them as ill-disciplined and poorly armed but he later recognized that they were 'a brave and hardy people'. Some of Amar Singh's men were Gorkhas from the Nepal hills, but many others were drawn from Kumaon and Garwhal, lands his army had occupied. These were considered lesser men when compared to those from the middle hills of Nepal.

Closely allied with Ochterlony was his friend, William Fraser, a talented and adventurous Bengal civil servant and political agent. He, too, was familiar with the northern hills, having been an Assistant Resident at Delhi, where he had formed a friendship with Ochterlony. Fraser was an opinionated extrovert, a brilliant scholar, imaginative and vigorous, a soldier manqué, and like Ochterlony, greatly influenced by Mughal culture. He adopted local dress and customs and, also like Ochterlony, possessed several local wives with whom, it was reputed, he had fathered 'as many children as the King of Persia'. Fortuitously, he commissioned from Mughal painters in Delhi an extravagant and valuable collection of watercolours of colourful Indians of the time, now known as the Fraser Album. This collection included pictures of the soldiers of the Gorkha Army now in the possession of the British

Gurkha Museum (*see* plate section). As an aside, his brother James was a gifted artist and produced a number of distinguished aquatints of India and Nepal. During the Nepal wars William greatly admired the courage and endurance of the Gorkhas, and both he and Ochterlony proposed that the Company assemble several thousand Gorkha prisoners and deserters into an irregular force. During the war some of these irregulars were given to Frederick Young to command, albeit with mixed results, but after the war some of the better irregulars were to serve on a more established basis.

Frederick Young hailed from Donegal and was well known to both Ochterlony and Fraser. At the age of fifteen he had won a cadetship in the Honourable East India Company. At interview he was apparently asked whether he was ready to die for King and Country. Having replied in the affirmative, Young was told, 'That will do.' Would that I could have joined the 2nd Goorkhas quite so easily! He arrived in India in 1800, was posted to a Native Infantry Battalion and was to remain in India without a break for 44 years. He saw early service in the Mahratta Wars and had taken part in a three-year expedition to Java, where he was appointed ADC to another Irishman, the wild and colourful General Rollo Gillespie. Subsequently he was to accompany the General as a staff officer on his ill-fated journey to Nepal and to command one of the first groups of irregulars raised by Fraser.

To campaign against the Gorkhas the Company assembled a formidable force from the Bengal Army and divided it into four separate columns. In total it consisted of 30,000 regular troops, 60 guns and 12,000 auxiliaries. Logistical support included 1,100 elephants and 3,600 camels, and thousands of camp followers swelled the numbers yet further. The wonder was not that these columns moved slowly in the rough and hilly country, but that they were able to move at all, for the Bengal Army was more used to operating on the plains than in the hills.

The British force was opposed by a Gorkha army of only some 12,000 men. But the Gorkhas knew the country and proved adept at building stockades and forts that dominated the passes into their country, around which they moved with great alacrity. The four columns of the British force advanced simultaneously into the hills – two columns in the east and two in the west. The quality of the British Generals in command of the columns was mixed, and the Bengal Army proved largely inadequate for the challenge. The Gorkhas put up a tough fight and drove back three of the four columns. In the east, the two columns were deployed to mount a threat to the central authority in Kathmandu. Of their commanders, Major General Bennet Marley had a nervous breakdown and deserted the field, and Major General John Wood ambled indecisively. In the west, two further columns moved into the occupied territories of Garwhal and Kumaon. They were commanded respectively by the wild and impetuous General Rollo Gillespie and the skilfully determined Major General David Ochterlony. Gillespie, his column having secured Dehra Dun, was killed while personally leading a disastrous and costly assault on one of the well-built Gorkha forts at Kalunga in the hills above Dehra. This fort had contained a hardy garrison of some 650 Gorkhas, including a number of brave women. Gillespie's first costly attack had been beaten off and on the second attempt he was shot through the heart. The General died at the side of Lieutenant Frederick Young, and the assault again stalled.

Kalunga was the first major engagement of the Anglo–Nepalese war and it had all the flavour of the stiff fighting that was to come. But in the far west General Ochterlony, a decisive, audacious and energetic commander, proved himself capable of defeating the Gorkhas. By dint of hard marching he outmanoeuvred the Gorkha General, Amer Singh, gained a significant victory at the Malaun fort and eventually forced the Gorkhas to succumb and sue for terms. Ochterlony demanded the surrender of all the territories that Gorkhas had occupied. These stringent demands proved unacceptable to Bhim Sen back in Kathmandu, and so the war continued. In January 1816, Major General Ochterlony launched a new offensive campaign, this time in the east, where Generals Wood and Marley had failed. Outflanking Gorkha defensive stockades by a daring 25-hour march, Ochterlony fought a decisive battle at Makwanpur on the way to Kathmandu. The Gorkhas, fearful for the safety of their capital, surrendered, and the war was over.

In March 1816 the antagonists signed a peace treaty at Segauli, close to the Nepali border with India. After a general clause promising peace and eternal friendship, the treaty required the return to the Company of all conquered territory, including Sikkim, Garwhal and Kumaon, as well as much of the Terai, and a general withdrawal of the Gorkhas back to Nepal's original boundaries. Much later, the surrendered lands in the Terai were returned to Nepal in the aftermath of the Indian Mutiny, in appreciation of the assistance provided to the British by Nepal. Additionally, the Treaty provided for an exchange of envoys – thus a British Resident would be established in Kathmandu.

A good deal of Gurkha mythology originates in these wars, but it was clear from a variety of sources that the British recognized the fighting qualities and the general military ingenuity of their Gorkha opponents. Ochterlony, Fraser and Young were all clearly impressed. So was Ensign John Shipp, who fought at Makwanpur with the 87th Foot (the Royal Irish Fusiliers). While he regarded the Gorkhas as a cruel, barbarous and savage people, he also wrote in his much-quoted memoirs:

> Those we were dealing with were no flinchers; but on the contrary, I never saw more steadiness or bravery exhibited by any set of men in my life. Run they would not; of death they seemed to have no fear, though comrades were falling thick around them, for we were so near that every shot told.

Of course, it is sometimes the case that those recording their own military exploits tend to exaggerate the strength of their adversaries. Nonetheless, Shipp's views seem to match those of many other participants in the campaign, so that at least his general thrust should be accepted.

It was soon recognized that the irregular forces that had been raised with mixed success throughout the war now needed to be put on a more formal footing. Some of these early irregulars were hill Gurkhas from the Magar and Gurung tribes, many of them were worthwhile prisoners of war, others were deserters, Kumaon and Garwhal hillmen, and there was a good deal of riff-raff. The Governor General, under pressure from Ochterlony and Fraser, was persuaded that some of these men should be formed into three battalions; one of these would be the Sirmoor Battalion and it would be commanded by Frederick Young.

'Give me the authority', Young wrote to Ochterlony, 'to release our prisoners and tell them they are free men. I undertake to raise a body of soldiers that will not disgrace you, or the country, or myself.'

It was agreed.

THE SIRMOOR BATTALION

The competence and loyalty of the Gorkhas were quickly established, and in 1815 three Gurkha units were formed. These included the Sirmoor

Battalion, soon to be based at Dehra Dun. Six months later, Frederick Young reported that his Battalion was fit for active service. He wrote further that although the Gurkhas were Hindus they were not fastidious; they were loyally attached to British service, to which they looked for protection; in their cantonments they were orderly and well behaved, and on active service vigilant and bold. These are characteristics of the Gurkha soldier that would certainly be recognized two hundred years later.

Frederick Young was to command his irregular unit of the Bengal Army, the Sirmoor Battalion of Goorkhas, for twenty-eight years, building them into a formidable and disciplined force. He led them to win their spurs in a major engagement at Koonja in 1824, when after a forced march of 36 miles in 12 hours the Battalion overcame a superior force of *dacoits*, well-armed terrorists, to win the day. Later, the Battalion was to earn its first Battle Honour at the successful siege of Bhurtpore in 1826, and further honours followed, particularly during the Sikh wars at the battles of Aliwal and Sobraon in the 1840s, where the Goorkhas' service was much commended. The Battalion had begun to make a name for itself, campaigning with versatility not only in the hills but also on the plains.

In addition to his role as Commandant, Frederick Young developed Dehra Dun as a cantonment for his Sirmoor Battalion, building it into something of a paradise in the shadow of the magnificent Mussoorie hills. His Regiment was to be based there for over 130 years until Independence and Partition, forever sallying forth on various campaigns, and over the years additional land around the cantonment was either purchased or granted to the Regiment. Aside from soldiering, Young possessed a considerable hinterland. He was the first person to grow tea and potatoes in the Himalayas and he also imported from England a pack of hounds that he formed into a regimental hunt, which he led regularly around Dehra. In addition to commanding his Battalion, he was the Magistrate, Collector and Surveyor of Dehra Dun. Not least, he married a Colonel Bird's daughter and sired eight children. So his time in Dehra Dun was far from idle, and his Goorkhas prospered.

Chapter 4

Delhi and a Rite of Passage

Rumour is fleet of foot and swift on her wings.
—Virgil

THE SOFT BEAT OF AN OMINOUS DRUM

Together with the Indian historian Squadron Leader Rana Chinna, who knows more about the Indian Mutiny than most, I trekked up the path that leads to the hog's back Ridge above Old Delhi which runs along the north-western outskirts of the city far from the grandeur of Lutyens' New Delhi. We were following the route that Charles Reid and the Goorkhas of his Sirmoor Battalion had taken in 1857, on their way to face the mutineers of the East India Company's Bengal Army who had invested Delhi so strongly. It was the Regiment's performance on the Ridge that was to firmly establish the Gurkhas' reputation for fighting fidelity. It was to set the seal on their pride of place in the forefront of a new Indian Army – a force that was to rise phoenix-like from the ashes of the East India Company's old and discredited Bengal Army.

My arrival in the Regiment had awakened me to the important place that 'Delhi' held in the history of the 2nd Goorkhas. It was also symbolic of the whole future of the Gurkha soldier's service in the armies of India and Britain. I now wanted to see at first hand where my Regiment had earned its most famous Battle Honour and to piece together what happened there in a year when the East India Company faced its greatest challenge; how a once proud Bengal Army rebelled against its British officers, and the Company's hold on much of India lay in the balance.

The Mutiny was the 2nd Goorkhas' (then the 'Sirmoor Battalion') rite of passage, a major test of its character and its loyalty to the Crown and a chance to demonstrate more widely its military credentials. I read and absorbed Major Charles Reid's diaries and letters, in which he recorded, largely as it happened, the formidable service the Sirmoor Battalion that he commanded had rendered to the British and the debt owed to 'Reid's Goorkhas' for their resolute defence of the Ridge.

The Ridge walk today is well trodden and somewhat nondescript, given the historic events that once engaged it. Many of the buildings of Reid's time on this commanding position have gone. While still somewhat free of urban development, the Ridge is now heavily overgrown and sadly littered with rubbish. As we walked up in the early hours of the morning, elderly joggers earnestly covered the ground in front of us, clapping their hands as they did so, presumably to improve some sluggish circulation. Monkeys fed on the sides of the broad track that follows the line of the Ridge. A vast tangle of jungle now covers the ground between the Ridge itself and what little remains of the walls and gates of Shahjahanabad – Old Delhi.

Pausing on our walk, I considered with Rana Chinna what had led to the catastrophic Mutiny. What was the genesis of the sedition that had long simmered, largely undetected and unacknowledged, among the Army's so-called native ranks? What were the mutineers' motives, incomprehensible to the East India Company officials and the British officers of its Bengal Army? Certainly, regimental officers had huge difficulty in accepting that the men with whom they had served for so many years, in whose loyalty they had the utmost confidence and in whom they were so proud, could possibly prove themselves unworthy of that confidence.

It was a hundred years since Robert Clive's victory at Plassey in 1757 over the Nawab of Bengal, his French allies and the State ruler's armed forces. This had allowed the Company to take control of this huge part of the Indian sub-continent and extend their interests further. In the century since Plassey there had been several mutinies of varying gravity. Mostly the causes had been disputes or grievances over the Army's complex system of pay and allowances; the authorities were often insensitive to these matters, yet the soldiers of the Bengal Army were essentially mercenaries. They had a loyalty to the colours of their regiment inculcated by their officers, but loyalty to King and Country was a European concept about which the sepoys of the Bengal Army knew little. Such mutinies were in part an extension of pay bargaining. Commanders who trampled lightly over the sepoy's perceived monetary grievances, or took him for granted, did so at their peril. More often than not such grievances were locally resolved, albeit with often ruthless punishment.

In 1806 the Company's accelerated expansion brought about by direct annexations or alliances with local rulers, coupled with its Army's reputation for military excellence, had brought its position in India to an historic high point, and the utter fidelity of its soldiers was taken for granted. There then came a particularly savage mutiny at Vellore in Madras, the first large-scale rebellion by its sepoys against the Company. With hindsight, it is perhaps to that moment that historians could trace the soft beat of an ominous drum that was to summon up the terrible Mutiny some fifty years later. A thoughtless order designed to make the soldiers look more English prohibited the wearing of caste marks in uniform. Proposed alterations to the pattern of the turban and other changes to the dress code offended religious sensibilities and created strong resentment among the Company's Hindu and Muslim soldiers. Together with some political subversion, these measures set off a conflagration that had been smouldering for some time. In what was clearly a planned uprising, native troops of the Madras Army garrisoning Vellore fell upon the British garrison troops at the city's fort and killed fourteen British officers and 115 other ranks before order was restored.

Leading that restoration was the energetic bully, Colonel Rollo Gillespie of 19th Light Dragoons, at the head of a detachment of his regiment; the same officer was later to fall during the Nepal wars, when his reckless impetuosity led to his untimely death. At Vellore eight years earlier he delivered harsh, deliberate and vengeful retribution: 350 mutineers were killed when the fort was retaken; after trial, nineteen more were executed, five were transported and three regiments were disbanded. Too late, the orders that had led to the outbreak were rescinded. But a growing insensitivity to Indian religious and cultural practices was to be a factor in the far wider and more serious conflagration of 1857.

In 1824 there had been a further and equally worrying incident at Barrackpore, a large military cantonment on the outskirts of Calcutta. This was an event that once again demonstrated apparent British insensitivity to the religious sentiment of their sepoys. Several regiments of the Bengal Native Infantry had concerns about orders to travel overseas by ship to the port of Chittagong and thence to Burma. Such a journey was across the 'black sea' against the code of their caste. After remonstrations they were instead ordered to march, but then there arose more grievances about a lack of transport for personal effects, and the regiments refused to set off. Attempts to resolve the dispute failed, the regiments were ordered to lay down their arms, and when this order, too, was refused, they were surrounded by loyal regiments and two battalions of British infantry. After a final ultimatum the mutineers' camp was attacked and around 180 sepoys were killed. Most of the remaining mutineers were captured, and eleven ringleaders were hanged. Not surprisingly, there was widespread criticism of the manner in which the mutiny had been handled and of its costly repression. Barrackpore was to enter the growing archive of incidents that led directly to the uprising in 1857.

Equally profoundly, and particularly in the Bengal Army, it was clear that confidence in the invincibility of the Company's armies was on the wane. There had been dismay stemming from some poor military performances during the Nepal wars and the calamitous outcome of the First Afghan war. With the growing centralization of Army administration, the power of commanding officers had been reduced and with it their discretion to deal with grievances on the spot. Generally, the whole machine had grown stiff and impersonal, and some of the best officers had been creamed off from their regiments for political service. There was less tolerance of Indian ways, a creeping influence of Christianity. The original Company dogma that there should be no interference in religion was being ignored, as evangelical missionaries openly preached in markets and bazaars. Commanders were often too old, in a system which rewarded length of service over military competence. Officers were losing contact with the soldiers they led, and the system had in parts become complacent and stodgy. An arrogance bred of power began to beset the Company, an overweening sense of hubris destined to meet its nemesis.

In 1849 the Commander-in-Chief in India, General Sir Charles Napier, a great and discerning general as well as a firebrand of extravagant rhetoric, had investigated morale in the Bengal Army, particularly those serving in the newly annexed Punjab. He concluded that several regiments might mutiny and decided, using his own discretion, to restore in newly conquered provinces certain allowances, the loss of which had provoked discontent. Subsequently, the Governor General, Lord Dalhousie, took exception both to Napier's statement on mutiny and the trespassing on his financial prerogative. Following an acrimonious public row, Napier, the most talented general officer in India, resigned. His loss was widely regretted, and his prediction of approaching danger was to prove all too prescient.

Other signs and portents that all was not well abounded, but rumour and warnings were brushed aside. After over a hundred years of fidelity, surely there was ample reason for confidence in the Company's armies? But below a veneer of peace and calm lurked dangerous fault lines that were to lead to terrible and savage events.

More perceptive officials such as Napier and the proconsul Sir Henry Lawrence knew that something was wrong, even if the specific causes could not be identified. British rule, with its immense weight, alien religion, racial arrogance and meddling missionaries, had become increasingly unpopular. Some former rulers of princely states had longstanding grudges against the Company. In the cantonments and bazaars, in regimental lines and grog shops, rumour followed rumour. Across Bengal mysterious night runners were delivering *chapattis* to military cantonments and elsewhere, with instructions to bake five more and pass them on in pyramid fashion to further stations. Whatever this phenomenon meant, it seemed symbolic of a gathering storm and fed a growing sense of unease.

Mysterious fires were also appearing, sparked by fiery arrows shot into the thatch of officers' bungalows. At the end of 1856 in the Calcutta money markets, like all exchanges the first place to pick up vibrations of trouble, the Adjutant of the 44th Native Infantry noticed that all his Indian officers were cashing in their company bonds in favour of gold *mohurs*. Enquiries amongst the officers produced evasive answers. If anything was discovered it was lost in the general swirl of events, the wild rumours and perceived attacks on religion and caste, twisted news spreading like a virus through much of Northern India.

There was a final catalyst, a last contrived excuse perhaps, for the explosion that was about to occur, and one which would enter the public mind as the major cause of rebellion. It was the issue of cartridges for the new Enfield rifle. The smooth bore musket known as the Brown Bess was still the standard weapon of the British Army, but its range was short, its loading cumbersome, and the rifle was more efficient. But it was a slow business to reload a muzzle-loading rifle. First the charge of powder had to be rammed in; then, since the bullet must fit the rifling snugly, it had to be tapped in with a mallet. Until someone could come up with a quicker way of loading, the musket was preferable for close order battle and had remained the preferred weapon.

Now the whole Army in India was to be re-armed with the new Enfield rifle – it was still a muzzle-loader but its loading procedure was quicker, its range longer and its accuracy greater. There was a cartridge made up of powder only and a separate bullet, greased so that it could more easily be forced down the barrel. This was wrapped in a piece of cloth smeared with a lubricant which helped the loader ram the cartridge home. The end of the cartridge away from the bullet had to be broken immediately before loading to enable the charge to ignite. The standard drill was to do this with the teeth. In England the cartridge was greased with tallow and there was no doubt – in spite of reservations in some quarters as to its wisdom – that the tallow used on the new cartridges contained the fat of cows or, probably, of pigs. This was obviously offensive to the religious susceptibilities of both Hindus and Muslims. In spite of new orders allowing battalions to make their own arrangements for the lubrication of cartridges, rumours had already begun to fly. A toxic atmosphere started to spread amongst the units of the Bengal Army, and rumours surrounding the new cartridges certainly reached the Sirmoor Battalion of Goorkhas in its lines at Dehra Dun.

A small group from the Battalion, an advance party of instructors, had been sent on detachment along with similar parties from many Company and Queen's regiments to the musketry school at Ambala for training on the new rifle. Dislike of handling the new greased cartridges was openly expressed there, and the Goorkhas, becoming aware of some mutinous and insubordinate talk, requested that they be allowed to pitch their camp alongside British units. On return to Dehra Dun they reported back what they had picked up to their Commandant, Major Charles Reid. They themselves had no problems in handling the new cartridges.

REBELLION AND MUTINY

Once again in the cantonment town of Barrackpore on the outskirts of Calcutta there was a challenge to the Army's authority. On the morning of 29 March 1857, Mangal Pandy of 34th Native infantry Regiment – his name was quickly adopted by the British soldiery as their nickname for all mutineers – ran amok while high on drugs. Shouting mutinous oaths, he fired at the British Regimental Sergeant Major and the Adjutant. Both grappled with him, as the twenty sepoys at the Quarter Guard stood by seemingly unconcerned. An order to the Guard to seize Pandy was ignored. On 6 April Mangal Pandy was court-martialled and two days later was hanged in front of the formed ranks of the whole garrison. A week later, Issuri Pandy, the commander of the Quarter Guard, was also hanged.

Disaffection now spread. It burst into flame in the Divisional barracks of Meerut, close to Delhi. Orders to handle the greased cartridges were disobeyed, and courts martial ensued. Those found guilty were paraded in front of the whole garrison, which included two well-armed Queen's regiments, 60th Rifles and 6th Dragoon Guards, on the flanks and unarmed Indian regiments in the centre. Sentences ranging from ten years hard labour to life in remote penal camps were announced. The prisoners were shackled and marched away, but an ominous restlessness remained on the parade ground. On the night of Sunday, 10 May the town erupted into violence. The 3rd Cavalry broke into the gaol and released the prisoners, Europeans were slaughtered, fire and murder spread as the town fell into the hands of the mutineers. Only the news of the approach of the British 60th Rifles to take back control of the city gave the mutineers pause, and then as one they beat a path to Delhi, some 40 miles to the south-west. The local commanders lamentably failed to order an immediate pursuit to save the city, when some bold and energetic cavalrymen might possibly have saved the day. The British had been caught off balance, and their initial response was neither speedy, aggressive nor effective.

The significance of the walled city of Delhi as a rallying point for the mutineers was clear enough. For 300 years it had been the fortress of the Mughal Emperors, and it was here within his gilded palace inside the Red Fort – itself contained within the walls Delhi – that the last of them, Bahadur Shah Zafar, King of Delhi, sat reading and writing poetry. He was now a pensioner of the British, a direct descendant of Ghengis Khan but a white-haired and bearded 82-year-old impotent royal sage, who had seen his dynastic position humiliatingly eroded by the expanding British and their armies. His power now extended no further than the gates of his palace. But if the Mughals had lost power, their name still carried great prestige. Etched on the entrance to the audience chamber of his palace built by an earlier predecessor, Shah Jehan, were the now somewhat ironic lines of the famous thirteenth century Delhi poet, Amir Khusrav: 'If there be a paradise on earth it is here, it is here, it is here.'

It was to Delhi that the mutineers headed, led by the Bengal Cavalry unit, 3rd Dragoons from Meerut, galloping across the bridge of boats that spanned the River Jumna, entering the city and pleading with the Mughal King to lead the rebellion – a leadership that he eventually and reluctantly gave. Well might he write his couplet:

> The Englishmen who conquered Persia and defeated the Tsar of Russia have been overthrown in India by a simple cartridge.

The looting and killing now began; the small British garrison was slaughtered, and before long a ravaged city had fallen to the mutineers. Throughout the coming days and weeks numerous mutinous regiments were to march into Delhi to swell the numbers. They came with their colours flying and their bands playing British airs. A 'devil's wind' had blown, and with few exceptions the whole of the once great Bengal Army had been taken by it. With the reluctant blessing of the last Mughal, and in due course under the elected military leadership of a Subedar of Artillery, the self-styled General Bakht Khan, a battle-hardened veteran of the Afghan war with forty years of British service, the force at its height was to reach well over 30,000 armed and trained sepoys. At their disposal, despite the gallant destruction of the main magazine by its British officers, were vast quantities of guns, muskets and ammunition.

CHARLES REID'S SIRMOOR BATTALION

Three days after the outbreak of rebellion at Meerut on 14 May 1857, a tired and exhausted Indian cavalry trooper pushed his horse through the bazaars of Dehra Dun and made his way to the lines of the Sirmoor Battalion. He brought dramatic news and orders for Major Charles Reid, the Commandant: he was to march his regiment of Goorkhas immediately to Meerut, 100 miles to the south. There was no time to wait for carriages to convey tents and baggage. The Battalion would have to move on light scales with just what the soldiers could carry on their backs, together with sixty rounds of ammunition in pouches. Two elephant-loads of spare ammunition would bring up the rear. The Sirmoor Battalion's response to the rebellion of the Bengal Army, its military rite of passage, had begun. Its involvement in this most terrible of all imperial wars was to prove decisive for the Battalion, the British and their mutinous adversaries.

Major Charles Reid was an outstanding and experienced officer in every way, courageous, shrewd, competent, tough and resilient, and much liked and respected by his Goorkha soldiers. He had entered East India Company's service as a 16-year-old Ensign in 1835 and was initially posted to the Bengal Army's 10th Battalion of Native Infantry (interestingly, named *Duffel ka paltan* – Duffel's Regiment) before joining the Sirmoor Battalion in 1840. He had given distinguished service with his Goorkhas at the battles of Aliwal and Sobraon during the Sikh wars, during which he suffered the sobering experience of having his horse shot from under him on two separate occasions. He was twice mentioned in despatches and had taken command of the Battalion at Sobraon when Captain Fisher leading the Battalion was killed. He had been selected to command the escort to Dost Mahomed, the exiled King of Kabul, when he was detained in Mussoorie during the First Afghan War. He was called back for attachment with his 10th Native Battalion for the Burma war in 1852, during which he was given brevet promotion. He was thus a tested and experienced operational commander. But never before had his qualities of leadership, courage and toughness, together with those of his men, been as sorely tested as they were to be in the months ahead.

From the moment that he received orders, Charles Reid kept a detailed diary chronicling the events of the Battalion's advance to Meerut and its subsequent battles on the Ridge at Delhi. This diary, together with certain letters he wrote about the campaign, gives a clear account and insight into the significant part his Sirmoor Battalion and its Goorkhas played in suppressing the Mutiny and the eventual defeat of the rebels. Privately published a century later by the Regiment, the diary still reads as freshly today as when it was written. Even allowing for possible hyperbole in the recording of events, it is now widely regarded as an accurate description of the Siege of Delhi and vouched for by others. It is much quoted in the many accounts of the Mutiny.

Rereading Reid's diary, I continue to be deeply shocked at the sheer level of violence perpetrated by both sides in this terrible and iniquitous conflict. But it also engenders much admiration for the courage of Reid and his Goorkhas in the most demanding of circumstances. The Sirmoor Battalion was the first Native Regiment into the field and the first to pull a trigger against the mutineers. Reid himself was a calm, brave and decisive leader and throughout the campaign showed a ruthless determination in dealing with the mutineers and others taking advantage of an increasingly chaotic situation. Given that the account was written on a daily basis, and between gaps in almost constant fighting, his diary entries demonstrate a remarkable insouciance and calm. In the face of the continual stresses and strains of close-quarter battle and the incessant artillery bombardment that was to dominate his life and those of his Goorkhas, Reid kept his diary for the next three months. It begins with the arrival of the message from Meerut:

> About noon on 14 May I received an express from Head-Quarters, directing me to march with my Regiment, to Meerut, to aid the Europeans at that station in supressing the mutiny of the native troops. Four hours after receipt of the Commander in Chief's order the Regiment was on the move.

Not surprisingly, given the rumours of disaffection within the Army, the issue of the cartridges and the prevailing 'devil's wind', these orders did not come as a complete surprise to Reid. He had already laid on contingency plans for a possible move to Meerut with the Engineer Commander at Roorkee, the formidable Sapper, Richard Baird Smith. It was Baird Smith who was later to provide the technical genius for the Engineers' critical role in the final storming of Delhi. Reid had arranged to have fifty boats ready at Roorkee to move the Battalion on the recently completed Ganges Canal more speedily to Meerut. But before reaching Roorkee he heard of possible mutiny amongst some Engineers. Reaching the outskirts of the town he saw several sappers moving back and forth among his men and observed some insolence and a note of defiance among them. He asked a couple of his men what the sappers had said to them, and the Goorkhas replied that the sappers had wanted to dissuade them from going to Meerut; one of the Goorkhas had replied that the Regiment was going wherever ordered and that they 'obeyed the bugle call'!

On 24 May, having made good progress in his fleet of boats in the searing heat, Reid landed his Regiment at one of the canal stations opposite Boolundshur. He had orders from General Hewett commanding the Meerut Division to try to save the treasure of which a company of 9th Native Infantry had charge. He discovered that the treasure was gone, the company having walked off with it to Delhi. Several cryptic entries in the diary give a sense of the Battalion's progress and challenges:

> May 24. About an hour after my arrival my picquets reported that a body of cavalry was advancing. They turned out to be 400 of the Rampoor Horse. I saw at once by the look of these gentlemen that they were rather shaky.
>
> May 28. The Rampoor Horse not to be trusted. I'm watching them. My Goorkhas in high spirits and ready for action.
>
> May 29. The Rampoor Horse mutinied last evening. Have sent them to the right about. I was just about to attack them in their camp when I was informed, they had taken to their heels; they have gone to Delhi, I imagine – a good riddance. Why were they ever sent here? A great mistake.
>
> May 30. The heat is frightful. We marched twenty-seven miles along the left bank of the canal; men dead beat, hot wind blowing all night. Bivouacked under a few thin baubul trees at 11am on 31st. Resumed march at sunset, and after marching the whole night and until 10am on 1 June I eventually reached Brigadier Wilson's camp.

Brigadier Archdale Wilson was a garrison commander at Meerut serving under General Hewitt. Later, after the departure of earlier commanders

through sickness or death, he was to command, with varying degrees of
success, the Delhi Field Force on the Ridge and through to the final capture
of the city. The Brigadier had already faced down two attacks by the mutineers
and was extremely pleased to see the Sirmoor Battalion. His whole force
turned out and cheered the Regiment into camp.

As Reid progressed towards Delhi, further skirmishing and hard
marching followed, and on 7 June the Battalion reached Alipore, some seven
miles short of Delhi. Here he met up with a force heading for the city under
the command of Major General Sir Henry Barnard:

> June 7. Marched into camp but not a cheer for us; on the contrary all
> looked upon the Goorkhas with suspicion which was very discouraging
> after what my little fellows had already done. I was not questioned
> myself but several asked my officers whether they thought the Goorkhas
> were to be trusted; when I was told this, I said, 'Time will show.'
> So suspicious was the General of the Goorkhas that he actually had a
> camp pitched for us on the extreme left of the line with the Artillery close
> to us ready to pound us if we misbehaved.

On 8 June the force left Alipore and took part in an attack against a strong
rebel position about seven miles from Delhi at Badli-ke-Serai that guarded
the approach to the Ridge. After two hours fighting the enemy were driven
from their position to the city walls, with the loss of thirteen of their guns.
The Sirmoor Battalion reached the Ridge at 1.00 p.m. and was directed to
occupy Hindoo Rao's house, the key forward position, some 1,200 yards
from the city walls.

The battle at Badli-ke-Serai gave the British control of the Great Trunk
Road and with it command of communications to the north and west, as
well as clearing the way to the Ridge. The Ridge was then an almost bare
and rocky hill feature about four miles in length running north to south,
at a distance of between half a mile and two miles from the northern walls
of the city. Between the Ridge and the walls of Old Delhi the ground was
rocky and rugged, with some steep faces and ravines and covered with scrub.
The River Jumna protected the Ridge's left flank and ran to the east of the
city's walls. The right flank was guarded by the Jumna Canal (*see* plate
section). The British encampment lay on the reverse slope of the Ridge, and

the strength of the Field Force encamped there was around 4,000 men. On the forward slope, Hindoo Rao's house was the large empty mansion of a Mahratta chief, originally built as his private house by the former Resident at Delhi, William Fraser, the same Fraser who had encouraged the enlistment of Goorkhas into British service during the Nepal wars.

What might William Fraser have thought to see the Goorkhas now occupying his old Palladian mansion on the Ridge? The house itself had been built on the site where the Mongol emperor Timur had pitched his tents during his sack of Delhi in 1398, when a single day of slaughter cost the lives of 100,000 Hindus and condemned the city to two centuries of desolation. This seemed to me to put the agonies of the Mutiny in some sort of historical perspective.

Hindoo Rao's house, the main picquet nearest to the city, was throughout the siege occupied by the Sirmoor Battalion. It became the object of almost every attack by the mutineers. Within the compass of Reid's position also came the *Sabji Mundee* – a group of buildings that served as a vegetable market, to the south and astride the Grand Trunk Road. The city itself was protected by seven miles of wall, 16–24ft high with ten massive gates and numerous gun emplacements and bastions. The walls themselves were surrounded by a ditch 25ft wide and 20ft deep and half encircled by the unfordable River Jumna. It would be a formidable task to take the city by storm and one that would need heavy artillery, which the British did not yet possess, to breach the walls. Within the city lived over 150,000 people – about half were Hindu and half Muslim.

The immediate objective of General Barnard and his modest British Field Force on the Ridge was not the capture of the city. With the men and materials at his disposal this would have been an impossibility. It was a limited occupation, hardly a siege, but a position that overlooked Delhi and from where an offensive defence and preparations for an assault could be undertaken while awaiting reinforcement. For it was clear that once the walls were breached, large numbers of troops would be required for the house-to-house fighting that would surely follow. Even though a number of young and ambitious officers were urging General Barnard to mount an early coup de main assault, he was sensibly persuaded against it. The city was the most defensible in all of India.

On reaching their position on the Ridge, the Sirmoor Battalion was soon in action, as Reid's diary records:

> June 8. Had just made ourselves comfortable when the 'alarm' was sounded. In ten minutes, the mutineers were seen coming up towards Hindoo Rao's House in force. I went out with my own Regiment, two companies of Rifles, and two guns of Scott's Battery, and drove them back into the City. This was not accomplished until 5p.m. so that we were under arms for sixteen hours. Heat fearful, my little fellows behaved splendidly, and were cheered by every European Regiment. It was the only Native Regiment with the force, and I may say every eye was upon it.

A valuable reinforcement for the Field Force arrived on 9 June in the shape of the Corps of Guides, which in the coming weeks was to share much of the fighting with Reid's Goorkhas. This Corps was composed chiefly of Sikhs and Punjabis but also possessed a 100-strong Gurkha company.

Throughout the rest of June, the Sirmoor Battalion was in the thick of the fighting, constantly under attack and suffering a steady drain of casualties. Between 8 and 23 June the Battalion losses totalled 103 killed and wounded out of a starting strength of 490. Reid recalls that on 13 June there was another attack on his position launched from the city by about 5,000 mutineers headed, curiously, by the 60th Native Infantry led by their *Sirdar Bahadur*, the senior Native officer. Reid let them come to within twenty paces of the main picquet before his Battalion and the 60th Rifles opened fire and the artillery let fly with grapeshot. Then two companies rose up and charged the rebels, who beat a rapid retreat. The *Sirdar Bahadur* was killed by Reid's orderly, Sepoy Lalsing Thapa, and Reid himself took the ribbon of the Order of British India from the *Sirdar*'s breast.

Two days later, Charles Reid's force was in action again, beating off an attack by some 6,000 rebels with severe losses, and on 17 June came a further attack, as well as orders for offensive action:

> June 17. About 3pm a 32-pounder round shot came smashing into the portico of the house which the officers occupy killing ensign Wheatly, 54th, who was doing duty with my Regiment, a Havildar, and four of my men and wounding three of my men one of whom, Ticca Ram, died in the evening. (This little fellow was one of the best shots in the regiment.

He had killed 22 tigers in the Dhoon.) Nine killed and four wounded by one round shot, and regimental colour cut in two.

One of the toughest days on the Ridge followed on 23 June, the centenary of the Battle of Plassey:

> June 23. The mutineers about 12 o'clock made a desperate attack on the whole of my position. No men could have fought better. They charged the Rifles, the Guides and my own men again and again and at one time I thought I must have lost the day. Thousands were brought against my mere handful of men, but I knew the importance of my position and was determined to do my utmost to hold it until reinforcements arrived. I drove the enemy out of Subzee-mundee no less than six different times and at length succeeded in establishing a small force in the place. We were fighting hard until sunset, when the mutineers gave it up as a bad job, they retired leaving about 800 killed and wounded on the field. The loss in my own Regiment in three weak companies, 36 killed and wounded of my little fellows.

Of this action the official history of the Mutiny records:

> The 60th Rifles went gallantly to the attack and the Gurkhas and the Guides vied with them in sturdy unflinching courage to the last.

Attacks continued on an almost daily basis throughout the rest of June and July, heightened by the arrival of the mutinous Bareilly Brigade and the formidable Subedar Bhakt Khan, who was to assume command and give the mutineers some new inspiration:

> July 10. We had another grand scrimmage yesterday; the old story, an attack on my position. The enemy were about 8,000 strong and fought desperately. We drove the enemy before us through the Jungle and down the Grand Trunk Road. My own Regiment eight killed and twenty-six wounded. The total loss in my Regiment up to this date, 173. High time I got some more men. Our spies say their loss was very great.

The ebullient Charles Reid was constantly in the front line commanding not only his Sirmoor Battalion but detachments of 60th Rifles and the Guides as well as the guns, and continually in action. Indeed, it says much for the respect in which his qualities of leadership were held that he was

continually placed in command of this mixed force. Together with his
Goorkhas he was now well known to the mutineers, who singled out his force
for attack. In the face of all this, his general sangfroid was quite remarkable,
as was his ability to ride his luck as far as personal safety was concerned.
On 15 July he was attacked again and had a lucky escape when three of his
officers were wounded and he himself was struck on the shin by a spent ball,
while a 24-pounder shaved his head:

> July 19. The Pandies made their twenty-first attack on my position
> yesterday. They swore all kinds of things on the holy waters of the Gunga
> that they would have my post and that before sunset the people in the
> city would see me – the Prince of Devils, as they call me in the green
> Turban – hung in the Chandee Chowk.

The Chandee Chowk was the main thoroughfare in the walled city and led
directly from the walls to the Lahore Gate and the Red Fort. The losses
in his Battalion had by now been so heavy that Reid was waiting anxiously
for reinforcements which he had requested from Dehra Dun. Towards the
end of July, he heard that a draft of ninety-one men was approaching, and
on 29 July the Battalion's wounded men left in a large convoy for Ambala.
The Battalion's effective strength was now down by 200 men, and there was a
new threat: cholera had spread from the city to the Ridge, and one of the first
to die was the Sirmoor Battalion's Adjutant, Lieutenant Sutherland Ross.

There was no let-up for Reid and his Sirmoor Battalion, and he was
soon in action again and once more riding his luck:

> August 1. The enemy came out in great force yesterday. Round shot,
> shell and musket balls come phit, phit, phee, phish past my old head, but
> still it is all safe on my shoulders. The escapes I have had are perfectly
> wonderful. People look at me after every engagement and say, 'What
> are you still untouched?' Thank God for thus sparing me. Hope to keep
> my old head on my shoulders for some time yet; anyhow until I have
> seen the imperial city fall. A 24-pounder shot just came through one of
> the upper rooms and killed one of my poor fellows. The poor fellow cut
> completely in two.

Spies operating within the city now reported that the rebels were planning
an overwhelming attack on the day of the Muslim festival of Eid, which

signals the end of Ramadhan fasting. On the evening of 1 August Reid's Gurkha lookouts on the top of Hindoo Rao's house reported that the whole of the city was turning out:

> August 3. The whole force, in all about 20,000 came straight at my position. I was prepared for them. At dusk the enemy brought up their guns, supported by a very large force. They were very desperate indeed. Before 12 o'clock we had driven them back half-a-dozen times, I began to think we had got rid of our friends; but shortly after the moon rose, up came fresh troops from the city bugling and shouting on all sides. This sort of thing went on the whole night, but I managed to hold my own. Thus ended the great Eed attack, being number twenty-four on my position.
>
> August 5. The mutineers had an inspection parade this morning outside the Ajmere Gate. We heard their bands playing some lively airs, such as 'Cheer, boys, cheer', 'The girls we left behind us', 'The British Grenadiers', etc. The feeling which existed between the men of the 60th Rifles and my own men was admirable; they called one another 'brothers', shared their grog with each other, and smoked their pipes together . . . they had fought side by side for so long that they became quite attached to one another. My men used to speak of them as 'our Rifles' and the men of the 60th when mentioning the Goorkhas, 'them Gurkhees of ours'. There was a good deal of rivalry. My men would never allow that they were in any way inferior to the Rifles.

At the end of the 'Eed' battle, Reid recorded that he came across a Goorkha boy squatting behind a rock with a rifle; it appeared he was a Line boy who had come down with a draft from Dehra Dun. His father had been on duty in a defensive position, and the boy was assisting in getting out his cartridges when his father was killed. The boy then went to one of the 60th riflemen and helped him to load quickly. Later in the action, he had been wounded and showed Reid four holes where a bullet had gone through the fleshy part of both thighs without doing serious injury. Reid enlisted him on the spot in spite of his being only fourteen.

The Regimental History records that of the twenty-five Goorkhas at Delhi who were awarded the Indian Order of Merit for their gallantry on the Ridge, twelve were Line boys, and Reid extolled their virtues: 'The esprit de corps shown by these Line boys throughout the Siege was wonderful.' Line boys were the sons of serving soldiers, born and brought up in Dehra

Dun and thus supposedly knowing nothing of the struggles and hardships of life in the hill villages of Nepal. Even one hundred years later, Line boys educated in Malaya or Hong Kong were regarded with suspicion by some in the Regiment as being too clever by half and not amenable to the same discipline as hillmen. I shared the views of Charles Reid on the value of these boys, with their education and some mastery of English, even if they sometimes needed more careful leadership and management than boys recruited direct from the hills. They were just as physically tough as their peers from Nepal, and a decided asset.

Further desultory attacks and some offensive actions by Reid continued throughout much of August. At the same time, he recorded in his diary that constant work and exposure to shelling in the monsoon rains that had now overtaken the heat were, not surprisingly, beginning to tell on some of his Goorkhas. Many were in hospital with a fever that had gripped the Ridge. Uniforms were in tatters, boots mildewed by the wet. Sunstroke, too, had taken its toll, and the stench of death in the breathless monsoon air pervaded the Ridge. The summer plague of flies clustered over the 'putrid corpses of dead men and animals which lay rotting and unburied in every direction'. The Ridge had become 'a steaming bog'.

On 7 August a column of reinforcements from the Punjab arrived on the Ridge under the command of the formidable and charismatic Brigadier John Nicholson – the 'Lion of the Punjab'. His presence invigorated the senior Field Force leadership which, following the death of General Barnard through cholera and the departure of two successors, was now in the hands of an exhausted Brigadier Archdale Wilson.

Imperial in appearance, arrogant in manner, ruthless in action, in many respects psychopathic in his approach to soldiering, and with the quality of mercy never entering his soul, Brigadier John Nicholson's imposing character was soon felt by the Field Force. Charles Reid was initially less impressed: 'I have never seen a man I disliked so much at first sight. His haughty manner and peculiar sneer I could not stand.' But within a week they were sitting on top of Hindoo Rao's house and surveying the battlefield together. The strength of the Field Force on the Ridge was now about 12,000, but with a large proportion laid low by disease or wounds. The forces in the city below were reliably estimated at 30,000. Nicholson was to provide the impetus to turn defence into an assault.

On the final day of August came the last of twenty-six attacks on Reid's position. Prior to the attack, a spy had brought Reid a copy of a written order from the King to the mutineers offering the same reward for every Goorkha head as for the head of an English soldier, 10 rupees. This demonstrated the high esteem in which the Goorkhas were held as adversaries. These attacks were repulsed, and now the end for the mutineers was not far off. Intelligence suggested that they were already slipping away from the city and that their morale was low.

On 10 September Nicholson and Reid had a very narrow escape when standing on the roof of Hindoo Rao's house looking out towards Delhi. While discussing the long-awaited assault on the City and Reid's role within it, a shrapnel shell burst over them. Three balls struck Reid's telescope, a Goorkha sitting at his feet lost an eye and another Goorkha to the rear was hit in the chest. Subsequently, the battered telescope found its way on to a plinth in our officers' mess, where I often used to inspect its shell-battered shape. Once again, good fortune had travelled with Charles Reid.

Preceded by a week of constant artillery bombardment, the British assault was planned for 14 September under command of Brigadier Nicholson. Using a breach made by Richard Baird Smith's Engineers at the Cashmere Gate, a simultaneous entry by three columns of troops was to be launched. Meanwhile, a fourth column under Charles Reid was to attack the Kissen Gunj suburb south of the Jammu Canal – still held in force by the mutineers. His column would then enter the city at the Kabul Gate to link up with Nicholson. A fifth column was in reserve. Reid's column was composed of 200 men of his own Sirmoor Rifles, plus detachments of the 60th Rifles, the 61st and 75th Foot, Coke's Rifles, the Kumaon Battalion of Gurkhas (later titled 3rd Gurkha Rifles) who had arrived with Nicholson, 1st Fusiliers and a battery of Royal Horse Artillery. In addition, there were the 1,600 men of the Jammoo contingent – a mixed cavalry and infantry force with four guns sent by the Maharajah of Kashmir – some 2,500 men in all. Reid had protested about the mix of units he had been given and he also had grave reservations about the untested Jammoo contingent: 'I don't much like the look of them; I only hope they will obey orders.' Reid's fears were far from groundless.

At 0400 hours Reid's fourth column formed up on the Grand Trunk Road forward of the Subzimandi picquet with the Jammoo contingent on the left and awaited the signal to advance – the blowing of the Cashmere Gate. A further worry then befell Reid – his guns had failed to arrive – but he nevertheless felt compelled to advance as planned. The courageous Engineers having breached the gate, the Sirmoor Rifles and the 60th Rifles led the way forward. As they advanced, a strong force of mutineers from Kissen Gunj and reinforced further from the city fell upon the Jammoo contingent, routing it completely. In the roar of musketry they bolted, losing their guns to the rebels in the process. In the midst of this difficult situation the gallant Charles Reid, attempting to read the confused battle by forward reconnaissance, was wounded in the head and carried from the battlefield by his Goorkha orderly, Lalsing Thapa. He ordered his second-in-command, Captain Lawrence, to take over command. In the melee the column was being forced back to the Ridge before managing to hold the line at the forward positions of the Sabjee Mundee and Hindoo Rao's house. From there it invested the Kissen Gunj and captured its guns and mortars. The remaining three columns eventually penetrated the city, albeit with some 1,200 casualties including the death of the commander, John Nicholson – a sad loss to the force.

Two days later, the enemy had retreated from the Ridge, and within a week, amid savage house-to-house fighting, much looting, murder and ill-discipline on the part of some troops, caused not least by the loss of so many senior officers, the city fell. Great stores of liquor were found by the assaulting troops, and after the deprivations of life on the Ridge and the terror of the assault, the temptations were great. By 20 September a ruined Delhi, with all its imperial prestige and symbolism, was back in British hands, and the Mutiny had been struck a mortal blow. Shah Bahadur Zafar, his sons ruthlessly murdered in an uncalled-for act of vengeance by Major William Hodson, was banished to spend his last days in Rangoon. He eventually left Delhi in a humble bullock cart escorted by the cavalry. The British had achieved their costly 'retributive justice'.

The losses in Reid's fourth column, as elsewhere, had been very severe, almost one third of the column's strength. The Sirmoor Battalion's casualties, inclusive of the final assault, had been particularly heavy. They totalled 327 all ranks out of the 490 who had entered the Siege in early June. Eight British officers out of nine had been killed or wounded. Of the other two Corps that had fought alongside the Sirmoor Battalion under Reid's command and had borne the brunt of the fighting forward of Hindoo Rao's house, the 60th Rifles' losses were 389 out of 640 men, and the Corps of Guides lost 303 out of 550.

REFLECTIONS ON THE RIDGE

When Charles Reid recovered from his wounds he revisited the Ridge. He reflected on what he saw and the service his Sirmoor Battalion had given to save the day at Delhi and allow the successful assault on the City, thus playing a significant part in bringing to an end, in due course, the tragedy that was the Indian Mutiny. He wrote after his visit:

> When I look at the ground round about Hindoo Rao's House – ploughed up with shot and shell, fragments of which still lay upon the ground although cartloads had been removed – it appeared a miracle that I stood there gazing upon the scene where I had seen my troops driving the enemy before them, and again retreating under a burning sun, a deadly fire of artillery and of musketry, and a vastly superior force I exclaimed, 'Can it be – is it possible – am I really a living being after all I have gone through?'
>
> I cannot close without expressing my heartfelt gratitude to all officers and men who served under me from first to last. Their courage and endurance, and their cheerful obedience to all orders they received, won my esteem, and I have to thank them for the high honour I have received from Her Most Gracious Majesty. Without such men I never would have held the position entrusted to me.

Having charted the fortunes of his Battalion in that terrible summer of 1857, one can only admire the resilience and fortitude of Reid and his Goorkhas as they battled the mutineers of the Bengal Army through the height of an Indian summer and the subsequent monsoon. It had been a formidable feat of arms to finally reinvest Delhi.

For today's historians, Reid's diary offers little of sentiment; in cataloguing the losses he makes no mention of where the remains of his soldiers are buried, no mention of grieving wives and families or how the news of casualties was relayed to 'next of kin', if it was relayed at all. In the hills of Nepal, perhaps, it might have been known that men were 'lost'. But within the Regiment's home at Dehra Dun there was certainly a strong sense of community, so perhaps I am misjudging events, and Gurkha widows and orphans did receive some modest welfare. I like to think that was the case.

Continuing my own walk with Rana Chinna along the line of the Ridge I could only imagine the panoramic views of the walls and gates of Shahjahanabad – Old Delhi – that would have been enjoyed by the Field Force. In Reid's day, from the roof of Hindoo Rao's house there would have been a clear picture of Delhi's ramparts across the sloping ground that led down from the Ridge. It was up this slope that the rebels launched so many of their brave but forlorn assaults on Reid's embattled position around Hindoo Rao's house. Today, vegetation and the destruction of much of the walls make it difficult to picture the scene that became so familiar to the Sirmoor Battalion and the rest of the Field Force encamped on the Ridge.

Just occasionally I caught a tantalizing glimpse of the city through the trees, and using my field glasses I could just make out the red sandstone walls of the Red Fort built by the Mughal Emperor Shah Jehan in the seventeenth century, a building second in architectural importance only to his Taj Mahal at Agra. Even Christopher Wren would have been in awe of the Mughal builders.

On the north side of the Ridge in the middle of the track still stands the well-maintained Flagstaff Tower, in which the frightened European women and children who fled from Old Delhi sheltered from the fighting before fleeing into the countryside. It is not difficult to visualize the fear that must have gripped them, confined within its bare walls. The remains of Hindoo Rao's house, once William Fraser's fine Palladian mansion with its Scottish features and overlooking his beloved Delhi, have now been incorporated into a seemingly ramshackle Indian hospital – albeit one, I am told, with a fine medical record. Auto-taxis and pedal rickshaws carrying patients and medical staff arrive and depart in profusion. Hard as I looked, I could find few signs of its former use as the main defensive picquet of the Delhi Field Force, the base for the Sirmoor Battalion.

Suitably close to Hindoo Rao's house and just before I reached the Sabjee Mundee – the vegetable market that marked the southern right-hand boundary of the British position – is the Mutiny Memorial. This is a sandstone Gothic tower erected on the Ridge in 1863 to recall the British and Indian soldiers who died fighting the rebels. Surprisingly, the original

(*Above*) Hong Kong Border Observation Post in a MacIntosh Fort manned by
2nd Goorkhas, 1979. Watercolour by Ken Howard.

(*Below*) A village in Western Nepal. Watercolour by Ken Howard.

(*Above*) The Gurkha contingent marches past Horse Guards, Whitehall in the Coronation Parade, 2 June 1953.

(*Left*) 2nd Goorkha pensioners. The author with Captain Bhagtasing Pun MM, former Japanese PoW aged 101. Bhagtasing also marched in the Coronation Parade, above. Behind are three retired 2nd Goorkha veterans. L to R: Captain Ganesh Gurung, Captain Karnabahadur Thapa and Captain Ramkaji Gurung.

(*Above left*) Colonel Jimmy Roberts, 2nd Goorkha paratroop commander in Burma, mountaineer, founder of modern tourism in Nepal and breeder of rare pheasants.

(*Above right*) Major Bhimbahadur Thapa, 2nd Goorkhas paratrooper and Company Commander during the Malayan Emergency.

(*Below left*) Lieutenant Colonel Digby Willoughby, 2nd Goorkhas, a fine soldier and romantic gallant.

(*Below right*) Major Bishnu Pun, 2nd Goorkha Rifleman and Royal Gurkha Rifles Major, Company Commander and Queen's Gurkha Orderly Officer. Son of Captain Bhagtasing Pun.

(*Left*) The hazards of travel in the hills of Nepal. A ravine bridge is navigated by a heavily laden porter.

(*Below*) The painting depicts the signing of the Treaty of Segauli in 1816 that concluded the Anglo-Nepal war.

THE TREATY OF SAGAULI
1816

(*Above left*) An early Goorkha sepoy of the Sirmoor Battalion, c. 1817.

(*Above right*) An officer of the Sirmoor Battalion, 1827.

(*Below*) The main picquet of Hindoo Rao's House on the Ridge at Delhi, 1857, with survivors of the Sirmoor Battalion, later the 2nd Goorkhas. They repulsed twenty-six separate rebel attacks on their position.

(*Left*) Major Charles Reid (later General Sir Charles Reid), who commanded the Sirmoor Battalion of Goorkhas at Delhi.

(*Below*) The battle of Kandahar, 1880. A 2nd Goorkha rifleman, Indebir Lama, captures an Afghan gun. (*From a painting by Colonel E. A. P. Hobday*)

(*Above*) Trouble on the North-West Frontier. Mahsud and Waziri tribesmen, 1930s.

(*Below*) Gurkha machine gunners on the Frontier.

(*Above left*) Following an Investiture by the Queen, three men of the Royal Gurkha Rifles proudly display their Military Crosses, awarded for gallantry in Afghanistan in 2008, in the forecourt of Buckingham Palace. L to R: Lance Corporal Bhimbahadur Gurung, Lance Corporal Mohansingh Tangnami and Lance Corporal Agnish Thapa.

(*Above right*) Lieutenant Colonel Gez Strickland, awarded the Distinguished Service Order for his leadership of a Royal Gurkha Rifles Battlegroup in Afghanistan. He is now a Major General and Colonel of his Regiment.

(*Below left*) Corporal Hari Budha Magar of the Royal Gurkha Rifles. He lost both his legs to an improvised explosive device in Afghanistan and plans to climb Everest in 2019. (*By kind permission of Corporal Hari Budha Magar*)

(*Below right*) A contemporary Gurkha of the Royal Gurkha Rifles in Afghanistan – Colour Sergeant Suman Sherpa.

(*Above*) Gurkhas in trenches on the Western Front, 1915.

(*Below*) The 1st Battalion, 6th Gurkha Rifles attack Turkish positions and reach the crest of the Sari Bair feature at the Dardanelles, 9 May 1915. Painting by Terence Cuneo. (*The Royal Gurkha Rifles*)

(*Above left*) General 'Bill' Slim, Commander of the Fourteenth Army in the Burma campaign.

(*Above right*) Havildar Bhanbhagta Gurung VC visits the 2nd Goorkhas in Hong Kong, where his three sons are all serving in his regiment. The Queen's Truncheon is beside them, held in its centrepiece.

(*Below*) Gurkha riflemen clear a Japanese trench in fighting around Imphal during the Burma campaign, 1944.

Image: © Gurkha Mus

(*Above*) General Montgomery, Commander Eighth Army, flanked by General Horrocks, examines a Gurkha rifleman's kukri in North Africa.

(*Below*) Gurkhas in action in North Africa.

Distinguished 2ⁿᵈ Goorkhas at the Battle of Wadi Akarit.
All three commanders were awarded the Distinguished Service Order and
a further sixteen 2ⁿᵈ Goorkhas were decorated for valour.

(*Above left*) King George VI in the forecourt of Buckingham Palace invests Subedar Lalbahadur Thapa of the 2ⁿᵈ Goorkhas with his Victoria Cross won at the Battle of Wadi Akarit in 1943.

(*Above middle*) Lieutenant Colonel James Showers, Commandant 1ˢᵗ Battalion.

(*Above right*) Brigadier Os Lovett, Commanding 7 Brigade.

(*Below left*) Major General Francis Tuker, Commanding 4ᵗʰ Indian Division.

(*Below right*) Major Monty Ormsby, later Commandant 1ˢᵗ Battalion, 2ⁿᵈ Goorkhas when the author joined the Regiment.

Pensiangan, North Borneo (now Sabah). The author's 'A' Company base during Confrontation.

A tough 2nd Goorkha rifleman during Confrontation – Rifleman Jamansing Gurung.

Lieutenant Colonel 'Birdie' Smith, who commanded 1st Battalion, 2nd Goorkhas after Johnny Clements. He lost an arm in a helicopter crash in Borneo and had a courageous fighting record.

(*Above*) A mobile Gurkha patrol apprehends a Chinese illegal immigrant attempting to cross the border separating Hong Kong from China, 1980s.

(*Below*) 1st Battalion 2nd Gurkha Rifles on riot control duty in Nathan Road Kowloon, Hong Kong during the Star Ferry Riots, April 1966. A foretaste of the Cultural Revolution disturbances one year later.

(*Above left*) Sir Claude Macdonald, British Minister in Peking in 1897: 'imperfectly educated, weak, flippant, garrulous, the type of officer rolled out a mile at a time and then lopped off in six-foot lengths'. Sir Claude negotiated the lease of the New Territories to Hong Kong from China for 99 years that caused much later difficulty.

(*Above right*) The author with Major General Zhou Borong of the People's Liberation Army while attending a course together at the Royal College of Defence Studies in London, 1988.

Major General Duffell, with the Governor of Hong Kong, Sir David Wilson, and Baroness Dunn, a leading Hong Kong politician, businesswomen and fellow member of the Governor's Executive Council, 1990.

A *Dai Fei*, fast speed boat used by Chinese criminal elements to smuggle luxury motorcars out of Hong Kong into China.

Strong bonds. A British Platoon Commander, Captain Connolly, and his Platoon Sergeant, Sergeant Bahadur Budha Magar, together in Afghanistan.

The earthquake of 2015 did untold damage in Nepal. A hill boy stands beside all that is left of his village home at Barpak, western Nepal. (*By kind permission of Johnny Fenn*)

A Gurkha welfare pensioner and his wife stand in front of their new house built by the Gurkha Welfare Trust to replace the home destroyed in the earthquake.

British inscriptions are still there on their eight marble plaques around the spire, with tables of statistics itemizing each unit's casualties starkly set in Gothic trefoil. They include the sad figures of the Sirmoor Battalion's losses. Below the British inscriptions is another tablet erected by the Indian authorities that reads:

> The 'enemy' of the inscriptions on this monument were those who rose against colonial rule and fought bravely for national liberation in 1857. In memory of the heroism of these immortal martyrs for Indian freedom, this plaque was unveiled on the 25th anniversary of the Nation's attainment of freedom 28th August 1972.

For reasons that I can't quite explain, the whole structure had a slightly macabre and dissonant air, and we hurriedly pushed on to Old Delhi itself. On our way we passed the Sabjee Mundee, which continues to flourish as a vegetable market. Reaching Old Delhi, we confirmed that much of the surrounding wall and its formidable gates had gone. The city authorities, no doubt recognizing its tourist value, have rebuilt the Cashmere Gate. The Jumna River has been redirected several hundred yards away from the city's walls, and the bridge of boats that once echoed to the clatter of rebel cavalry hooves entering the city is no more. Shah Jehan's magnificent Red Fort with its imposing and vast sandstone walls stretching a mile and a quarter in circumference, from where Shah Bahadur Zafar held reluctant sway over the mutineers, still stands intact and placid. It is a remarkable monument to the Mughal Empire, although much of its internal architectural glory has gone. From its ramparts every year on Independence Day the Prime Minister delivers his address to the nation. It all contrasts strongly with the less ornate, less oriental, if no less emphatic, New Delhi of Lutyens.

Central to Old Delhi remains the Chandi Chowk, the main thoroughfare to the Red Fort. In Mughal times it was the city's commercial heart and a street to rival the world's finest boulevards. Today it is crowded and dilapidated, its once gilded mansions broken and sad, echoing with turbulent noise and trading bustle, covered in tat and rust. Down its dark byways and alleys a multitude of jewellers and traders still ply their business. Perhaps the ghosts and spirits of the terrible Mutiny still stalk its gutters. Along this thoroughfare had come Brigadier John Nicholson's assaulting column, and a curtained tablet in one of the alleys reveals where he fell, mortally wounded and unable to witness the recapture of the city as the remaining British columns followed after him amid scenes of terrible carnage and pillage. Lieutenant Fred Roberts (later Field Marshal Earl Roberts) of 8th Foot described his grim route along the Chandi Chowk after the assault:

> A veritable city of the dead . . . dead bodies were strewn about in all directions, in every attitude that the death-struggle had caused them to assume, and in every stage of decomposition . . . Here a dog gnawed at an uncovered limb, there a vulture, disturbed by our approach from its loathsome meal, but too completely gorged to fly fluttered away to a safer distance . . . Our horses seemed to feel the horror of it as much as we did, for they shook and snorted in evident terror.

The British Army had learnt a lesson that was to be relearnt by armies over the two and a half centuries that followed, in such diverse battle-grounds as Stalingrad, Mosul and Syria. Fighting in an urban jungle may increasingly be the norm. Traditional front lines and manoeuvre across open ground are of the past, and the city will increasingly be the battlefield. Command and control in such a place, as Nicholson found, is difficult; the defender determines tactics; civilian suffering is magnified; and the environment soaks up fighting manpower with costly casualties.

I emerged from Old Delhi via the Cashmere Gate and crossed the road, pleading successfully with hand signals to the taxi and rickshaw drivers to let me pass, and entered the British cemetery through its iron gates. It is a mournful site, a tangle of unkempt growth strangling once proud gravestones and memorials, many of them fallen or broken. These mark the burial places of many of the British officers and men who fell during the great Siege, and eventually I found John Nicholson's grave. It is a large engraved stone slab surrounded by an iron picket fence in this melancholy and somewhat desolate place. As I contemplated the memorial, a gentle, ragged sweeper appeared, armed with a whisk of a brush; softly he lifted out one of the pickets and delicately slid himself inside, then proceeded to sweep the gravestone with his whisk before withdrawing in the same manner. He did not stop for a rupee, and I know not on whose behalf he cleaned the tomb or why he chose the moment I was there.

For another nine months until July 1858 the Sirmoor Battalion remained stationed in the Red Fort as garrison for the city of Delhi, while the Goorkhas recovered from their exertions and the toll the Siege had taken. The official Delhi historian summarized the contribution the Goorkhas had made:

> The Sirmoor Battalion, which formed part of the main picquet (Hindoo Rao's House), was never once relieved during the whole siege and was assisted by the 60th Rifles, the Guides Corps, with detachments of other infantry regiments. It sustained and defeated twenty-six separate attacks on the Ridge, and, moreover, made two attacks on the enemy's position at Kissen Gunj.
>
> The Sirmoor Battalion was the only Regiment of the whole force which was exposed to constant fire, Hindoo Rao's House being within perfect range of nearly all the enemy's guns, and was riddled through and through with shot and shell. For a period of three months and eight days the Regiment was under fire morning, noon and night.

As a reward for this sterling performance, the Crown granted the Battalion the rare distinction of carrying a third Colour. This was to be inscribed in Persian, Hindi and English with the word 'Delhi'. Shortly afterwards, when the Battalion's title was changed to the Sirmoor Rifle Regiment, and it not being the custom for Rifle regiments to carry Colours, it was replaced by a Truncheon. An extra Jemadar was authorized on the Battalion establishment to carry it on parade. Two further cherished official rewards were also granted: the Regiment was to adopt the red facings worn by their friends the 60th Rifles – a sartorial flourish reflected by '*lali*', the red piping still worn around service dress collars of all ranks; and the sepoys of the Regiment would henceforth be called 'riflemen' like their comrades in arms on the Ridge, the 60th Rifles. The British had every reason to be grateful to the Sirmoor Battalion and its staunch Goorkhas.

As for the vanquished mutineers, their campaign had not appeared to be driven by any articles of faith beyond a hatred of the British. Nor did they appear bent on the creation of any sort of unified Indian nation state, which then, ethnically, politically or culturally, did not begin to exist. In fact, many Indians helped to put down the revolt. Further, the Company Presidencies of Bombay and Madras remained calm – if the rebellion had spread there, India would almost certainly have been lost to the British. The country as a whole did not rise up against the British.

The direct military causes of the mutineers' defeat were many: tactically, the rebels had no experience of handling large bodies of soldiery; they were badly organized above company level and had inferior weaponry; and they failed to fight a supporting guerrilla campaign attacking British rear areas or lines of communication. Brave as they were at Delhi, with their internal discipline holding strongly, their constant frontal attacks, rather than probing the British lines on the reverse slope of the Ridge, proved disastrous and caused severe losses. They were beaten in detail. They seemed to have no overarching strategy; rather it appeared to be made up as they went along, and in the end, the lack of it sealed their fate.

The fall of Delhi did not end the Mutiny; it was to be nearly two years before Cawnpore (Kanpur) and Lucknow were relieved, vengeance extracted, other towns and forts gradually reoccupied, the last gun captured and the last rebel held by the British, before the Governor General was able to declare on 8 July 1859 a 'State of Peace'. The losses on both sides in this bloody insurrection had been shocking; the massacres of European men, women and children by the mutineers were matched only by the indiscriminate killing of Indian soldiers and civilians by the vengeful British soldiers.

More widely, the Mutiny sounded the death knell for the East India Company's rule of India. The Government of India Act of 1858 transferred the governance of India from the Company to the Crown, and the Governor was replaced by a Viceroy. With the dissolution of the Company came a reorganization of the financial and administrative systems of India. A programme of reforms, greater religious tolerance and closer integration of Indians into the Civil Service were key tenets of the new policy. Caution and a measure of conciliation were the order of the day. It was a profound watershed in the history of the British in India.

Equally important was the reorganization of the Army. A new Indian Army was slowly built up, with reforms in both recruitment and culture designed to prevent any repetition of the rebellion that had so shattered the Bengal Army. Centres of recruitment shifted and new ethnic groups that had proved their worth in the Mutiny were increasingly to be enlisted. The recruitment grounds of Oudh and its adjacent provinces, with their Brahmins, Rajputs and high-born Muslims, were largely replaced by the Punjab, the North-West Frontier and Nepal, with their more flexible

Sikhs, Pathans and Gurkhas. Talent and seniority were to be better balanced. Commanding officers were to wield more power, and officers of merit would remain with their regiments. In due course, and thanks in no small part to their distinguished service at Delhi, Gurkha battalions were to be raised from the ruck of the Sepoy battalions, created Rifle Regiments and more of them raised. By the turn of the century Gurkhas had become a special corps of ten Rifle Regiments each of two battalions. They were now well established in the new Indian Army, unencumbered by caste or taboo and with their own consecutive numerical titles. All were clad in Rifle green. In this way did the Sirmoor Battalion, along with its 'lali' and Truncheon, become the 2nd Gurkha Rifles. In due course it was to earn further distinction.

In the fullness of time the dismal and battered city of Delhi, with all its ghastly material and human debris, returned to some degree of normality, and refugees were allowed to return. In 1911 the city replaced Calcutta as the capital of the Raj, and Edwin Lutyens would design and build New Delhi, a city possessed of the same architectural stamp of authority once held by the Mughals, their Red Fort and Old Delhi, albeit an authority that was to prove just as illusory. In some matters, old or new, Delhi would never be the same again; in the wake of the Mutiny, Hindu and Muslim had moved far apart, and this, inexorably, would steer the city towards the violent and radical change wrought by Partition ninety years later. It was a change that would also affect the Gurkha soldier.

Chapter 5

The Great Game

THE NORTH-WEST FRONTIER

Aside from its exploits on the Ridge at Delhi, the early history of the 2nd Goorkhas' imperial campaigning – and that of the Gurkha regiments as a whole – was dominated by Afghanistan and the North-West Frontier. There were other campaigns around the corners and borders of India with names now lost in the mists of an imperial past: Aliwal and Sobraon during the Sikh Wars; Lushai, where Donald McIntyre won the Regiment's first Victoria Cross; and Manipur, Tibet and Gyantse, to name but a few more. But the North-West Frontier was the great physical bulwark that guarded the gates of India and thus demanded special attention. The potential vulnerability of this wild, barren and mountainous region linking central and southern Asia loomed large in British imagination, given the threat posed by a burgeoning Russian empire already moving steadily eastwards. Extending west beyond the Frontier itself was Afghanistan – the buffer state that separated two vast empires and very much in Britain's arc of interest, so the Emirs of Kabul needed to beware of flirting with the Tsar. A glance at the Battle Honours emblazoned on the Regimental drums and recorded on our shoulder belt badge tells part of the story: Kabul 1879, Kandahar 1880, Afghanistan 1878–80, Tirah, Punjab Frontier, Afghanistan 1919. In the last two hundred years the Gurkha rifleman has soldiered four times on behalf of the British Crown in the beautiful, dangerous and perfidious country of Afghanistan – always at some cost and never for much discernible gain.

In the minds of many, in Victorian times and beyond, the Frontier has had a certain romantic and legendary appeal: the wild grandeur of its mountains, the shadowy intrigue of British and Russian espionage – Younghusband, Kipling and his Kim, and the Great Game, certainly a forerunner of the Cold War. Aside from the Afghan wars themselves, campaigning on the Frontier was perennial against the Pathan tribes, Semitic in origin, Muslim in religion, Pushtu in speech – the Mahsud, the Afridi, the Waziri and fifty others, an ethnological jigsaw that spreads from the Frontier itself right through southern Afghanistan. The tribesmen were continuously on the rampage, invading the Plains or raising Jihads. These were lean sinewy men with gaunt faces and high noses and cheekbones, men who moved with a long, slow, lilting gait, a rifle – 'a ten-rupee *jezail*' – forever slung across their shoulders. The Pathan accepted no master and gave no quarter. These were a proud and independent people, physically tireless, natural tacticians with an ability to strike hard and fast if their enemy dropped his guard; men with a taste for violence, forever driven by vendettas, and ruthless with prisoners – 'save one round for yourself' was the traditional advice. Custom and law here proclaimed the *lex talionis*, an eye for an eye and a tooth for a tooth. Hard as the ground itself, they were a dangerous battlefield adversary.

A glance at a map reveals the striking grandeur of the region's geography. Central to Afghanistan and the barrier between east and west is the snow-clad Hindu Kush – the killer of Hindus – that runs south-west down from the Pamirs into the heart of Afghanistan, with its capital Kabul at the southern edge of the range. It is this dominant feature that formed the dividing line between British and Russian spheres of influence. It is a formidable range,

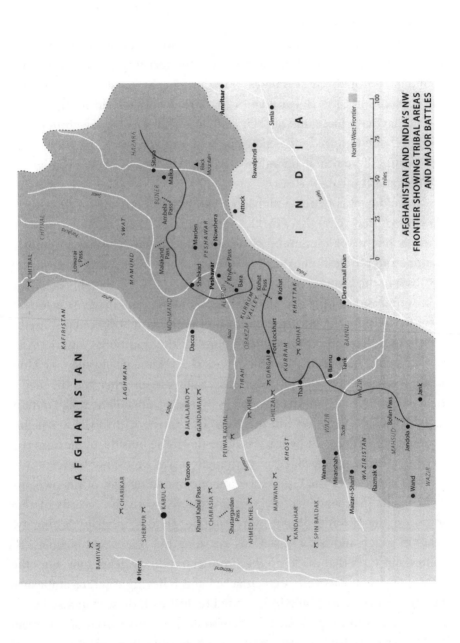

AFGHANISTAN AND INDIA'S NW
FRONTIER SHOWING TRIBAL AREAS
AND MAJOR BATTLES

North-West Frontier

0   25   50   75   100
           miles

600 miles of high summits and deep valleys covered with much forest, its main ridges 15,000 to 20,000ft high. Its passes are at best inhospitable and in winter impassable.

Then east from the Hindu Kush runs another chain of mountains – the Safed Koh and the Sulaiman Range, the territory of the North-West Frontier. Through these ranges run the lengthy passes – the Khyber, the Kurram and the Bolan, names that are deeply etched in history and even today have lost none of their potency. Travel east again through this territory, one hundred miles more or less, and you reach the Indus River that forms the cultural boundary between the North-West Frontier and the Plains of India to the east.

No soldier was better designed or equipped to operate on this North-West Frontier than the Gurkha rifleman. He had demonstrated his obvious talent for mountain warfare in the Anglo–Nepal wars, and his stamina and physical robustness ensured that he would always be intimately involved in the Frontier as well as Afghanistan itself. Further, his excellence at scouting and sniping and ability to tackle climbs and descents made him ideal for fighting the unruly, cunning and unforgiving tribesmen. I used to see these skills demonstrated many times in the traditional Gurkha *Khud* race that has been run throughout Gurkha regimental history. In Hong Kong the soldiers would pit themselves against each other and the men of their neighbouring Gurkha regiments by racing up a 700ft rocky outcrop suitably called 'Nameless', in the New Territories. It involved a gruelling running climb followed by fearless leaps down the hillside, often from rock to rock, at amazing speed. I always thought it was a most noble race.

The histories of the Gurkha regiments, including that of my own, and right up to Independence in 1947, are littered with the records of their tours on the Frontier. Some were routine periods, perhaps lasting two years in rough and isolated stations guarding the passes and picquets, the routes and forts that made up the Frontier's military geography. On other occasions, when garrisons were attacked and relieving columns ambushed, punitive expeditions would be mounted to deal with those responsible.

Regiments moving to the Frontier would generally march up the major trails and routes that led to their stations. These vulnerable columns, complete with baggage trains, would progress in a fairly slow and deliberate manner, moving with an advance guard to mount picquets on the high ground to their flanks as they went. These could be hazardous operations in themselves, since the slightest neglect of precautions or lack of alertness would invite the remote, proud and independent Pathan to make a murderous dash, seize valuable weapons and then to melt away. Every move of picquet parties up the high ground needed protective cover from machine guns and mountain guns.

Frontier hostilities were continual and, unlike the wars in Afghanistan, were a general feature of service and campaigning in India. On occasions, major forays and uprisings by the Pathan demanded a huge commitment of force to contain them. The Tirah campaign 1897–8 lasted eighteen months and was probably the most serious in the Frontier's history of conflict. The Afridi and Orakzaies tribes had occupied the Khyber Pass, captured within it the military post at Landi Kotal and were raiding into British India. It was clear that serious campaigning would be required, and before long, 40,000 British and Indian troops were committed, served by a supply train of 60,000 camels, mules and oxen. The 2nd Goorkhas, commanded by Colonel Eaton Travers, were brigaded with their old friends the Gordon Highlanders, with whom they had previously campaigned. In the course of that campaign the 2nd Goorkhas were to be engaged thirty-two times in battles with the tribesmen and fight nineteen rearguard actions. Three months into the campaign, on 20 October 1897, the most serious of these engagements occurred at the village of Dargai, where the two regiments of Highlanders together with the Dorset Regiment and others were ordered to occupy its dominating heights at 6,000ft. It soon became apparent that these heights were occupied by several hundred well-armed Afridi based in loop-holed *sangars* (stone-built temporary shelters), and a very harsh battle ensued. As the regiments assaulted, the enemy waited for them to rush across an open saddle on their approach. The 2nd Goorkha history records:

> The men scrambled up the few yards of shale and coarse grass which separated them from the glacis in front, and pouring over the top, came in view of loopholes above. Instantly the whole line of sangers burst into smoke and flame, and a torrent of bullets from front, right and left tore through the ranks; men literally fell in heaps and the stony slope was strewn with killed and wounded.

Sixty 2nd Goorkhas fell at this point but, urged on by the wounded Piper Findlater of the Gordons playing strongly, eventually the heights were taken and the piper had his Victoria Cross. Subedar Kirparam Thapa was first man to reach the top along with a mass of Gordons, but by then the enemy had wisely left. In the spirit of comradeship the wounded Gurkha riflemen were carried down from the heights by their friends in the Gordon Highlanders. There would be several months more of campaigning before the tribesmen sued for peace. It was a costly affair for both sides.

Forty years on, in 1936, campaigning on the forbidding hills of the Frontier had largely settled into a fixed pattern of stereotyped drills that were a complete anathema to the new Commandant of the 1st Battalion, 2nd Goorkhas, Lieutenant Colonel Francis Tuker, a Regimental officer since the First World War and destined to make a name for himself as a Divisional commander in the Western Desert. On arrival he lost no time in shaping his Battalion for a fresh style of Frontier soldiering. Dehra Dun was an ideal location for training, with its bare and forested hills, broad and narrow rivers, deep ravines and desert plain, and here he put his officers and the Gurkha soldiers through their paces and injected some new thinking into Frontier operations. The Battalion trained hard.

Tuker deplored the traditional style of a Frontier column trickling its ponderous way along the valley bottoms, posting picquets to the left and right to protect themselves, with a huge caravan of camels and mules stretching back for miles, advertising their presence wherever they went. He wanted to break out of stereotyped drills and he brought a new and innovative approach to campaigning.

Tuker's tactical style was one of vigorous offensive, patrolling and skirmishing by day and particularly by night. His riflemen would wear noiseless Afghan sandals, they left back at base the heavy, shiny bayonets that glinted in the sun and they dulled the brasses on their equipment. The approaches to their picquets would be constantly ambushed from varying positions. These ambushes would regularly change their positions and do so at night. His mantra everywhere was for surprise and to keep the enemy guessing. Tuker moved his Battalion by night and he utilized every one of his Gurkha soldiers' natural talents.He demanded greater mobility, better communications and improved marksmanship

In 1937 the Army was faced with an increasingly belligerent Fakir of Ip and thousands of his Wazir and Mahsud supporters, together with Afghans from across the border. Increasingly confident, tribesmen were spreading sedition, inciting insurrection, attacking and mauling Indian battalions. Roads and bridges had been destroyed, and sniping was a regular occurrence. All the while, offensive action in response was governed by political considerations that forced the Army to act with considerable restraint. In certain areas troops could only fire when shot at, and it seemed that every tactic of effective Frontier campaigning was proscribed by political restrictions, which were well known to the tribesmen, who took full advantage.

When the 2nd Goorkhas arrived to join others on the Frontier in 1937, the Battalion was ready to put their Commandant's new thinking and training into action. Undeterred by political constraints, Tuker's bold and aggressive tactics soon began to reap dividends. Successful ambushes forced the enemy to recognize that they now faced a bold and aggressive adversary, and they began to do all they could to avoid the Gurkhas. The Battalion's innovative forward policy and its mantras of secrecy and surprise that Tuker called the 'salt of battle' began to bear fruit and quickly caught the eye of forward-thinking soldiers in Delhi such as Auchinleck. The lessons that Tuker had inculcated into his Battalion were to be taken forward with much effect by his 1st Battalion in the iron battles they were to fight in the Western Desert three years later. There, Francis Tuker, his talents recognized and duly promoted, would be their Divisional commander. But before we look at something of those testing battles, we should consider the wars that took the Gurkha soldier into Afghanistan.

THE FIRST AFGHAN WAR 1839–42

It is beyond the scope of my story to deal with all the political and military complexities that gave rise to the totally unnecessary, hugely damaging and highly expensive first Afghan War. It was a war that was to cost the East India Company not only vast amounts of blood and treasure, but cause grave reputational damage and, not least, hasten the Indian Mutiny. Further, it was not a happy experience for the Gurkha soldier trapped in it. The First Afghan war was an attempt by the Governor General, Lord Auckland, to install the former Emir, Shah Shujah, on the Afghan throne in place of Dost Mohammed, who had supposedly courted the attention of the Russians.

In spite of the Russian threat having largely receded, a grandiloquently titled 'Army of the Indus' of 21,000 British and Indian troops drawn from the Bengal and Bombay Armies (participating regiments were purportedly selected by the drawing of lots) set out from the Punjab in December 1838 to effect this change. A train of 38,000 camp followers travelled in their wake. By late March 1839, the British Force – it contained no Gurkha regiment (perhaps fortuitously, they had been unlucky in the draw) – had passed through the Bolan Pass and entered Afghanistan. In August, following a decisive victory over Dost Mohammed's troops, Shujah was enthroned in Kabul. Dost Mohammed, after a fruitless guerrilla campaign, was captured and exiled to India in late 1840. Under an escort commanded by Lieutenant Charles Reid, who several years later was to lead the Sirmoor Battalion to the Ridge at Delhi, the Emir was taken to Mussoorie, where he would spend his exile.

In addition to the 'Army of the Indus', Shujah, with the help of the British, recruited 6,000 Indian mercenaries as a personal army – Shah Shujah's Levy. This force included a Gurkha regiment of some 700 men raised exclusively for the invasion and, separately, a unit of Engineers, 'Broadfoot's Sappers', which contained some 200 Gurkhas who were to distinguish themselves in the defence of Jallalabad. The men of the Gurkha regiment were specially recruited, but they were trained and led by senior ranks from two Gurkha regiments, including the Sirmoor Battalion, who each provided as volunteers, three Havildars (Sergeants), four Naiks (Corporals) and six sepoys. They were all promoted one rank and given extra pay, but they would have been wiser to remember the old army adage of never volunteering for anything, for they were to suffer greatly. Titled the 4th Regiment (Light Infantry), the specially raised Battalion was commanded by a British officer from the Bengal Army, Captain Codrington. By all accounts the Levy as a whole was full of ne'er-do-wells and soldiers of fortune, and its efficiency declined rapidly the longer it remained in Afghanistan. The Gurkha regiment itself seems to have been a mixed bunch. Beyond the contribution of the Sirmoor Battalion to the 4th Regiment as an element of the Levy, I have found it difficult to piece together an accurate picture of this hybrid Battalion, but they were clearly raw and inexperienced.

Once Shujah had been installed in Kabul, the majority of British troops returned to India. William MacNaughton, the Company's political officer – reportedly 'a man without ballast' – allowed his remaining soldiers, some 4,000 of them, to bring in their families to improve morale. All this gave the impression that here was an army of occupation – a presence that was deeply resented by the Afghans, who also had little respect for the arrogant Shujah. The association by men of the British Force with local women was also deeply offensive to the Afghans. The British garrison was located in a cantonment to the north-east of Kabul, and Shujah's Gurkhas were based at an outpost at Charika, some 40 miles from the city.

In due course Afghan dissatisfaction gave vent to an uprising against the British. In a deteriorating security situation, amid much murder, cruel violence and mayhem, William McNaughton was killed and his body dragged through the streets of Kabul before being publicly displayed in the bazaar. Faced with a situation that they were no longer able to contain or control, the British negotiated a humiliating agreement to leave Kabul, in exchange for an Afghan promise of safe exodus out of the country. Meanwhile, the Gurkhas, besieged together with their families by 20,000 Afghan rebels, were either captured or shot, and their Commander, Captain Codrington, was killed. His Adjutant, Lieutenant John Haughton, managed to escape from Charika having been wounded and losing an arm in the process, amputated by the surgeon at Charika without anaesthetic. He was to be taken hostage by Dost Mohammed's son, Akbar Khan, who had led the uprising.

The story of the terrible retreat from Kabul is well known. On 6 January 1842 the withdrawal of the British contingent began. It numbered about 16,500 all souls, of whom 4,500 were military personnel and their families, and the rest camp followers. Unable to reach the relative safety of Jalalabad, all would either freeze to death in the bitter Afghan winter or be shot, stabbed or cut down by marauding Afghans. Some were taken prisoner and sold as slaves or held hostage. As depicted in Elizabeth Butler's famous painting of the scene, only Assistant Surgeon William Brydon of the main party would reach Jalalabad alive. A few nights later, a few hardy Gurkhas also reached sanctuary, and it later transpired that perhaps a few hundred men, women and children had been taken prisoner by the Afghans. It was a singular disaster for British arms, matched only by the fall of Singapore one hundred years later.

Retribution quickly followed. Major General Sir William Nott, John Nott's great-great-great-grandfather, an energetic, independent if somewhat cantankerous General, was still in command of the British garrison at Kandahar. Back in India, General Pollock was put in command of an army of retribution of some 8,000 men. By September 1842, both Generals having fought successful battles against the Afghans, the army reached Kabul, where a punitive policy of destruction and retribution was enacted and many hostages rescued. These included the Gurkha adjutant, John Haughton, who managed to gather up 165 Gurkhas from the bazaars and hills whither they had fled or been taken prisoner and sold as slaves. Before the joint force arrived, Shah Shuja was gunned down by an assassin just outside the city. A month later, having rescued the prisoners and demolished the city's main bazaar, Generals Pollock and Nott and their troops withdrew from Afghanistan by way of the Khyber Pass. In a final ironic twist to this unhappy campaign, the British released the deposed Dost Mohammed and restored him to his position as the Emir of Kabul, where he remained for the next twenty years. Their former protégé lay dead in a roadside ditch.

The 2nd Goorkhas' Regimental History records that on conclusion of the Afghan War thirty-six surviving Gurkhas from the 4th Regiment of Shah Shujah's Levy and George Broadfoot's Engineers were, on return to India, drafted into the Sirmoor Battalion. Whether these survivors included any of the original party of regimental volunteers, there is no record and the Regimental History offers little help. But it would seem that something like 400 Gurkhas of the Levy perished at the hands of the Afghans. As many were to learn, it is always easier to enter Afghanistan than it is to leave it. Although not members of a formal battalion of the Bengal Army, it was a salutary experience for the Gurkhas.

As an aside, my old regimental colleague John Nott reflected in his autobiography that there were some parallels between the service of his ancestor, General Sir William Nott, and his own service some 140 years later as Secretary of State for Defence:

> Both of us became involved in a colonial war – his role was to maintain the integrity of the British Empire in India; my small part was to resist aggression in almost the last outpost of Empire; the Falkland Islands. The First Afghan War was provoked by the expansionist ambitions of Russia in Asia; my two years in the Ministry of Defence were overwhelmingly concerned with resisting the expansionist ambitions of Russia in Europe – the Cold War. When my grandfather [sic],

as Commander of the Kandahar Army, recovered Afghanistan for the British in 1842, he did so in opposition to the Afghan tribes; in 1982, at the height of the Cold War I cooperated with the CIA to arm these same Afghan tribes against the Russians. Now the sun has set on the British Empire and the Russian Empire has collapsed, not least because of the Soviet bloodletting in Afghanistan.

THE SECOND AFGHAN WAR 1878–80

In the four decades that followed the first disastrous war, the British adopted an isolationist policy of 'masterly inactivity' towards Afghanistan; but with Russian expansionism in the east, that policy would change. The Viceroy, Lord Lytton, and the British Government were to adopt a harder line, and a 'forward policy' – forward of the Indus River – was in the ascendant. Dost Mohammed had died in 1863 and following various internecine struggles was succeeded by one of his sons, Sher Ali. Relations between the Viceroy and the new Emir were uneasy. A series of diplomatic exchanges of an increasing bellicose nature caused discord to grow, and matters reached a climax with the news that Sher Ali, albeit under some pressure, had accepted a Russian mission in Kabul. This delegation was soon to depart, but the damage had been done. Lord Lytton demanded that a British envoy be received in Kabul, and when that envoy, Major Cavagnari, was refused entry at the Khyber Pass, the die was cast.

Following the Mutiny and the reorganization of the Indian Army, there were now five Gurkha regiments, all of which were to be involved in the forthcoming operations in Afghanistan. The 2nd Goorkhas, with a newly bestowed royal title 'The Prince of Wales's Own', had, in April 1878 been part of an Indian Army Expeditionary Force of 7,000 men sent to Malta, and subsequently to Cyprus, at the time of the Russo-Turkish war and general instability in the Near East. In the end the Regiment saw no action, but it did not return to India until October of that year, by which time events in Afghanistan had moved on. Within three weeks of reaching Dehra Dun the 2nd Goorkhas were off to the North-West Frontier; but in the light of their late arrival in this first phase of the war, the Regiment was stationed, 'in crowning positions', on the heights of the Khyber Pass, and in reserve.

On 21 November 1878 a British force of some 30,000 men and 144 guns in three military columns entered Afghanistan. On the left, moving from

Quetta, was the Kandahar Field Force under Major General Donald Stewart, and his command included the 1st and 3rd Gurkhas. Local Major General Frederick Roberts (he was still a Major in his own Regiment) led the central column designated as the Kurram Field Force, with the 5th Gurkhas under command. On the right was the Peshawar Field Force led by the one-armed Lieutenant General Sir Samuel Browne, designer of the famous belt; with him marched the 4th Gurkhas. Sher Ali, hearing that the British were on the march, decided to flee and look for Russian support and appointed his son, Yakub Khan, as regent. By February of the following year Sher Ali was dead.

Neither Stewart nor Browne met significant opposition. Stewart's force eventually reached Kandahar unopposed, and after some trouble in the Khyber Pass, Browne's troops reached Jalalabad. But Roberts had a more difficult task in the higher reaches of the Kurram Valley. Here his passage on the only route forward was blocked by a large element of the Afghan Army in strong defensive positions on heavily wooded slopes at 9,400ft, around the summit of the pass named the Peiwar Kotal. Roberts' force was the smallest of the three columns with only 3,200 men, and apparently many Kurram locals had already told Roberts that his diminutive and smooth-cheeked 5th Gurkhas would be no match for the tall, bearded Afghan warriors.

Given the strength of the opposition and the results of his own reconnaissance, General Roberts decided on a feint and a surprise flanking attack in an attempt to turn the Afghan position. Setting off at 2230 hours, Roberts himself led the flanking force under cover of darkness on a 12-mile trek through the most difficult terrain in absolute secrecy and in bitter cold. Meanwhile, he had left signs, messages and false trails suggesting that his force would launch a frontal assault. As that frontal feint went in with major artillery in support, Roberts' force, consisting in the main of the 5th Gurkhas and the 72nd Seaforth Highlanders, assaulted up the perilous slopes and hooked into the right flank of the Afghans. In the close wooded country the Gurkhas were able to get within 50 metres of the defenders before they were spotted. General Roberts, in his memoir *41 Years in India*, wrote of the battle:

> The Gurkhas, forgetting their fatigue, rapidly climbed the steep sides
> of the mountain and, swarming into the first entrenchment, quickly

cleared it of the enemy, then guided by the flashes of the Afghan rifles, they pressed on, and, being joined by the leading company of the 72nd, took possession of a second and larger entrenchment 200 yards higher up. Without a perceptible pause, the Highlanders and the Gurkhas together rushed a third position, the most important of all, as it commanded the head of the pass. The Kotal was won.

Some sixteen hours after setting off, the position belonged to Roberts, and the Afghans, with some eight regiments and eighteen guns and possessing all the ground advantage, had been routed. Success was due to the subtleties of Roberts' plan of attack and the aggression of his two regiments of Highlanders. After the battle, the 5th Gurkhas suggested that their lighter casualties were the result of Afghan fire going over their heads, while the taller Seaforths were not so lucky. So much for the diminutive size of the Goorkhas!

I have always admired the large-scale painting by Vereker Hamilton, now hanging in the National Army Museum in London, which depicts the assault at Peiwar Kotal by the Seaforths and Gurkhas, side by side. Peiwar Kotal was to be the first of many battle honours awarded to the 5th Gurkhas. In addition, Captain John Coke won a Victoria Cross for saving the life of a fellow officer during the assault (the first of seven VCs to be won by the 5th Gurkhas over the next sixty years). Five 5th Gurkhas were awarded the Indian Order of Merit at Peiwar Kotal, and it became a legendary battle.

General Roberts and his force pressed forward into the Kurram valley, and the Gurkhas again distinguished themselves when acting as a guard force to the rear of the column. Roberts recorded:

The tail of the column was followed and much harassed by the enemy but they were kept at bay by the steadfastness of the gallant Gurkhas and so successful were they in safe guarding the baggage that not a single article fell into the hands of the tribesmen.

With the three Field forces now established in Afghanistan, and the greater part of southern Afghanistan in British hands, a demoralized Yakub Khan agreed to negotiate. A treaty was signed at Gandamak between the Emir and the erstwhile British envoy, Major Sir Louis Cavagnari, that would allow his mission to be received in Kabul and his safety ensured. By 24 July it was installed, but disaster followed. By 5 September, in spite of much bravery on the part of his escort of Guides, Cavagnari and the whole of his party were dead, massacred by some thousands of the Emir's unpaid soldiery. News of this terrible event, brought by a secret agent, quickly reached India. General Roberts was on leave at Simla, but a flurry of orders followed, and Roberts, reinforced, was ordered to advance to Kabul to avenge the massacre. General Stewart was to stand fast at Kandahar, and a further column would occupy the Kurram in place of General Roberts.

Roberts quickly set off with his newly titled Kabul Field Force, which once more included the 5th Gurkhas and the Seaforths. Meanwhile, General Bright and his Second Division were to advance through the Khyber Pass into Afghanistan prepared to reinforce General Roberts if necessary. With Bright went the 2nd Goorkhas, who were to see a good deal of fighting before eventually joining Roberts' Field Force in Kabul.

After battling with the Afghan Army Roberts reached Kabul; the British held the capital city and, following more ruthless retribution for the death of Cavagnari, Roberts effectively became the new Emir. Unhappily for the Afghans, the British were going to stay in a country that was far from stable. Meanwhile, Ayub Khan, the Governor of Herat, had been rejected by the British as a possible Emir and was stirring up trouble. The Field Force wintered in Kabul and were constantly in action around the country. In July of the following year there came a serious setback when a brigade of the Kandahar Field Force was attacked at Maiwand, eighty miles west of Kandahar, by the superior forces of Ayub Khan. Despite inflicting 2,300 casualties on Khan's forces, the British were defeated and over 900 were killed, the survivors escaping to the British-held fortress of Kandahar, where they were besieged. There was no Gurkha regiment with this force. The news of the disaster at Maiwand quickly reached Roberts at Kabul, and a relief column consisting of three brigades and totalling some 9,700 men, plus 8,000 followers and a similar number of pack animals, was formed. This force included the 2nd Goorkhas, commanded by Arthur Battye, as well as the 4th and 5th Gurkhas. It set out on 9 August 1880 on a remarkable and renowned march of over 300 miles in summer heat of 110° and over inhospitable mountain and desert. It lasted twenty-one days with only two halts before reaching the demoralized garrison at Kandahar, and a thousand of Roberts' men were laid low by the rigours of the march. Encamped on hills outside the city, Roberts learned that Ayub Khan had raised the siege and was entrenched some three miles to the west. Following a brief skirmish with Afghan troops Roberts decided to engage him without delay.

The battle of Kandahar took place on 1 September and was a sharp engagement lasting a few hours. Shortly after 9.00 a.m. Roberts' 40-pounders opened up on subsidiary Afghan positions, the start line for the attack having been secured by the 4th Gurkhas. The assault itself was led by the 2nd Goorkhas and the Gordon Highlanders, who were to fight together again at Dargai twenty years later. The fighting was severe as they cleared the early positions with bayonet and *kukri*. Charging on and reaching the main position and the enemy's guns, much hand-to-hand fighting ensued, but after a sharp struggle, a further charge by the two Highland Regiments proved decisive and the day was carried 'in most dashing style'. Thousands of Afghans broke away in disarray.

The 2nd Goorkhas' Regimental History records that a rifleman, Indebir Lama, reached one of the Afghan guns first and springing on it waved his cap, crying out in Hindi, 'This gun belongs to my Regiment – 2nd Goorkhas – Prince of Wales's!' He then thrust his cap down the muzzle in order to ensure that there should be no dispute as to future ownership. It's a good story and probably true, for the gun taken at Kandahar was presented by the Government to the Regiment. Today it stands in front of the guardroom of the Royal Gurkha Rifles barracks at Shorncliffe. Roberts' losses were 40 killed and 228 wounded – losses considered small for such a decisive victory. Later, they buried 600 Afghan dead. The Gordons' Commanding Officer was killed and Colonel Battye was wounded in the right shoulder, which suggests that commanding officers were certainly well forward leading their men.

The Second Afghan War was over, and the last British forces left Afghanistan in April 1881. The whole campaign had cost them 50,000 casualties from disease and enemy action, much treasure and the enduring enmity of the Afghan people. Strategically, it would have been much more valuable to have retained the Afghans as allies in the face of a perceived Russian threat. Such an option, if it realistically existed, proved elusive.

With its reputation much enhanced, along with those of the other Gurkha regiments, the 2nd Goorkhas left Afghanistan at the end of September and reached Dehra Dun a month later. They had been campaigning for thirteen months at the cost of sixty-three all ranks lost. Medals and clasps, including a special Bronze Star cast for participants in General Roberts' great march, new Battle Honours and a generous subscription from the people of Dehra Dun together with a liberal grant of leave were the 2nd Goorkhas' rewards.

THE THIRD AFGHAN WAR 1919

A varied set of circumstances, many of them historical, came together to cause yet another conflict between British India and Afghanistan in 1919, a war that lasted only three months but would involve several Gurkha battalions. In general, relations between British India and Afghanistan had been relatively placid since the end of the Second Afghan War. Britain, through the payment of a large subsidy, had retained control of Afghan foreign affairs, and the country had remained neutral during the First World War, although Turkish agents had attempted to foment trouble on the Frontier. However, in spite of much of the British and Indian Armies campaigning abroad, the Frontier had generally remained calm at a time when trouble could have caused difficulty.

This outward calm was shattered in February 1919 by the assassination of Emir Habibullah and a resultant power struggle for succession. Amanullah, Habibullah's third son, seized the throne and soon demanded total independence for Afghanistan and freedom from the restrictions imposed by the British on his foreign policy; a demand that the British declined to meet. Looking for a diversion from internal strife and unhappiness at this ruling, Amanullah decided to invade India.

Amanullah had watched Gandhi-inspired nationalist disturbances in India and sensed that Britain's position was in decline and the time for action was right. Unrest was particularly prevalent in the Punjab, where rioting was rampant and led to the lamentable bloodbath that occurred in Amritsar on 13 April. There Brigadier General Dyer, personally commanding a squad of fifty soldiers armed with rifles, including twenty-five recruit riflemen from the 9th Gurkhas as well as Sikhs and Pathans, in an act of gross misjudgement bordering on lunacy, ordered his soldiers to open fire without warning on an illegal assembly of several thousand people hemmed in at the Jallianwala Bagh. This killing of 379 unarmed people including women and children and wounding of hundreds of others deeply shocked India as well as people in Britain. It was to damage British reputation in India for years to come, and Amanullah and his bellicose supporterts saw it as a further example of British decline and decadence.

At an extremely difficult time, with post-war demobilization under way and large numbers of troops deployed on internal security duties, the Army gradually prepared itself for another conflict with Afghanistan. The Afghan forces, some 50,000 strong, were in reality no match for the Indian Army, even if they could possibly also count on the loyalty of up to 80,000 Frontier tribesmen. The Afghan Army was not ready for war, and they failed to recognize the new potency of the Royal Air Force and its Handley Page bombers. Nonetheless, the Afghans concentrated their forces at two of the main entry points to India, the Khyber and Kurram passes, while a third prong pushed through the Bolan pass and threatened the town of Quetta. In an attempt to control the area of the Frontier, they crossed the border into India. After several fierce engagements in the area of the passes that involved, amongst others, battalions from five different Gurkha regiments, the Afghans were in retreat. Ironically, one of the most successful British Force Commanders was Brigadier General Dyer, but his performance in the field was not to save him from the Hunter Inquiry into events at Amritsar, and he was found culpable and forced to resign. Amanullah, realizing that the Indian population were not going to rise up in support and having experienced the lethal quality of Royal Air Force bombers, sued for peace before air power threatened Kabul.

The final war against Afghanistan for the old British Indian Army was over. But it had encouraged dissident Pathans of the Frontier, especially the warlike Mahsud and the tribal peoples of Waziristan, to continue to cause trouble. The Gurkha battalions would soon be back on the Frontier, and lawlessness would occupy them up to the Second World War and beyond. In the fullness of time, Gurkhas would also return to Afghanistan.

THE FOURTH AFGHAN WAR 2001–?

These are early days to describe the Gurkhas' contribution to campaigning in what might be described as the Fourth Afghan War, and my familiarity with the campaign is limited. It began in the aftermath of the 9/11 attacks on America that Osama Bin Laden effectively launched from Afghanistan. Historians have yet to cast their judgement on the final outcome of the complex operations that have lasted, in one form or another, from the autumn of 2001 to the present day. In the course of this lengthy campaign, Gurkha units have completed twenty-four separate tours in that benighted country, and both battalions of the Royal Gurkha Rifles have campaigned successfully once again. Gurkha deployment has not been without significant cost, engaging the forces of the Taliban in that difficult and dangerous environment, and casualties have been many. Today, sustained combat operations by British forces have largely finished, and most of them have been withdrawn, but the Army, including the Gurkhas, still provides a strong protection force, rotationally, in Kabul. It cannot be said that a totally stable and peaceful Afghanistan has been achieved or that the Taliban has been beaten. In the end, it may be that some sort of peace accord will come to pass, but history does not provide much promise. A new 'Great Game' may be running but, as always, no country has the means to impose its will on Afghanistan.

The history of the Royal Gurkha Rifles, now twenty-five years old, has yet to be written, but in due course some of the pace and intensity of their involvement in this latest of Afghan wars will be revealed. Some of our Gurkha soldiers have already produced popular memoirs, and regimental magazines give something of the flavour of these operational tours. Initially, I sense in talking to those involved that there was a steep learning curve as soldiers experienced the heaviest set of engagements for the British Army since the Korean War. Professionally, the soldiers had to come to terms with operating in an all-arms environment with a heavy air dimension and in regular contact with the enemy. Gradually they became more comfortable and confident as each tour progressed, and they soon got on top of it. This was a journey that all regiments of the British Army experienced. The Royal Gurkha Rifles were tested, one or two men were replaced, but their record has been an extremely impressive and enviable one. The list of gallantry medals and commendations won at every level from Commanding Officer down to junior rifleman is long, the will to win was certainly there, as was a fine fighting spirit. Further, the Gurkha soldier, perhaps uniquely, was able to establish a remarkable affinity with the local people of Afghanistan. He seemed able to communicate in Pushtu, and his familiarity with village farming life and his style gave him a distinct advantage in winning hearts and minds.

Perhaps one account of gallantry in Afghanistan in 2010 will suggest that the contemporary Gurkha soldier more than matches the courage of his predecessors. Acting Sergeant Dipparsard Pun of the 1st Battalion was the sentry in a fortified compound in the village of Rahim Kalay in Helmand Province at a time when his platoon was absent on patrol. He noticed the Taliban approaching his base and edged forward on to a low roof, taking his rifle and a heavy machine gun with him. He came under attack from some thirty Taliban shooting from every quarter, some of them no more than fifteen yards away. Rocket-propelled grenades struck the building behind him while others flew overhead. The Taliban were attempting to climb the wall of the compound, one succeeding and getting no further than five yards from him. He fired a grenade launcher underslung from his rifle and then engaged the enemy, first with his machine gun and then his rifle and other assorted grenades. In the course of the attack, which he repulsed alone, he fired 250 rounds of machine gun ammunition, 180 rounds of rifle ammunition, threw six phosphorus grenades and six high explosive grenades, fired five underslung grenades and, in a final act of defiance, with no ammunition left, hurled a sandbag and his machine gun tripod at the Taliban. All this brave defence saw off singlehandedly an attack by thirty well-armed men, who sustained heavy casualties. Sergeant Dipprasard was awarded the Conspicuous Gallantry Cross – the first occasion that this prestigious medal, second only to the Victoria Cross, had been awarded to a Gurkha soldier. Both Dipprasard's father and grandfather had served in Indian Army Gurkha regiments and both had also won awards for bravery.

The citation for the Distinguished Service Order awarded to Lieutenant Colonel Gerald Strickland, who commanded the 1st Battalion Battle Group to which Dipprasard belonged, sits well alongside that of one of his Sergeants.

Distinguished Service Order – Lieutenant Colonel Gerald Strickland

The Royal Gurkha Rifles

Commanding Officer, Afghanistan, April – September 2010

Despite suffering significant casualties, Lieutenant Colonel Strickland ·has fought an unrelenting battle to stabilise a key rural area of central

Helmand. Strickland and his Battlegroup have achieved a remarkable success in tipping the balance against the insurgents thus giving Afghan Governance a real opportunity for success.

Based on what was the most challenging of areas, comprising of scattered settlements and few roads, whose inhabitants were easy prey to insurgent intimidation, the police had little control and the government no influence. Displaying flawless judgement, he identified the key villages he needed to hold and then fought an aggressive campaign to seize control of them and build and secure roads between them to establish freedom of movement for the population.

Throughout all the setbacks and many challenges he faced, Strickland motivated his men with a steely sense of purpose. They did not falter. As he built check-points he patiently reached out to the local communities and won over their support. The expansion of government control of his area was slow and gradual but it was irresistible and within months Strickland achieved his goal; the local insurgents began to feel intimidated.

It has been his professional performance in Afghanistan, as well as his earlier contribution in other campaigns, that over the last twenty-five years has built the Gurkha soldier a strong and respected position in the heart of the British Army.

Chapter 6

Iron Wars

In the faint slumbers I by thee have watch'd
And heard thee murmur tales of iron wars.

—Shakespeare, *Henry IV, Part 1*

REMEMBRANCE

Every year, in the second week of November, a group of us, both serving and retired members of the Gurkha Brigade, assemble on the Thursday morning before Armistice Sunday in the gardens of Westminster Abbey. We are joined by representatives from every regiment in the British Army, including many that no longer exist, as well as those from the other two Services, for the planting of small wooden crosses in the Field of Remembrance. Medals, poppies, a rich variety of regimental headdress and a few bowler hats predominate, and the gardens themselves are covered with a vast swathe of small crosses. The Gurkha Brigade has an allocated plot in the south-west corner of the gardens.

The year 2018 marked the centenary of the end of the Great War, so that year's ceremony assumed greater significance and saw a larger gathering. In addition to the thousands of individual crosses there were larger ones for each regiment; crosses to mark the dead of two world wars and numerous other campaigns. Regimental Colonels hammered these larger crosses into individual unit plots. On Big Ben's stroke of eleven the bugles sounded the Last Post, and a two-minute silence followed. Reveille then broke the reverie, some appropriate words from the Dean followed and Prince Harry toured the garden, meeting regimental representatives.

Within our group were two serving Gurkhas, the Queen's Gurkha Orderly Officers – historic and coveted appointments that date back to the reign of King Edward VII. The appointment was immortalized in Kipling's story *In the Presence*, in which the King's Orderly Officer, Subedar Major Santabir Gurung of the 2nd Goorkhas, stands vigil at the King's lying in state. Today, these officers attend the Queen at her Investitures and on other royal occasions. The appointments are held for a year by two outstanding regimental officers. Their presence at the ceremony in their immaculate dress uniforms, their gold aiguillettes worn with a flourish, always draws much appreciative attention, and Prince Harry paused with them for photographs. Having trekked in Nepal and served with the Regiment as a Forward Air Controller on operations in Afghanistan, the Prince knows the Gurkha soldier well. 'When you know you are with the Gurkha, I think there is no safer place to be', he memorably remarked on his return from that experience. He seems to bond easily with the soldiers and particularly with our disabled wounded, who have been enthusiastic competitors in the Prince's Invicta Games for worldwide disabled veterans.

The ceremonies at the Field of Remembrance over, our group sets off round Parliament Square, up Whitehall and past the Cenotaph, for a short parade at the Gurkha statue, 300 yards away in Horse Guards Avenue. Just before turning right from Whitehall we pause at Raleigh Green, opposite Downing Street, to allow representatives of the 6th Gurkha Rifles to lay a wreath at the base of the statue of their most distinguished officer, Field Marshal Slim. The Gurkha statue itself, a permanent memorial to Gurkha service, stands four-square opposite the north entrance to the Ministry of Defence; the soldier's watchful gaze seems directed through the Horse Guards arch and across the expanse of the parade ground itself to the Guards Memorial on the edge of St James's Park. The figure on the plinth of Portland stone serves as a reminder to all those entering and leaving the Ministry, as well as others who pass by, of the contribution the Gurkha soldier has made to the defence of the realm.

It is a strong and powerful statue – one and a half times life size – in the style and dress of a Gurkha rifleman of the 1920s. The figure, with his upright rifle centrally held, stands at ease but alert and ready. Philip Jackson, the sculptor, based his work on a similar figure sculpted after the First World War by Richard Goulden for the Gurkha Memorial in India. I had long admired the original plaster maquette for that work, which stands half way up the Gurkha staircase in the Foreign Office. The Queen unveiled the new statue to much acclaim in 1997, and as Colonel of the Royal Gurkha Rifles I accompanied her as she inspected the Regimental Guard of Honour found for the occasion. At the statue's foot, members of our group representing each of the historic Gurkha regiments laid a wreath.

Finally, that year, two days later, on Sunday, a contingent of eighty retired Gurkhas, officers and soldiers, including myself and twenty 2nd Goorkha pensioners, assembled on Horse Guards Parade in readiness for Remembrance Sunday's Cenotaph Parade. It's a lengthy process; we reported at 9.00 a.m., but it was nearly midday before our Gurkha contingent, having entered Whitehall at 10.00 a.m., started to march. We needed to wait for the Royal Family, Ministers, Service Chiefs and other good and great to place their wreaths. Perhaps some thirty contingents had gone before us, and behind us were many more. Overall, some 10,000 men and women, mostly stalwart and proud veterans, marched, followed, especially in 2018, by another 10,000 members of the public. It was reassuring to hear the applause of the crowd which seemed to rise as we passed; our old men's paces were steady enough to the beat of the military bands, and our Gurkha hats made us readily identifiable. As I marched down the broad thoroughfare of Whitehall, where I had watched the Coronation procession all those years ago, I ruminated about my Regiment's service in the two world wars; those iron wars in both of which the Gurkha soldier, at some cost, made a strong and distinguished contribution. Among all the honours, the victories, the occasional setbacks and defeats, some episodes have always struck a particular chord with me. These fragments seem to be illustrative of the Gurkha soldier's wider contribution.

THE FIRST WORLD WAR 1914–18

On an extremely cold and wet Sunday towards the end of January, I drove the sixty miles from Calais to the crossroads and roundabout at Port Arthur, on the edge of the village of Neuve Chapelle. This village and its surroundings were the scene of the first large-scale battle fought by the Indian Corps as a single formation, in March 1915. The bitter weather that I experienced on my visit seemed appropriate, for it made me appreciate just what these soldiers had faced on their introduction to the Great War. Here, by the side of the crossroads – ground which the 2nd Battalion of my Regiment had crossed on their way to assault the Germans – stands the elegant memorial dedicated to the Indian soldiers who lost their lives in the battles of the Western Front in 1914 and 1915 and have no known grave.

The memorial is Indian in style, a sanctuary enclosed within a semi-circular wall, with a lotus-capped high column in the foreground, flanked by two carved tigers guarding the memorial. Engraved on the stone panels of the memorial walls, and grouped by regiment, are the names of some 5,000 officers and men of the Indian Army who fell in a succession of engagements, at Neuve Chapelle and elsewhere on the Western Front. Across three of the stone panels that decorate the walls are the names of 185 officers and men of the 2nd Goorkhas. Alongside them are the names of the riflemen who belonged to five other Gurkha regiments, together with men from the Punjab, Garwahl, the Frontiers, Madras and Burma and all the many regiments – and Indian labourers – who served in the Indian Corps. A further separate panel lists the men of many Indian regiments who died as prisoners of war and are buried at Zehrensdorf, near Berlin. Eighteen men of my Regiment are listed on that memorial. Some of the Gurkha prisoners held in Germany suffered from tuberculosis, and under a compassionate Anglo-German agreement they were moved to Switzerland and placed in a sanatorium under the care of Swiss doctors and the Red

Cross. They were greeted with much good cheer by the Swiss people, but I was unable to discover whether any 2nd Goorkha riflemen gratefully drew that fortunate straw.

As I was visiting, the wind howled and the continuous rain had already turned much of the heavy black soil of the region into a muddy quagmire. This area is part of the dull, flat farmland of North-Eastern France that lies close to the border with Belgium, immediately south of Ypres. It is largely featureless, save for old coal-mining slag heaps, and is peppered with small villages, substantially rebuilt in the wake of the pummelling each received in two world wars. They looked neglected and forlorn on that Sunday afternoon. No grand chateaus, cathedral spires or enticing bistros graced this somewhat bleak landscape. A few old broken German bunkers still decorate the fields to remind the visitor of what had happened there. Wrapping myself up warmly, I attempted to identify the ground over which my Regiment had fought in their various engagements with the Germans at Neuve Chapelle.

On 12 October 1914, the SS *Angora*, having left Bombay in late September, docked in Marseilles. On board were some 720 officers and men of the 2nd Battalion, 2nd Goorkhas, including a large draft from the 1st Battalion, one of the six Gurkha battalions that belonged to the Indian Corps, commanded by Lieutenant General Sir James Willcocks. They had been sent to France to reinforce the hard-pressed and exhausted British Expeditionary Force (BEF). The Battalion was part of the Meerut Division and together with the 1st Seaforths, 1st Battalion 9th Gurkhas, and 6th Jat Light Infantry, they made up the Dehra Dun Brigade. Although some of the soldiers had seen active service on the North-West Frontier or in other more modest Indian campaigns, the Gurkha riflemen were totally unfamiliar with the climate and terrain of France or the rigours of European warfare, and they were, initially at least, ill-equipped for the Western Front when compared to their British counterparts. They were certainly ill-matched with the superior numbers and weaponry of the Germans. Further, many men of the Indian Corps, including the Gurkhas, had only the vaguest notion of what the war was about, and little sense of the geography of the broader battlefield. While strongly loyal to their regiments and their British officers, and bound together with innate discipline and regimental comradeship, they nonetheless had less patriotic commitment than the men of the BEF.

The Gurkha battalions, along with the rest of the Meerut Division, were generously received by the French, with expressions of high Gallic expectation in the local press for their coming performance in battle; an expectation that would shortly be tested in extreme circumstances. By the time of the arrival of the Indian Corps, much of Belgium and large parts of France were already occupied by the Germans, and the Gurkhas' area of operations was to be just south of Ypres, where the Corps' first battles against the Germans had already taken place. It was here, in the drab countryside surrounding Neuve Chapelle, that the defensive line of General Haig's First Army, which included the Indian Corps, would be held, to prevent the Germans seizing the Channel ports of Calais and Boulogne.

Following preliminary preparations, briefings and kit issues and a cursory introduction to the French character, the Battalion entrained and moved north from Marseille. Then, on 28 October, they received orders to march at once for the front and take over trenches from the Northumberland Fusiliers, just short of Neuve Chapelle. This village, a salient pushing into the British line, had just been occupied by the Germans, who were pressing forward with constant attacks and bombardments. While moving to these trenches, the Battalion came under fire for the first time and suffered their initial casualties – four men being wounded. The Gurkhas found their designated trenches in bad condition and generally too deep for their shorter frames, and the Battalion, under sporadic fire throughout, spent the first day in the line improving them and repairing the battered parapets that offered little protection. To the great regret of the Battalion, and while this work was proceeding, Major Neil Macpherson, in command of the forward companies and whose father, General Sir Herbert Macpherson, had won a VC during the Indian Mutiny, commanded the Regiment and was a battlefield commander in the Second Afghan War, was shot through the head and killed, as were two riflemen. Others were wounded.

The countryside around Neuve Chapelle seen by the Gurkha soldier in his first engagement during that cold winter of 1914 was much as I saw it over a hundred years later – a flat desolate plain, with small scattered villages and farms standing in a sea of mud, and pools of stagnant water filling the numerous shell holes. The high water-table made the digging of deep trenches very difficult, and heavy rain would soon turn them into muddy excavations; the communication trenches were often no more than

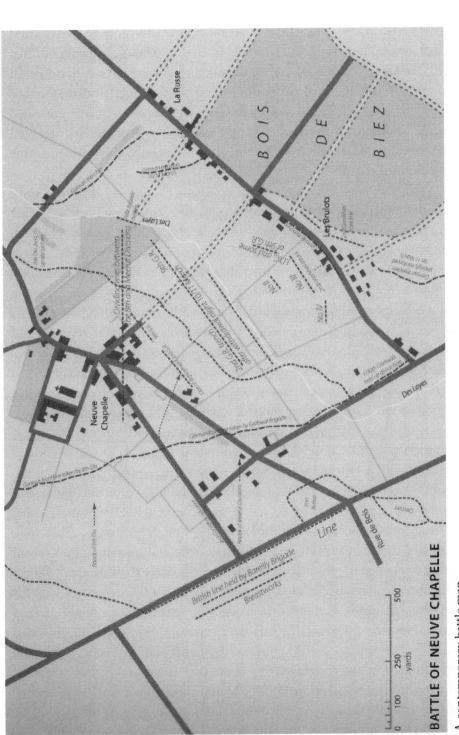

BATTLE OF NEUVE CHAPELLE

A contemporary battle map.

bottomless streams. The riflemen were regularly knee-deep in water, and if a man was wounded and fell, he would often drown before he could be lifted out. Walking over this ground in the middle of winter it was not difficult to imagine that life in these positions had been distinctly uncomfortable. This waterlogged ground and its drainage ditches and streams presented a real challenge to the Indian Corps, being devoid of much cover and strategically dominated from German positions on Aubers Ridge to the east, some three miles beyond the village.

Over the next few days, while continuing work on their defensive position, including the construction of new communication trenches, the Battalion was subject to bombardment of gathering intensity by high explosive shells. The German trenches were only some 100 yards distant and in some positions no more than 30 to 40 yards away, with the Battalion's forward company trenches forming a dangerous salient. On the morning of 2 November the enemy opened the day with heavy shelling on to those forward Gurkha positions; violent explosions obliterated the trenches and blew men high into the air, while others were buried alive. Survivors of this murderous assault sought cover where they could, as the Germans followed up their barrage with an infantry assault into the collapsed trenches. In this serious position, and against superior numbers, some robust counter-attacks were launched with much hand-to-hand fighting and further casualties. The Battalion's Commandant, Lieutenant Colonel Charles Norie, a veteran with a Distinguished Service Order won and an arm lost on the North-West Frontier, gathered the Battalion's reserve of one and a half companies and attempted to regain the line. Although inflicting some damage on the Germans, within 150 yards of the front trenches they were brought to a standstill by heavy German rifle and machine gun fire and were compelled to retire. Towards evening, the brave Commandant, amidst much confusion, once again attempted to launch a counter-attack with his reserve, but in the face of further losses the shaken survivors were forced back. Not surprisingly, as friends were scythed down, their officers killed and the forward positions subjected to fearful bombardment, some men ran to the rear and sought shelter where they could find it; but in general the companies held reasonably steady, and there were many brave actions by individual riflemen. At dawn the following morning, in the face of the weight of their casualties, the Battalion was ordered to retire and refit.

It had been a most testing start to the Battalion's campaign in France, as indeed it had been for much of the Indian Corps. Although the Battalion's sector of the line was invested for a time, it did appear that the general stubbornness of the Gurkhas and their British officers, together with their own heavy losses, had caused the Germans to withdraw to their own trenches during the night. The casualties from this grim opening affair were gross. Easily identified by the enemy, every one of the British officers in the forward companies had been killed. Of the twelve British officers who started out for Neuve Chapelle, seven were lost and a further one wounded, together with four Gurkha officers killed and three wounded. Additionally, 132 Gurkha soldiers were killed, wounded or missing; many of those missing had been buried alive during the heavy bombardment, while others had been taken prisoner. The scale of the losses and, critically, the annihilation of the Regiment's British officers, familiar faces to all ranks and bringing some cohesion to the battle, must have been sobering to say the least, and would have had a telling effect on the riflemen. The damage was not confined to the 2nd Goorkhas. All the other Gurkha battalions, and indeed most of the units of the Indian Corps, were to suffer similar losses in their introduction to the alien inferno of European warfare. Once out of the line, the Battalion reconstituted itself and prepared for the next challenge.

During the Battalion's period out of the trenches a singular event occurred when, on 12 November, the Indian Army's most famous and much decorated soldier, Field Marshal Lord Roberts VC, with whom the Regiment had served both on the Ridge at Delhi in 1857 and in 1880 on his famous march from Kabul to Kandahar, as well as in the subsequent Kandahar battle, paid a memorable visit to the Indian Corps. Contemporary reports suggest that his visit made a deep and encouraging impression. Sadly, however, when inspecting the Indian and Gurkha troops and seeing they were not wearing greatcoats, he discarded his own; in the cold conditions he contracted pneumonia and died a few miles away at St Omer two days later, much mourned by all. 'No other English soldier has commanded such measure of human affection,' wrote the Secretary of State for India to the Viceroy.

That winter cold also took its toll on the Gurkha soldier, many of the riflemen in the trenches suffering from frostbite and trench foot. As a precaution, at night men wore sandbags full of straw on each foot and leg, and whale oil well rubbed in to the limbs also helped. Lice, fleas, rats and the smell of death stalked the trenches. I very much felt that cold as I tramped around the village, and I could only admire the fortitude of the riflemen as they withstood both the elements and the enemy. It was with some relief that I regained the sanctuary of my warm motorcar – a privilege, I fear, denied to the men of the Indian Corps.

On 20 December the Battalion was back holding the line once more in the area of Neuve Chapelle, where it experienced two more days of severe battling. The German sappers managed to explode a mine under a forward company position and followed it with a sharp and heavy assault; but although the immediate area of the explosion had to be evacuated, the other companies held firm and prevented the enemy from exploiting his initial success. After 48 hours of fierce and bitter fighting the Battalion handed over the sector and were relieved by the Royal Sussex Regiment. In this second costly spell in the line the Battalion had lost 132 officers and men, killed and wounded. These continuing and grievous losses were replaced by new drafts of men from India and returning sick and wounded; by mid-January the Battalion had almost recovered its original strength of 720 Gurkhas, but attrition on this scale must have been extremely hard to bear.

Battalions on the Western Front faced two great tactical problems. The first was how to break through the enemy's trenches, usually constructed in depth, against defensive fire coming from all sides, secure them, and then move on into the country beyond. In addition to skill and courage in hand-to-hand fighting, this required the preparation and delivery of a complex and heavy artillery bombardment prior to the assault, designed to pulverize the enemy defensive positions and destroy their protective wire, while protecting the advancing troops with a curtain of fire. That fire would then lift rearwards, to prevent enemy reserves from re-occupying positions lost and launching counter-attacks. The second great problem was the difficulty of communication with and between the assaulting troops, when radios were far too cumbersome to be carried. Given that few battle plans survive contact with the enemy, the ability to pass information, adjust and issue new orders once an attack was under way, coordinate with flanking units or rapidly change the direction of travel, was limited largely, to flags, runners and line. All too frequently, thin field telephone line to the forward troops, if it existed at all, was destroyed by enemy artillery fire. Any sort of effective mobile command finished where the line ended.

After a further period of rest and refit, the Battalion returned for the third time to the Neuve Chapelle sector. It was to take a prominent part in the first major offensive by Haig's First Army, of which the Indian Corps was part. The aim was to breach the German line, one and a half miles wide, in front of the village, before pushing on to capture the high ground of Aubers Ridge. The assault allocated to the Indian Corps focussed on German positions to the south and west of the village and was to be carried out in two stages. First, on the morning of 10 March there was to be an assault by the Meerut Division's Garhwal Brigade. Prior to that Brigade's advance, the battle would be opened at 0730 hours with a carefully prepared and complex salvo from 480 guns pounding two miles of enemy positions for thirty-five minutes. With one gun for every six yards of front, this reduced the village of Neuve Chapelle and the German front trenches to rubble. Then, as the barrage lifted to its next targets, the leading companies of the Garhwal Brigade, including a Battalion of 3rd Gurkhas, swarmed over their parapets and into the attack, crossing no-man's-land and leaping into the pulverized trenches to kill the surviving, shell-shocked Germans. Two hours later, the enemy's hostile front at the south corner of the village was in the hands of the Garhwal Brigade, and they had linked up with the British 8th Division on their left. Together they had gained the village itself.

Then, in phase two of the battle, 2nd Goorkhas, together with the rest of the Dehra Dun Brigade, were ordered to exploit this success and advance to capture the wood beyond the village, the Bois du Biez. A fragment of the outline orders for the Battalion gives something of the flavour of the day:

> The order of march will be: No 4 Company; No 3 Company; the Scouts; the Signallers; No 1 Company; No 2 Company; Machine Guns.
>
> Greatcoats will be worn and each man will carry 200 rounds of ammunition, his emergency ration, and tomorrow's cooked ration in the haversack.

As the 2nd Goorkha companies deployed for this phase they came under heavy machine gun fire and sustained casualties. Nevertheless, No. 4 Company, led by Major Donald Watt and Captain Alexander Dallas-Smith, who had brought up bridging material to assist with the crossing of the obstacle of Layes Brook that crossed their line of advance, bravely succeeded in reaching the edge of the Bois du Biez and dug in. As night came on, enemy firing subsided and the leading companies reported the wood clear of enemy. But as the Battalion was preparing to consolidate on its objective, orders were received to withdraw some 500 yards. There had apparently been regrettable delays in the advance of troops of the 8th Division of the British IV Corps on the left flank who had been checked by strongly held German positions. The Battalion was thus isolated and exposed on its flank.

Very early next morning, 11 March, orders were received to reoccupy the wood, but in the interim the Germans had reinforced their positions. There was a thick fog, and while companies were moving forward they again came under heavy machine gun fire from new enemy trenches, and the two leading companies were forced to retire again to the positions of the night before. During this attack, three riflemen, Manjit Gurung, Partiman Gurung and Ujarsing Gurung, particularly distinguished themselves by attending to the wounded and bringing them back under fire, while Hastabir Roka, although badly wounded, brought up machine gun ammunition across fire-swept ground. All were rewarded with the Indian Order of Merit.

At 2.00 p.m. the Battalion was warned to stand by for a fresh attack, but from that point until dark the enemy kept up heavy fire, and any movement brought casualties. The Battalion was then told to stand fast behind Layes Brook, and more bridges were sent up to be placed across the brook for a possible further attack. But at 1.30 a.m. next morning the Dehra Dun Brigade was withdrawn from the battle, suffering more casualties from enfiladed machine guns in the process. The Corps Commander, concerned at the level of casualties, decided to hold firm on what his Corps had achieved. Extremely heavy German counter-attacks were then launched on 12 March, all of which were held by the British line. Following German counter-attacks a fresh assault on the Bois de Biez was then planned but vetoed by General Willcocks – to General Haig's disappointment – and the Meerut Division ordered to consolidate on its new positions. A massed German counter-attack, described by those present as an astonishing spectacle, was beaten off by the Indian Corps, the Germans suffering massive casualties and breaking up in much disorder.

This closed the grim and somewhat inconclusive affair that was the Battle of Neuve Chapelle. It had, however, gained the British and Indian

Corps the entire village and a successful advance across a two-mile front to a depth of 1,000 yards. Modest it may seem today in the great sum of things, but this was the first time in the war that the German line had been breached, and the cost had been great. The Battalion casualties amounted to ninety-one killed, wounded and missing; in three days of fighting the Indian Corps as a whole had suffered 4,000 casualties, while an estimate of German losses puts them at not far off 18,000, and nearly 2,000 German prisoners had fallen into British hands. In spite of securing only limited objectives, it was seen as a huge victory for the Indian Corps, and a delighted General Willcocks declared, 'We had shown that the Indians will face any enemy.'

The 2nd Battalion was to remain on the Western Front, battling hard and fiercely in the general area of Neuve Chapelle, until the end of the 1915, when they sailed for Egypt, and the bulk of the Indian Corps left France for the Turkish front. La Bassée 1914, Festubert 1914–15, Givenchy 1914, Aubers and Loos, all embraced by France and Flanders 1914–15, were the Battle Honours for the Regiment that were to sit alongside Neuve Chapelle. It is salutary to record that by the end of that year the total casualties sustained in France by 2nd Goorkhas amounted to 560 killed, wounded and missing, coupled with an extended list of gallantry medals. Losses are no measure of battlefield efficiency, but the fact that the Battalion was able to suffer these casualties and remain, reinforced by battlefield replacements, a fighting unit, says much for the regimental spirit that sustained it. Of the many tributes in the wake of Neuve Chapelle I was drawn to a message from the Battalion's Brigade Commander, General Swinton Jacob:

> The Goorkha Battalions (2nd and 9th) had an opportunity of making up for the terrible ordeals they have been through in the earlier days of the war, and they took full advantage of it. Their spirits were high and nothing could stop their dash.

Aubers Ridge, the battle's original final objective three miles beyond Neuve Chapelle, was not to be captured until three years later – a sad and brutal commentary on the cost of every yard of ground gained in that terrible and costly war of attrition.

Although not part of the 2nd Battalion's fighting on the Western Front that was so indicative of the contribution made by all the Indian Corps' six Gurkha battalions, there is one incident I should record. There were many individual acts of bravery by Indian and Gurkha soldiers, but in the autumn of 1915 there was a significant act of valour at the Battle of Loos. Prior to the First World War, British officers from Gurkha regiments had won nine Victoria Crosses, but until 1911 soldiers of the Indian Army, for major acts of gallantry, were awarded the Indian Order of Merit. On the orders of the King, issued during his Durbar in India in 1911, this changed; all soldiers in the Indian Army became entitled to the award of the Victoria Cross, and Rifleman Kulbir Thapa, who served with the 2nd Battalion of the 3rd Gurkhas, became the first Gurkha to be so recognized.

Kulbir was the sole wounded survivor of an abortive wire-cutting party who, acting with unselfish courage, saved the lives of three other wounded soldiers. He had managed to fight his way through the German wire and into a trench, where he found a wounded private soldier of the Leicestershire Regiment believed to be Bill Keightley from Melton Mowbray. Keightley begged Kulbir to leave him, but Kulbir stayed for the rest of the day and that night until, under cover of early morning mist, he got Keightley out of the trench and through the German wire without being seen and left him concealed in a shell hole. Kulbir then returned twice to the wire to recover two wounded Gurkhas from his party. Finally he brought the three men to safety by carrying them on his back, one at a time, crawling across no-man's-land to Allied lines, all the while under fire. On the last occasion, German soldiers actually applauded his bravery as he returned for the third time. During the centenary events marking the Armistice I was much struck by the huge and poignant image of Kulbir sketched in the sand on the beach at Lyme Regis. He was one of a number of gallant Great War veterans briefly recognized in this fashion before the tide washed the portraits away. This was the 'Pages of the Sea' project designed by Danny Boyle to mark the 100th anniversary of the Armistice, and I have included a photograph of it in this book.

After the withdrawal of the Indian Corps from France, the Gurkha soldier was to serve in every other theatre of operations during the war. Regiments from France joined others already deployed from India to battle the Turks. There is no space to record the deeds of my 1st Battalion, who were to fight in Mesopotamia and Persia and even against the Bolsheviks until 1921, before they returned to Dehra Dun. Their casualties, amounting to 186 officers and men killed and 414 wounded, give an indication of the severity of their campaigning.

Stalemate on the Western Front led to the ill-fated amphibious expedition to Gallipoli, where three Gurkha battalions formed part of General Hamilton's force. History naturally focusses on the major contribution of the Australian and New Zealand troops, but Gurkhas, too, played a significant role. The 1st Battalion 6th Gurkhas was ordered to capture Sari Bair Ridge overlooking the Dardanelles – a key Turkish position. In a famous feat of arms, they alone reached the top of the Ridge, and the Turks ran. But the Gurkhas were in a parlous position; all the British officers with the exception of the doctor had been killed or wounded; there were no communications, and expected reinforcements failed to arrive; they were, lamentably, shelled by their own side. The Turks counter-attacked, and the Gurkhas, now resolutely led by their senior Gurkha Officer, were forced to withdraw. But there was at least one fortunate outcome. While attacking up Sari Bair Ridge the 6th Gurkhas were watched by a wounded officer of the Royal Warwickshire Regiment. Impressed by what he saw of the Gurkha riflemen in the attack, he changed regiments and joined the 6th Gurkhas. His name was Bill Slim. Many years later, as Commander of the Fourteenth Army, he was to turn defeat into victory in the Burma campaign of the Second World War, and with him were to march 35,000 Gurkha soldiers, including two battalions of the 2nd Goorkhas.

THE SECOND WORLD WAR

The demands of the Second World War on the Indian Army's Gurkha Brigade were many. Over the five years of the war, 130,000 Gurkhas manned and reinforced ten regular battalions and thirty-six more raised for the duration of the war, as well as many ancillary units. This overall total included two parachute units and three further battalions for the 2nd Goorkhas to add to their two regular ones. The pressure on the regimental centres responsible for the recruiting and training of these men was immense, as it was on their British officers, often straight from civilian life and granted emergency wartime commissions, to learn the language and lead them all.

It is beyond the scope of this book to record the fighting deeds of these many battalions, and a few brief details must suffice, save for the adventures of my own 1st Battalion, who marched with the Eighth Army in North Africa. So, my story is limited to one of the Regiment's many battles as it traversed the Western Desert with 4th Indian Division and fought over one of the great battlegrounds of the Second World War.

In August 1942 the Battalion, having initially travelled through some historic cities of the Middle East – Mosul, Baghdad, Basra, Abadan and Haifa, with an interlude in Cyprus – well trained and acclimatized but without huge excitement or serious battle, arrived in Egypt to join 7 Brigade of 4th Indian Division. The Division was commanded by the Battalion's old Commandant, the supremely able and deeply thoughtful commander, Major General Francis Tuker. Tuker's stress on the importance of mobility and surprise when commanding the Battalion on the North-West Frontier was to serve the Battalion and his Division in good stead in the months of fighting ahead.

As a character, the Divisional Commander in many ways contrasted sharply with Montgomery, his Army Commander. Tuker's personality was somewhat withdrawn and intellectual, but if he lacked flamboyance he certainly had the interests and welfare of his men at the forefront of his mind and was deeply appreciative of the fighting qualities of the soldiers he commanded. He was never prepared to squander their lives unnecessarily and was much respected for his tactical acumen. He was greatly admired by his Division.

Commanding the 1st Battalion was one of its most dashing and legendary regimental officers, the last of those who had fought in the Great War. Os Lovett was a man of great physical strength and energy and possessed of an iron will; he evinced, it was said, 'the unmistakable characteristics of leadership'. He also possessed a fine reputation as a horseman and polo player and had been renowned when a younger officer as a general hell-raiser with a fat portfolio of unpaid bills. His officers and soldiers would have followed him anywhere. The Battalion had arrived in the Desert at a propitious and electric moment. Tobruk had fallen, the First Battle of Alamein and its architect, General Auchinleck, had come and gone; Lieutenant General Bernard Montgomery had arrived to reinvigorate and command Eighth Army with orders to end the war in North Africa; Rommel and his Afrika Corps were on the offensive; and the Second Battle of El Alamein awaited.

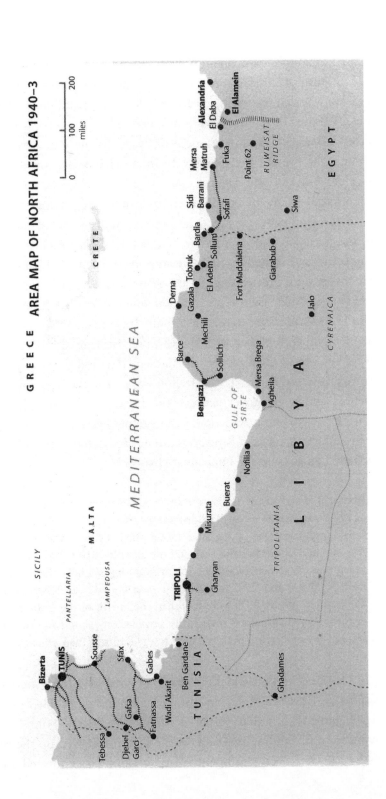

AREA MAP OF NORTH AFRICA 1940-3

GREECE

CRETE

MEDITERRANEAN SEA

SICILY

PANTELLARIA

MALTA

LAMPEDUSA

Bizerta
TUNIS
Sousse
Sfax
Gabes
Ben Gardane
Tebessa
Djebel Garci
Gafsa
Fatnassa
Wadi Akarit
Ghadames

TUNISIA

TRIPOLI
Gharyan
Misurata
Buerat
Nofilia

TRIPOLITANIA

LIBYA

Aghelia
Mersa Brega
Bengazi
Solluch
Barce
Mechili
Derma
Gazala
Tobruk
El Adem
Bardia
Sollum
Fort Maddalena
Giarabub

GULF OF SIRTE

CYRENAICA

Jalo

Siwa

Sidi Barrani
Sofafi
Mersa Matruh
Fuka
Point 62
El Daba
Alexandria
El Alamein

RUWEISAT RIDGE

EGYPT

0   100   200
miles

The Battalion's campaigning had started with a shocking disaster. On 28 August, at a reception camp near Cairo, an officer from the Royal Engineers was demonstrating to the whole of the Battalion's Headquarter Company the art of arming land mines; with other mines lying at his feet he inserted a detonator and, seemingly unaware that he was instructing with live mines, he pressed the plunger. In the terrible explosion that followed, sixty-eight Gurkha officers and men were killed outright and eighty-five were injured, many being blinded or losing limbs. Only twenty-eight men of the Company remained unhurt. Aside from the shocking human cost, the Battalion had, at a stroke, lost many of its specialists: the carrier platoon, drivers, signallers and the mortar and anti-tank platoons – the tragic losses were greater than in any of the Battalion's subsequent battles in the Desert. Such are the great misfortunes of war, but it required much fortitude and leadership to recover rapidly from that awful event.

In September, together with the rest of 7 Brigade, the Battalion moved forward into the centre of the El Alamein line and on to a promontory known as Ruweisat Ridge. The Battalion was now in the front line of a major battlefield and began to experience the harassing fire and Stuka attacks that were part of the unwelcome privilege of that role. Something of the flavour and character of this position, to be repeated in much of the Desert campaign, comes from the Divisional History:

> Except in a few sandy hollows, there was no cover. A slit trench could only be cut with an air drill out of solid stone. A shallow saucer-shaped sangar preserved the appearance rather than the reality of protection. The sun beat upon the solid rock and the glare struck the eyes like a knife. Every passing vehicle ploughed dust into the air, to choke the mouth and nostrils. Water and fuel were precious and issued sparingly. Yet all the dangers and discomforts were less than the horror of the clotted masses of flies which maintained their filthy siege as long as warmth was in the air. This living carrion pestered men to the limits of their endurance.

On 23 October the Battle of El Alamein opened, and from the Battalion's positions on Ruweisat Ridge an unforgettable scene unfolded to the crash of 1,200 guns; then, following fierce armoured battles, 4th Indian Division, moving from its holding position on the Ridge, followed up the retreating Axis forces. Os Lovett's rampant roving columns encountered a long line of retreating Italian infantry with their carriers and, beating off their escort of light tanks, captured over 2,000 men including the Divisional Commander. The Battalion had started its fighting with an early success, and the Eighth Army's victory at El Alamein was very welcome to a British people long starved of good news.

In the ensuing six months the Battalion built a firm reputation for itself, operating with particular dexterity and distinction as Montgomery's Eighth Army pushed its way, somewhat ponderously, back across the desert over which it had originally retreated. Mersa Matruh, Tobruk, Gazala, Benghazi and Tripoli – all returned to Allied hands before the Eighth Army entered Tunisia. Evidence of the sterling quality of the Battalion's performance was the promotion of Os Lovett to the command of 7 Brigade, within 4th Indian Division, while James Showers, descended from a long line of distinguished Indian Army soldiers, took command of the 1st Battalion. By March 1943 Rommel, in ill-health, had left the theatre and handed command of his Afrika Korps to the experienced Colonel General Hans-Jurgen Von Arnim; the reduced Axis forces took up a holding position on the strong Mareth Line, some eighty miles inside Tunisia. In Eighth Army's biggest operation since El Alamein, and after a series of battles and counter-attacks including an outflanking assault by 4th Indian Division, the Axis forces were edged out of their position. By the end of March Von Arnim had conducted a fighting withdrawal some forty miles further back into Tunisia to Rommel's favoured and stronger defensive position astride the Akarit line.

The Wadi Akarit position lay on a rough east-west line some twelve miles wide, running inland from the Mediterranean coast before reaching an impassable salt marsh that then stretched for some 120 miles beyond. The position started with four miles of flat coastal corridor, followed by the deep trough of the Wadi Akarit itself, while at the point where the wadi became shallow and narrow it was protected by an anti-tank ditch and the steep-sided, low Roumana hills that served as flank guard to the coastal strip. At the far end, and before the oozy sloughs of the salt marshes were reached, was the Jebel Fatnassa massif, a steep, jagged 800ft feature, a tangle of escarpments, rocky spires, deep fjord-like chimneys and ridges, with precipitous approaches and considered to be impassable to attacking forces. The Akarit line was ideal for defence, and Rommel had reported to Hitler that it was virtually impregnable. There were no flanks to turn, and it seemed that a frontal attack against prepared defences was unavoidable.

Montgomery planned an initial frontal assault with 51st Highland Division, together with a number of armoured brigades on the right to break through on the coastal corridor; 50th Division would be in the centre and 4th Indian Division on the left, short of the Jebel Fatnassa and tasked to take the Roumana hills. This was exactly what the Germans expected Eighth Army to do and they deployed their forces accordingly. General Tuker bravely dissented from this plan – 'the second highest ground is no good' – and together with his Corps Commander, General Oliver Leese, persuaded Montgomery to allow 4th Indian Division to attack the Jebel Fatnassa itself, using his mountain-trained infantry – primarily the Gurkhas – to surprise the defence. Difficult as it was to take Fatnassa, if that position was won, the whole of the Wadi Akarit line would be dominated from on high and would give the British command of the rear of the Axis position. General Tuker's plan envisaged a silent night attack some hours before the main battle. Os Lovett's 7 Brigade, with the 1st Battalion in the vanguard, would first seize the main Fatnassa feature, while 5 Brigade, with a battalion of 9th Gurkhas, would follow through and swing into the rear of the German defences. A corridor would then be opened through which armoured forces could close for the kill before the enemy could disengage. After much consideration, Tuker's plan was adopted and Divisional responsibilities were adjusted accordingly. The formidable reputation of 4th Indian Division and its commander was at stake.

The Jebel Fatnassa massif was defended by the Italian XX1 Corps with troops of the 80th Infantry Division 'Trieste' and the German 164th 'Leichte Afrika' Division. On the days preceding the attack a large-scale sand map faithfully reproducing the Fatnassa feature was built; in Colonel Showers' battle orders the rifle companies were allocated their tasks, and every officer and NCO familiarized themselves on the model with the exact lie of the land.

On 5 April at 1900 hours the three-mile approach march began. C and D Companies led the way, with Colonel Showers and his small tactical headquarters echeloned between them; A and B Companies followed. At 2330 hours the leading elements crossed the start line, the dim silhouette

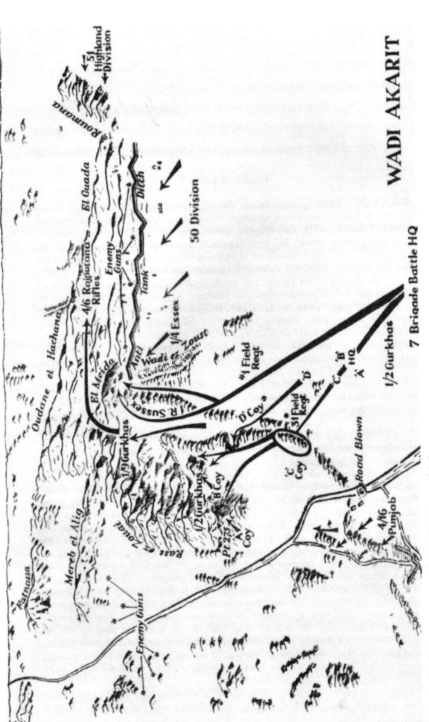

Battle of Wadi Akarit, 5–7 April 1943 Lines of Advance

(History of 4th Indian Division)

of Fatnassa appeared in front of the Battalion and the silent night attack was underway. Black clouds moved across the face of a sickle moon as D Company headed for the mouth of a rocky chimney between escarpments. The remainder of the Battalion swung slightly left.

C Company was first to engage with the enemy when a sentry gave the alarm before being cut down, and then riflemen, *kukris* in hand, surged up the escarpments. Before long, A, B and C Companies were all engaged in bitter hand-to-hand fighting, clambering up the broken ridges and seizing their early objectives. Meanwhile, D Company advanced on its critical mission in the corridor between escarpments to the left and right that led to the heart of the enemy's defensive position. It was vital that this passage be opened up so that the follow-on Brigade could pass through. The fate of the attack depended on rapid success in this chimney.

Subedar Lalbahadur Thapa, Second-in-Command of D Company, led the way with two sections of 16 Platoon, and extracts from the Subedar's citation that gained him his Victoria Cross tell the story:

> First contact with the enemy was made at the foot of a pathway winding up a narrow cleft. This steep cleft was thickly studded with a series of enemy posts, the inner of which contained an anti-tank gun and the remainder medium machine-guns. After passing through the narrow cleft, one emerges into a small arena with very steep sides, some 200 feet in height, and in places sheer cliff. Into this arena and down its sides numbers of automatic weapons were trained and mortar fire directed.
>
> The garrison of the outer posts were all killed by Subedar Lalbahadur Thapa and his men by kukri and bayonet in the first rush and the enemy then opened very heavy fire straight down the narrow, enclosed pathway and steep arena sides. Subedar Lalbahadur Thapa led his men on and fought his way up the narrow gulley straight through the enemy's fire, with little room to manoeuvre, in the face of intense and sustained machine-gun concentrations and the liberal use of grenades by the enemy.
>
> The next machine-gun posts were dealt with, Subedar Lalbahadur Thapa personally killing two men with his kukri and two more with his revolver. This Gurkha officer continued to fight his way up the narrow bullet-swept approaches to the crest. He and two Riflemen, (Riflemen Harakbahadur Gurung and Indrabahadur Gurung) managed to reach the crest, where Subedar Lalbahadur killed another two men with his kukri, the Riflemen killed two more and the rest fled. Subedar Lalbahadur

Thapa then secured the whole feature and covered his Company's advance up the defile.

This pathway was found to be the only practicable route up the precipitous ridge, and by securing it the Company was able to deploy and mop up all enemy opposition on their objective. This objective was an essential feature covering the further advance of the Brigade and of the Division, as well as the bridgehead over the anti-tank ditch. The ruthless determination of this Gurkha officer to reach his objective and kill his enemy had a decisive effect on the success of the whole operation.

Colonel Showers, hurrying forward, soon discovered that the assault had won home and that on the main feature all his Companies had accomplished their tasks at the first onset. As he returned to his battle headquarters he passed columns of 5 Brigade hurrying forward towards Lalbahadur's corridor. Two hours before Eighth Army's main attack was to go in at dawn, the vital high ground, the key to the whole position, had been seized, and the way to Tunis was open. The Regiment knew it had won a great battle, and General Tuker, inspecting the position taken by his old Battalion, marvelled 'at the skill of the men who captured the bastion of the hills'.

Following this much vaunted and highly publicized victory at Wadi Akarit for General Tuker's 4th Indian Division, with Brigadier Os Lovett's 7 Brigade and James Showers' 1st Battalion to the fore, all three 2nd Goorkha Commanders were awarded the Distinguished Service Order; and in addition to Subedar Lalbahadur's Victoria Cross, sixteen officers and men of the Battalion received decorations. Such was the significance of the victory. The cost to the Battalion of this key engagement was relatively light considering the strength of the position they had assaulted: five British officers and three Gurkha officers were wounded, fourteen Gurkhas were killed and thirty-two wounded. Os Lovett himself was wounded in three places by mortar fire during the battle but continued to command his Brigade until the issue was no longer in doubt. Not surprisingly, this lightning seizure under cover of darkness – a classic night attack – received worldwide acclaim; the Gurkhas caught the public eye and a brief dazzling spotlight was shone on them. It was a very satisfying vindication of General Tuker's plan.

Sadly, the success at Wadi Akarit could not be immediately exploited either by General Patton's 2 US Corps cutting into the Axis retreat from the rear, or the Eighth Army exploiting forward with 1st Armoured Division as Von Arnim and the remnants of his Afrika Corps retreated from the Akarit position. General Tuker's entreaty to 'get the whips out' went unheeded, and Montgomery in his characteristically deliberate way was unable to exploit the gap. After some initial counter-attacks on 4th Indian Division's positions that were repulsed, a day later, the enemy had vanished and the chance of a knockout blow was lost. Thus a decisive victory in North Africa was to be delayed, the 4th Indian Division picked up the trail again, and there was more fierce battling for the Battalion at Endaville with the First Army before Tunis was reached and the war in the Desert was all but over. Along with the Eighth Army and its 4th Indian Division, 1st Battalion had traversed over 1,500 miles of the Western Desert and fought with great distinction from El Alamein to Tunis. Of the Wadi Akarit battle Montgomery was to record in his diary: 'We had on this day the heaviest and most savage fighting since I commanded the Eighth Army. My troops fought magnificently especially the 4th Indian Division and the 51st Highland Division.'

One final and unexpected prize was won just as the campaign was ending. In early May 1943 the Battalion was rounding up the final remnants of the trapped Axis armies, just short of Tunis. Colonel Showers was moving amongst his rifle companies and, accompanied by his orderly, Rifleman Sarganah Limbu, climbed to the crest of a hillock to reconnoitre. Below him he saw a German officer beside a staff car which bore a flag of truce. On accosting this emissary, he was told that General von Arnim, Commander-in-Chief of the Axis troops in Africa, was to be found at the Headquarters of Afrika Corps near at hand. Showers described the aftermath of this encounter:

> Leaving the companies in position, I and my orderly got into the German staff car (very glad to sit down after our long and hot walk), drove up the road and up a side valley. Here hundreds of Huns had fallen in in rows. We got out of the car and walked to Von Arnim's caravan. I must have looked a grim sight, covered in dust and sweat, two days' beard, a plaster on a cut over one eye, a captured Luger pistol and a *kukri* on my belt, my orderly with his tommy gun at the ready, taking no chances. Real pirates we must have seemed to the neat German staff officers, but they were all most polite and punctilious about saluting.

A letter of surrender was despatched to General Tuker, who arrived on the scene and confronted his adversary. Noticing that von Arnim was armed he requested him to surrender his pistol, and Von Arnim threw it to the ground. When the terms of surrender had been arranged, the German Commander-in-Chief was driven away under a Divisional escort accompanied by Captain Monty Ormsby from the 1st Battalion. Meanwhile, Colonel Showers, rummaging in Von Arnim's caravan, found six bottles of Heidsieck champagne under the bed – a welcome bonus, as was the General's pistol which, together with his Mercedes staff car, eventually found its way to the Regiment's home at Dehra Dun. For the second time in less than a month the 1st Battalion was briefly international news as the press rushed to record the capture of the Commander-in-Chief and the surrender of the Afrika Corps. They lost no opportunity to link the victors of Wadi Akarit with the dramatic final scenes in the Western Desert.

On 19 June, rested after their exertions, 4th Indian Division was reviewed by King George VI along the hot and dusty Tripoli–Castel Benito road, where the Gurkhas were drawn up in two ranks on either side of the highway. With the King in his open car were General Montgomery and General Francis Tuker. Reaching Colonel Showers, the King and his accompanying generals dismounted and, after introductions, the King pinned the ribbon of the Victoria Cross on to the tunic of Subedar Lalbahadur Thapa.

Flushed with success, the Battalion then started to prepare for the grim challenges of the Italian campaign, but in North Africa, 4th Indian Division and not least its 2nd Goorkha riflemen had left their mark as they were to do again in Italy. As ever in battle, it was the man that had counted.

Later, Field Marshal Wavell was to write of Francis Tuker's 4th Indian Division:

> The fame of this Division will surely go down as one of the great fighting formations in military history, to be spoken of with such as The Tenth Legion, The Light Division of the Peninsula War and Napoleon's Old Guard.

The 1st Battalion was to continue campaigning for another two years. It fought its way up the spine of Italy and experienced the prolonged horrors of the battle for Monte Cassino where, as one Gurkha officer put it, 'even the brave faltered', and then the battles of the Gothic Line. After that, the internecine struggles in Greece were to occupy their attention until, after four and a half years' service abroad, they returned home to Dehra Dun, with a high and famous reputation won and many tales to tell.

THE BURMA CAMPAIGN

For the other 2nd Goorkha battalions, and for the rest of the Gurkha Brigade, the pendulum of battle was to swing back and forth, with some reverses and some good fortune. Outside of North Africa and Italy, the theatre of their endeavours was the Far East, for in December 1941 an expansionist Japan had entered the war on the side of the Axis powers. In one hundred dark days, Hong Kong, Indo-China, Malaya and Singapore, Siam (now Thailand), the Dutch East Indies and the Philippines had all fallen to a rampant Imperial Army.

In September 1941, in the face of the impending threat and fresh from a return from the North-West Frontier, the 2nd Battalion had been transhipped with two other Gurkha battalions from India to Malaya. It had then fought a series of costly delaying actions down the jungle-clad back of that country before reaching Singapore. There, on that so-called island fortress and without firing a shot at the enemy, the Battalion had been ordered, incomprehensibly, to surrender in a most humiliating defeat for British arms. For three years and more the remnants of the 2nd Battalion, along with so many others, would be prisoners of war.

To add to this serious setback for the Allies, on 19 January 1942 the leading division of General Iida Shojiro's Japanese Fifteenth Army crossed the border from Siam and invaded Burma. Here the Japanese aim was twofold: firstly, to cut off the flow of war material via the Burma Road into Nationalist China that was hampering their ambitious plans to complete their conquest of China; secondly, by occupying Burma, to place themselves at the gates of India and promote insurrection against the British Raj. The rich resources that lay within Burma itself, as elsewhere in South-East Asia, were an additional lure.

Burma is a huge country of arid plains, teak and bamboo forest, swamp and jungle, together with dense mountainous regions and great rivers that flow over 800 miles from the Himalayas to the Gulf of Siam. It is a harsh and was then a disease-ridden land with a debilitating climate, and it was now occupied by a fanatical enemy with dominance in the air – a challenging operational environment to say the least. The rivers of Sittang and Irrawady, the capital city of Rangoon and the lilting syllables of Mandalay, the Arakan and the Chindwin – these were names that might once have struck an irresistible, Kiplingesque image of tropical splendour; but, together with Imphal and Kohima across its border with India, they would soon carry a more sombre resonance as the battle honours of the regiments that fought in Burma. The Japanese Army itself was a formidable foe: seemingly impervious to death, fanatical in attack and hugely stubborn in defence.

The details of this most testing of campaigns, which was to last nearly four years, are largely for another place, and the barest of facts must suffice. At one time or another, twenty-seven Gurkha battalions fought in Burma. For the most part they were under command of General Bill Slim – a Gurkha Rifleman himself, and a consummate commander in every way. It was Slim, after a most unpromising start, with an 800-mile ignominious retreat to the borders of India, who was to fashion his Fourteenth Army into a most formidable fighting force and with brilliant generalship inflict a crushing defeat on the most resolute of opponents. The Gurkha soldier played a significant part in all of this – firstly, and defensively, during the Japanese dynamic advance, their capture of Rangoon and Mandalay and the early setbacks in the Arakan; and then in the British offensive that began with the battles at Imphal and Kohima and took the Fourteenth Army back through Burma, until the Japanese were finally vanquished.

A singular officer, a man of biblical features and rhetoric, eccentric and unpredictable, had also entered this grim theatre of operations – Orde Wingate. He planned and organized two expeditions by deep penetration forces behind enemy lines to harry and harass and tie down the Japanese. He called his men Chindits, the title being a corruption of the name given to the mythological winged creatures that guard Burmese pagodas – *Chinthe*. For the first expedition, Gurkhas provided nearly half the force of 3,000 men – the 2nd Goorkhas' 3rd Battalion and some 500 muleteers drawn from across the Gurkha Brigade. That first expedition lasting three months was expensive, the Gurkhas suffering 446 casualties and achieving little. The Regiment's Lieutenant Nicky Neill, commanding the Gurkha muleteers in one of the columns and who was to lead 2nd Goorkha riflemen in many jungle campaigns over the next twenty-five years, was a critic. Although admiring the overall concept, he thought the training ill-conceived, Wingate's man-management, aloofness and indifference to the fate of the wounded were poor, and the general preparation for the expedition inadequate. Others including General Wavell were more generous; not least, they realized the publicity benefits that accrued from the Chindits operating behind enemy lines, doing a great deal for morale at a time of many defeats.

The second expedition, almost a year later, was far stronger and included four Gurkha battalions. It was marred by the death of Wingate in an air crash, and some of the impetus of the Chindits went with him, but those four months of endless marching and fighting caused the Japanese to divert huge resources away from the crucial battles at Imphal and Kohima. Three members of the Gurkha Brigade were awarded Victoria Crosses for their gallantry as Chindits.

Before leaving Burma and as the 3rd Battalion made its way fighting down through that demanding country, there was one incident that needs recording. On 4 March 1945, as the campaign was reaching its final throes, the Battalion was involved in a seaborne landing in the Arakan to occupy a hill feature known as Snowden. Commanding the Battalion's B Company was Nicky Neill, who had experienced the first Chindit operation. The intimate details of what was essentially his battle need not concern us. Suffice to say that in the course of it there occurred an act of singular and premeditated bravery and leadership by a Gurkha – a rough, tough rifleman called Bhanbhagta Gurung. While assaulting Snowden, the company having suffered many casualties, Rifleman Bhanbhagta's section was pinned down by heavy Japanese machine gun, grenade and mortar fire; a tree sniper was also inflicting casualties. Bhanbhagta, unable to engage the sniper from the prone position, calmly stood up, fully exposing himself to enemy fire, and shot the sniper dead. Continuing the advance, the section was again pinned down, but without waiting for orders the intrepid Bhanbhagta dashed forward alone and attacked the first enemy foxhole to his front. Throwing in two grenades, he killed the two occupants. In the same manner he dealt with the next foxhole, killing two more Japanese with his bayonet. Two further foxholes that were still bringing fire to bear on his section were then dealt with by Bhanbhagta with bayonet and grenade. Then, continuing forward alone, he dealt with a fifth Japanese bunker.

Jumping on to its roof he flung two smoke grenades through the bunker's slit, and two Japanese, partially blinded by the smoke, rushed out and were despatched by Bhanbhagta with his *kukri*. A remaining Japanese inside the bunker was also dealt with by this tough and gallant rifleman. Bhanbhagta's brave and angry personal assault had inspired his Company and was to lead to the capture of the objective.

Bhanbhagta's courage earned him one of the nine Victoria Crosses awarded to the officers and men of the Gurkha Brigade in Burma. Years later, this indomitable soldier came to visit my Battalion in Hong Kong, where his three fine sons were all serving in the Regiment, and they were pictured all together (*see* plate section). They were a strong family.

The contribution of the Gurkha soldier to the final success of the Burma campaign had been enormous, but the cost was heavy: 2,600 Gurkhas were killed in action, including 113 of their British officers. It was a remarkable episode in the Gurkha soldier's history of hard fighting and sacrifice, a victory born of great resolution and endurance. The outcome of the Burma campaign has always been a contentious issue among military historians, but for all the subsequent tragedies of Burma, a victorious invasion by the Japanese would have been calamitous for the Allies and for India. It was the successful defensive battles at Imphal and Kohima in 1944, when the Gurkhas played a significant role, that prevented Japanese penetration of India and represented the turning point for British fortunes in the Far East. These battles produced the greatest defeat suffered by the Japanese Imperial Army at the hands of the British Indian Army and allowed the British to leave Asia with a measure of dignity, even if power in Burma was surrendered and the Chinese Nationalists were pushed by the Communists across the sea to Taiwan. As for the Japanese, their seventeenth century poet Matsuo Basho might characterize for them the meaning of their defeat in his haiku:

> Summer grasses…
>   all that is left of
>   the dreams of soldiers…

In 1995, fifty years on from that victory in Burma, the anniversary of the Japanese surrender was marked with a memorable parade in London. I watched it with thousands of others as a large column of veterans, including five of the six surviving Gurkha holders of the Victoria Cross won in the Burma campaign, paraded past the Queen in the Mall. During their visit to England I accompanied these fine Gurkhas – Agansing Rai, Gaje Ghale, Ganju Lama, Lachhiman Gurung and my old friend Bhanbhagta Gurung from the Regiment – to visit the President of the Gurkha Brigade Association, Field Marshal Lord Bramall, at his home in Surrey. It was a significant gathering in many ways, and one particular incident stays with me. Following copious drinks in the Field Marshal's garden we all set off for a popular Indian restaurant in Farnham, where we had reserved a large table. It was a happy, garrulous and drink-fuelled gathering that began to attract attention from the packed restaurant. The Field Marshal stood up, called for silence in the way that only Field Marshals can, and announced to the diners:

> Ladies and Gentlemen, I want to apologise for the noise, but you need to know that you are dining tonight with five holders of the Victoria Cross.

Immediately, and as one, the whole restaurant rose to its feet and greeted the Gurkhas with prolonged cheering. It was an entirely spontaneous response and it moved us all most greatly.

Chapter 7

Partition and New Beginnings

At the stroke of the midnight hour, when the world sleeps,
India will awake to life and freedom.

—Jawaharlal Nehru

The contribution that the 2nd Goorkhas had made to the Indian
Army's remarkable and voluntary effort in the Second World War
can be measured not only by its battle honours and decorations
but also by the work of the Regimental Centre at Dehra Dun. It was this
organization that recruited and enlisted, trained and administered the
11,000 2nd Goorkha riflemen who served in the Regiment during the war.
It expanded from its two pre-war regular battalions to a total of five with
the raising of a further three wartime battalions, and the other Gurkha
regiments would expand in similar fashion.

The recruits who helped to man the new battalions would also provide
the battlefield casualty replacements helping to maintain the fighting
battalions up to their wartime establishment. Many more were employed

in the Centre itself, preparing men for service, and externally, in the vast plethora of Army training establishments and schools and the support units of a myriad of headquarters and bases. Others volunteered for service in one of the two Gurkha parachute battalions or served as military policemen and in other roles. In addition, many pensioned veterans flocked to their old Centre to put their services at the disposal of the Regiment, just as they had done over eighty years before at the time of the Mutiny. These men all wore the *lali* with much pride and had been attested on the Queen's Truncheon. The regimental cadre of British officers was also greatly expanded with wartime and emergency commissions, so that in the course of the war some 350 officers' names were entered on the Regiment's rolls.

In September 1945, with the war over, the Gurkha regiments were all widely scattered, none more so than the 2nd Goorkhas. The 1st Battalion was in Greece and the 2nd Battalion languished in Singapore, recovering its strength in the aftermath of the Japanese surrender, free men again after over three harsh years in enemy captivity. The 3rd Battalion had landed in North Malaya to re-establish British authority and assist in the rounding up of Japanese forces. The 4th Battalion, having served on the Frontier and in Burma, had then been sent to French Indo-China to sort out the surrendered Japanese and establish law and order in the former French colony; then, having handed over responsibility to the French, it had been shipped to the more salubrious climes of Jesselton in North Borneo to supervise the repatriation of some 12,000 Japanese prisoners. The 5th Battalion remained on the Frontier, and hundreds of other 2nd Goorkhas were on detached duty in ancillary formations.

Gradually the battalions returned to Dehra Dun, to face much uncertainty. They returned to an India in increasing turmoil, with the prospect of civil unrest and communal violence as Independence and Partition loomed. The future of the Gurkha Brigade was unknown, and the prospect of post-war demobilization was for many Gurkhas an unhappy one. The desire to remain in the Army was strong, for men in service were relatively better fed, housed, clothed and paid than their civilian counterparts and for many, education, technical training and foreign travel were additional attractions. The pull of the Regiment – *in loco parentis* – was also strong. But as the Indian Army wound down in size, places in the regular battalions could only be found for about fifteen per cent of those returning from active service.

This, together with the imminence of Indian Independence, the abdication of British authority in Burma and the absence of definitive statements on the future of the Gurkha Brigade, seemed to suggest the end of an era and the possible dissolution of the long-standing partnership between Britain and Nepal. It became obvious, too, that India, and the Congress Party, increasingly recognizing their military prowess and lack of communal bias, would wish to retain the Gurkha regiments. Not surprisingly, the Gurkha soldier began to anticipate the end of his service under the British Crown.

The process of demobilization proceeded, with categories defined and quotas set. There were endless administrative obstacles to be overcome, but 400 to 600 men were released every month with their due gratuities and perquisites, and by the end of 1946, 7,000 men had been struck from the rolls. In January 1947 the Regiment's 5th Battalion was disbanded, and the 2nd and 3rd Battalions were amalgamated so that the memorable achievements of the 3rd Battalion, their unique service with the first Chindit expedition and in the Arakan, would live on in the body of the Regiment. For many of the Regiment's regular officers, having to implement these plans was a heart-rending business, dispensing with the services of men who had fought in the Western Desert, in Italy, in Burma and Malaya and elsewhere and who had proved themselves more than a match for Rommel's Afrika Corps and the Imperial Japanese Army.

In addition to the soldiers, some long-service officers, concerned for the future of themselves and their families and in some cases exhausted by wartime service, also began to slip away. Officers on leave in the UK were not allowed to return, no new commissions were granted, and this, too, began to have an effect on the senior Gurkha ranks. The 1st, 2nd and 4th Battalions were redeployed away from Dehra Dun on internal security duties as communal strife took increasing hold on a riven India.

In this febrile climate, in March 1947, Lord Louis Mountbatten arrived as the last Viceroy, with orders to move as quickly as possible to Independence. The final date was set for 15 August, and there was little time. At Army Headquarters in Delhi, the Commander-in-Chief, Field Marshal Auchinleck, and his pressurized staff grappled with vital issues: demobilization, the split of the Indian Army between India and Pakistan and a deteriorating internal security situation. Murder and arson were daily occurrences; the 1st Battalion's old Divisional Commander, Lieutenant

General Sir Francis Tuker, now Commander-in-Chief, Eastern Command and with security responsibilities that included Calcutta, was to write of 'unbridled savagery with homicidal maniacs let loose to kill and kill and maim and burn'. He had intervened to stop the killings in Calcutta, using both Indian and British troops, including Gurkhas.

Not surprisingly, with these challenges all demanding immediate attention, the future of the Gurkha Brigade seemed to some to be a lesser priority. In an information vacuum, rumour mills began their work, suggesting a possible split of Gurkha battalions, some to be retained as British troops while others would pass into service with the Indians.

Much has been written about the sensitive issue of 'the Opt' and the choice that the Gurkha soldier had to make as to where his future loyalties might lie. Some early delicate negotiations had taken place between the governments of India, Nepal and Britain in May 1947, and matters had been agreed in principle in a meeting between the British Chief of the General Staff, Field Marshal Montgomery, and Nehru in June. The final outcome of this work was contained in a signal received by all Gurkha units on 8 August:

> Future of Gurkhas. One. Following Gurkha Regiments have been selected to serve under HMG. Second (2) Gurkha Rifles less 4/2 Gurkha Rifles. Six (6) Gurkha Rifles less 3/6 Gurkha Rifles. Seventh (7) Gurkha Rifles. Tenth (10) Gurkha Rifles. Two. Remaining Gurkha Rifles and all war-raised battalions are being retained by the Indian Government. Retention of war-raised battalions may be temporary. Three. Announcement in Press probably tomorrow. Four. Further details follow.

In such peremptory and insensitive fashion, and without any consultation with Regimental Colonels or their representatives, did the British Government dispense with regiments of long and gallant service and fidelity. The whole exercise was poorly planned and shabbily executed. It seemed that, other than the 2nd Goorkhas, the remaining regiments had been selected by some faceless committee on the basis that each had a battalion in Burma; with their duties there ending in March, they could be extracted without replacement and, with some cost saving, sent directly to Malaya, where they were to serve as British units. For many the selection seemed to defy logic. Within the Brigade there were only two regiments out of ten, the 7th and 10th Gurkha Rifles, who recruited Rais and Limbus from Eastern Nepal, and thus the recruiting basis for each Army would be seriously out of balance. Further, no attention seemed to have been paid to the seniority of the regiments, those that had served Britain longest, or to special peculiarities such as the 5th Royal Gurkha Rifles possessing such a singular title. Every regiment seemed to have a complaint of some sort, and there was much resentment. The 2nd Goorkhas could consider themselves fortunate to have been selected, but the reasons for this were never recorded. It may be that General Francis Tuker exerted influence in the corridors of power – who knows? The Regiment certainly had a royal title and a distinguished provenance, but so did some others, not least the 5th Royal Gurkha Rifles. My Regiment certainly had a certain pre-eminent position within the Indian Army dating back to Delhi, and its performance in the Western Desert had brought it great renown. It was also affiliated to the distinguished British Regiment, the 60th Rifles, and that may have told.

In early August, immediately before Independence and in line with the wishes of the Nepali government, every Gurkha soldier was invited to complete a questionnaire that asked him to state whether he wished to serve with the British or the Indian Army, or leave the service altogether and return to Nepal. There were almost no details regarding terms and conditions of service – pay, pensions, family permission, leave, etc. Given that the answer was required immediately, it was soon apparent that the exercise was deeply flawed, and it was cancelled. It was held again in December, when these matters were clearer. On this latter occasion it had been decided, under Indian pressure, that only the men in those regiments earmarked for British service would participate. By this time, too, a Tripartite Agreement between the Governments of India, Britain and Nepal had been negotiated, and this formed the basis for future recruiting and laid down some broad parameters for Gurkha service in both armies; most terms of service had been settled.

But four months had dragged by, and between August and December there was much agitated discussion in the regiments designated for British service, and a good deal of truculence and anger in some quarters. There was no doubt that the march of events had damaged British prestige; Indians were the Gurkhas' neighbours and the country well known. It was suggested that there would be better opportunities for commissions with the Indians; many experienced British officers had left, and the whole exercise to formulate terms and conditions had taken far too long. In many cases, only sentiment remained. In this atmosphere, clerks and line boys, and other Gurkhas domiciled in India, sought to bring pressure to bear on regimental comrades to sway the vote in favour of India. There were threats and intimidation, and generally it was a most unhappy time. In the 1st Battalion there was a brief, uncharacteristic and unhappy demonstration by some 200 men objecting to a planned battalion move and refusing to go on parade. This was quickly and effectively dealt with by the Commandant, and General Tuker, now the Regiment's Colonel, addressed the Battalion in robust fashion; but the incident, much exaggerated externally as nervousness rose with rank, was indicative of general disquiet in the ranks. In the end, regimentally, seventy per cent of the men of the 2nd Goorkhas voted to join the British Army, but the overall percentages in the other three Regiments were far lower and collectively disappointing.

Against this background, the Regiment's 4th Battalion transferred to the Indian Army and became the 5th Battalion of the 8th Gurkhas. I visited that Battalion in November 2017, and it was obvious to me that they held their 2nd Goorkha legacy and provenance very dear. 'The Sirmoor Rifles' was carried forward as part of their regimental title, *lali* was everywhere, a faux Queen's Truncheon stood erect in the officers' mess, and pictures of Hindoo Rao's house on the Ridge at Delhi were on display in various messes, along with photographic portraits of former British Commandants.

In March 1948 the two battalions of the 2nd Goorkhas set sail for Malaya. A host of outstanding issues had been settled. The men who had opted for Indian service were sent on their way to their new regiments, those who opted for British service had been re-enlisted, sworn in and re-attested. The regimental land, properties and money had been largely sorted and safeguarded – albeit at some financial loss – and the Regiment, after 131 years at Dehra Dun, had been uprooted and had departed India for new adventures in Malaya. For the Gurkha soldier a distinguished era was over and a new one was about to begin. Meanwhile, in the British House of Lords on Friday, 18 July 1947 a piece of liberating legislation had been enacted that ended the British imperial dominion of India. Included in a sub-section the assent of the Parliament of the United Kingdom was given to the omission from the Royal style and titles of the words *Indiae imperator* and *Emperor of India*. It was indeed the end of an era.

Chapter 8

Emergency and Rebellion

The Jungle is Neutral.
—F. Spencer Chapman

THE MALAYAN EMERGENCY 1948–60

Following the sadness and drama of Partition and 'the Opt', in the early part of 1948 there occurred two significant events in the Regiment's history. Firstly, the two battalions, depleted by many enjoying hard-earned leave in Nepal as well as by those who had opted to remain with the Indian Army, left Bombay for Singapore. They sailed together on the P & O Liner *Strathnaver* and arrived on 11 March. The Regiment was still in the service of the Crown but now part of the British Army. Secondly, the Malayan Emergency – a military campaign that was to envelope and engage the Gurkha Brigade for the next twelve years – was about to begin.

For those who had long served in the 2nd Battalion there must have been a certain poignant irony in returning to Singapore. Just over two years previously they had completed three and a half years of captivity as prisoners of war of the Japanese. Peter Kemmis Betty was still with the 2nd Battalion, having begun his regimental service on the North-West Frontier before the war. He had been wounded and awarded a Military Cross during some desperate early battles on the Malayan Peninsula in 1941 and 1942. Then, following the surrender of Singapore, he had been incarcerated in the notorious Changi Jail, separated from his soldiers. Now, once again a Company Commander, he was heading back to Ipoh in North Malaya, where his Battalion was to be stationed. This was a town through which he had been forced to withdraw the remnants of his two Rifle Companies in the face of a compelling Japanese advance. His Battalion was to be billeted in Ashby Road Camp, the same place where some of the 2nd Battalion had previously been held as PoWs.

Also returning was another of the Regiment's PoWs, Rifleman Bhagtasing Pun. Following his incarceration and return to India he had been transferred to the 1st Battalion, only to find himself living in Singapore once again, albeit in more favourable circumstances. The 1st Battalion would be based in Singapore for the next ten years, although little enough of that time was to be spent in barracks.

Both Peter and Bhagtasing were men of immense charm and much fortitude, courage and stamina. In spite of their sufferings at the hands of the Japanese, they were both to reach a hundred years of age. As mentioned earlier, when I joined the Regiment in 1960, Peter was commanding the 2nd Battalion and Bhagtasing was a senior Gurkha Captain and a much-venerated figure in the 1st Battalion. They were to be engaging friends of mine for the rest of their long lives and great stalwarts of the Regiment.

This is not a definitive political or military account of the campaign, but it is fair to say that the Malayan Emergency was a rare successful post-war counter-insurgency operation, and in the end, saw the defeat of an attempted communist insurrection. Its genesis was in the Japanese invasion. The Malayan Communist Party, overwhelmingly Chinese in character, had with British help established an underground resistance movement – the Malayan People's Anti-Japanese Army (MPAJA) – deep in the Malayan jungle. A parallel civilian organization garnered supplies for the camps, found recruits and provided the funding and information to mount guerrilla activities against the Japanese. The British believed that in due course they would need to invade Malaya and that the MPAJA would be a valuable source of local support. By means of air supply drops and clandestine landings by submarine, the force was supplied with arms and ammunition. British officers from SOE's Force 136 – of whom the best known was Freddie Spencer Chapman – were also parachuted into the jungle to liaise with and further train the Chinese groups. By the end of the war the MPAJA would muster 7,000 armed followers.

Following the Japanese surrender in Malaya in August 1945 in the wake of the atomic bombs dropped on Hiroshima and Nagasaki, the need for an invasion to retake Malaya fell away, and the guerrillas were encouraged by means of financial inducements to hand over their arms. This amnesty was only partially successful, and thousands of weapons and much ammunition remained cached in the jungle ready for a Communist campaign against the British. Chin Peng, ironically an officer of the Order of the British Empire (OBE), was the Communist Party's Secretary General. He had spent the war in the jungle with Spencer Chapman and was now reactivating the jungle bases which he and his comrades had used in their operations against the Japanese.

In 1948 the armed wing of Chin Peng's party, totalling some 5,000 fighters and renamed the Malayan Races Liberation Army (MRLA), launched their campaign. Following principles developed by Mao Zedong, Chin Peng's objective was to drive the security forces back into the towns and create liberated areas. These would then serve as launch pads for further insurrection. They began by emerging from their camps deep in the jungle, attacking isolated rubber plantations and killing their European managers. Tin mines and police stations were also regarded as important targets; in addition, the Communist terrorists (CTs) ambushed and derailed trains. They were well armed, well organized and particularly ruthless. In the face of these attacks, in June 1948 the Government declared a state of emergency throughout Malaya.

As before, the Communists were supported by a larger group drawn from the Chinese community – the so-called Min Yuen (People's Movement). This group at the height of the Emergency numbered perhaps a quarter of a million people. They were drawn largely from an impoverished element

THAILAND

Alor Star
KEDAH

Sungei
Patani

Kulim
Baling
Grik

PENANG I.

KELANTAN

Lenggong

Kuala Kangsar
Sungei Siput
Gua Musang

TRENGGANU

Ipoh

PERAK
Cameron
Highlands

MALAYA

Jerantut

Slim River
Bikam
Frasers Hill

PAHANG

SELANGOR

SOUTH CHINA SEA

KUALA LUMPAR

Titi
Kuala
Klawang

Kajang

Bahau

Tampin

Seremban

*NEGRI
SEMBILAN*

Gemas

Port Dickson

MALACCA

Segamat
Labis

JOHORE

Muar

Yong
Peng

Kluang

Kota
Tinggi

Ulu
Tiram

Johore
Bahru

Pontian

SINGAPORE

0   50   100
miles

MALAYA 1948–66

known as 'squatters', who lived in makeshift huts on the edge of the jungle on land to which they had no title. Through intimidation or sympathy, they were the MRLA's lifeline providing, not least, information, supplies and further recruits. Tamil rubber tappers were also terrorized into supplying food and material assistance.

When I joined my Regiment, much of the chatter in the mess and with the Gurkha soldiers was about the Emergency and the various places that the Battalion had been based – the rubber estates and small towns from where the rifle companies and their patrols sallied forth to search for and hopefully kill the CTs who were inflicting so much damage on Malaya. There were endless tales, some much exaggerated no doubt, about engagements with the CTs, and a perennial topic for debate was how Rifleman X should have got the Military Medal and not Rifleman Y, 'but the Major Saheb didn't see what I did!'

I had already learned that the jungle was not a comfortable place in which to operate, and this was certainly the case during the Emergency. Primary jungle's protective canopy, often 150ft or more above the ground, shut out the light and restrained the undergrowth. Here the going underfoot was easier, and while still humid, it was relatively cool. But in other areas, particularly in range of any habitation, where the primary jungle had been cleared by slash-and-burn farming or logging and then abandoned, secondary growth quickly took over. Vines and creeper corkscrewing up trees and joining bamboo and trees, together with fern and thorn, created a dense understorey. The going was more difficult here, and a patrol's lead elements were often forced to cut their way through. This was both noisy and tiring. Additionally, close to rivers and streams the ground was often wet and swampy. Much patrol work took place in this secondary jungle, particularly in the southern Malay State of Johore, where the 1st Battalion largely operated.

Apart from the difficulties of the terrain, the jungle was host to other modest discomforts. Animals such as wild boar and rhino, although very occasionally sighted, did not generally pose a threat; tigers, although rare, could certainly be dangerous but tended to avoid humans; but leeches, centipedes, mosquitoes and scorpions certainly enjoyed our company. Snakes, too, were an occasional threat. Add to that the carriage of a heavy pack, weapons, ammunition and equipment, and movement in the jungle sapped the energy. Finally, apart from the sweaty humidity and the general fetid odour that seemed to pervade particularly secondary jungle, there was always the potential shock of a terrorist shooting at you. It was a stressful and rigorous arena in which to campaign.

The CTs lived deep in the jungle, appearing from time to time to commit atrocities, and in the initial phase of their campaign they held the upper hand. These were classic terrorists – hit-and-run gangs who struck hard, spread terror, then rapidly melted back into the jungle. They could emerge from their lairs at a time of their choosing, and they knew the environment in which they operated better than the Army. Initially, intelligence was poor, and it took some time for the Security Forces to come to grips with the challenge they were facing. This was as true for the Gurkha battalions as it was for the British and Malay troops. On arrival in Malaya the Gurkha regiments were under strength, with little experience of the jungle. There were many young, inexperienced soldiers, and they were operating in unfamiliar territory. Much training and preparation was needed.

Two Generals were to have an important impact on the successful outcome of the Malayan Emergency. The first Director of Operations was Lieutenant General Sir Harold Briggs. He quickly discerned that the link between the terrorists and their support arm – the Min Yuen – had to be broken. The Briggs Plan declared that all 'squatters' who were aiding the CTs had to be resettled into so-called 'New Villages', where they would be given plots of land to cultivate and protection from the predatory advances of the CTs. It all took time to take effect, but it forced the terrorists deeper into the jungle, where they might be supplied by aboriginal people or grow their own food but generally would be under much greater pressure.

Secondly, General Gerald Templar arrived in Malaya in early 1952. He was to prove, politically and militarily, a dynamic supremo – 'The Tiger of Malaya', a man who galvanized the government, its civil agencies and the military into defeating the terrorists, to a point that Malaya was able to hold free elections and achieve independence. His particular focus on 'winning the hearts and minds of the people' was one that was to find an echo during subsequent campaigns of the British and other armies.

This then was the background against which the Security Forces, including the Gurkha battalions, prosecuted their long, slow war of attrition against Chin Peng and his followers. As so often in the early days of a campaign, there were setbacks and casualties, a lack of solid intelligence and lessons learned the hard way. This was as true for the 2nd Goorkhas as it was for everyone else. Much of the story of the Regiment's involvement in the Emergency – not much different from other infantry battalions save that it went on for many years – was one of endless patrolling and ambushing; of brief sightings of fleeing terrorists before assaulting empty camps; of an endless deadly game of hide and seek, much weary patrolling and just occasionally the successful elimination of hard-core terrorists. A short description of some contacts with the enemy in the course of the Emergency might serve to illustrate something of the character of the Regiment's work.

One of the first areas that Chin Peng intended to liberate was Sungei Siput, north of Ipoh in Perak State, where the 2nd Battalion was stationed. It was here that the CTs had brutally murdered three planters on 16 June 1948 in their first act of terrorism; and the Battalion had been involved in follow-up operations since then. On 12 July Nicky Neill, of Chindit and Burma fame, and his Company achieved the first success for the Battalion and for the whole of the Gurkha Brigade in the Emergency campaign. An informer – a Chinese rubber tapper – had reported to the police in Perak that while looking for game tracks he had identified a CT camp occupied by fifty armed and uniformed terrorists. Brought to Nicky Neill's base, the informer offered to guide him through a rubber estate and jungle to the camp.

Setting off by transport at 0230 hours, Nicky Neill and his two platoons debussed at an agreed point and moved off through the rubber. It quickly became apparent that the informer had lost his way, but after some threats and some further searching in the dark, the track leading to the camp was identified. Moving slowly, Captain Neill put the informer in front of him and at about 0700 hours, just as the light was breaking the informer shouted, '*Rumah!*' (house) and, turning, ran away. Ahead Neill saw a large lean-to shelter with an *attap* (palm thatch) roof. Out of this burst men running in all directions, all dressed in khaki and without doubt terrorists. Neill instantly opened fire with his Sten gun and, using one full magazine, personally accounted for seven terrorists. Three others escaped despite a very rapid follow-up by the leading platoon. This was the first successful elimination of CTs in the Malayan Emergency, even if the numbers involved were not quite what the informer had suggested. Informers would often exaggerate terrorist numbers, anxious to please and perhaps collect a larger reward.

For some reason I never knew Nicky Neill well in the Regiment – our paths did not cross – but he had a formidable reputation as a fighting soldier from his time in Burma, and later he was equally formidable as Commandant of the 2nd Battalion in Borneo. His officers all swore by him. In the course of the Malayan Emergency he personally shot twenty-one CTs! Of course, we all wanted success for our companies when engaged on operations or in battle, but Nicky's personal enthusiasm and the absolute determination he brought to bear on killing the Queen's enemies were remarkable. I sensed his whole outlook had been coloured by his experiences in Burma, not least the legacy of the Tamandu battle, where Bhanbhagta had won his Victoria Cross and Nicky had lost so many men of his Company.

It was while operating in the Sungei Siput area that the 2nd Battalion suffered a very bad blow. A strong and heavily armed group of CTs wearing uniforms and steel helmets had set up a roadside ambush, into which a civilian lorry carrying twenty young and mostly newly joined riflemen drove. It was wet and, strictly against orders, the vehicle's canopy was in place. The lorry was caught in the fire of light machine guns and rifles which killed the driver; it then careered off the road into a drain and turned over, pinning the men inside. The terrorists poured fire into the vehicle, ten soldiers were killed and the remainder were badly wounded. The CTs escaped with the Gurkhas' weapons and ammunition. This was a sad and salutary episode for the Battalion, and not a mistake that was repeated.

I must turn now to Peter Richardson, whose lugubrious nature and fondness for whisky *pani* did not dampen his fellow officers' admiration for him. He was not, however, tolerant of young officers. Digby Willoughby had been posted to his B Company when he first arrived in the Regiment and had been unwise enough to arrive in Peter's company base on a Johore rubber estate carrying a guitar. Officer and musical instrument were quickly banished to a small backroom cupboard. But all that was some time after the episode that I shall recount. By early 1950 the Security Forces had begun to make some inroads into terrorist numbers, and the 1st Battalion was determined to eliminate 7 Company MRLA, known locally as the Labis gang, an active and particularly ruthless terrorist unit.

On the night of 4 January 1950, 7 Company had fired on the night mail train some three miles south of Labis in North Johore, causing casualties amongst the passengers. An immediate follow-up patrol by Lieutenant Tony Wright and ten men of the mortar platoon were themselves ambushed, the leading scout, Rifleman Bhaktabahadur Ale, was killed and Tony was wounded in the neck. After a brisk firefight the CTs retreated, and in the follow-up their tracks were eventually lost. The Labis gang remained elusive until 21 January, when Police Special Branch received information of a location where they might be in hiding.

Early in the morning of 22 January, 4 and 6 Platoon of Peter Richardson's B Company moved to a debussing point north of Labis where they were to lie up until about 0630 hours, when it was light enough to see. The location was an area of old and overgrown rubber trees bordered by swamp and paddy. Visibility was poor in the early morning mist. Peter led his company in extended formation through the old rubber searching for signs of the enemy. Suddenly Rifleman Bombahadur Gharti, in the section alongside Peter, saw a sentry ahead of him running towards a squatter's hut and immediately opened fire. The whole area now came to life as several other terrorists appeared, returning fire and throwing a grenade. Bombahadur immediately charged the enemy, firing his rifle and killing four terrorists. Peter himself was engaged by two CTs, both of whom he killed. Then he saw to his horror that another CT was attacking one of his men who had been close behind him, hacking him with a *parang*, a Malay knife. Peter killed the CT, but sadly Rifleman Hastabahadur Pun was badly cut about the head and died later.

Meanwhile, the CTs had tried to run off into the jungle beyond the old rubber, but led by Company Sergeant Major Bhimbahadur Pun, 6 Platoon carried out a flanking movement to cut off their retreat. Now the CTs' only escape route led through the paddy and swamp, where they ran into deadly crossfire from both of Peter's platoons. Later, the Company, assisted by some police, searched the whole area and recovered twenty-two bodies as well as many weapons and much ammunition. More bodies were thought to have disappeared in the swamp. Later, it was established that thirty-five CTs had been killed or mortally wounded. The extermination of 7 Company, including its Commander Yap Piow with a £585 reward on his head, helped to relieve terrorism in the Labis area. This was the largest number of terrorists killed in a single action in the entire Emergency.

Nearly a year and a half later, in May 1951, B company had another tough but ultimately successful engagement in the Labis area, resulting in twenty terrorists killed. On this occasion the terrorists showed distinct courage and discipline, and this made a great impression on Peter. He reported that the CTs were all dressed alike in khaki tunics and trousers, long puttees, hockey boots and khaki peaked caps with red star badges. Sadly, two of B Company's Gurkha riflemen were killed in the fight. This was the second most successful engagement in the Emergency. Whisky *pani* has much to commend it! Peter was awarded the Distinguished Service Order (DSO), and his Company Sergeant Major received the Distinguished Conduct Medal (DCM) for the earlier engagement.

Lastly, I should mention my old friend Bhagtasing Pun. Settling in with the 1st Battalion on arrival in Singapore, he proved adept at jungle warfare and was soon operating against the CTs in the jungles of Johore. Initially, and while men were bringing their jungle skills up to scratch, a specialist unit titled Ferret Force was set up to tackle the terrorists. Bhagtasing, together with a number of other Gurkhas from both battalions, was selected for attachment to this unit and he was to practise his jungle warfare skills throughout the Emergency. Reports on his performance told of a bold and determined leader, and there was an early commendation and recommendations for awards. He shot and killed his first CT with Ferret Force, and a subsequent series of successful engagements had established his reputation in the jungle by the time he returned to A Company. On 13 July 1951, and by now promoted Sergeant, he led an A Company patrol in the Jementah area of North Johore, locating a small occupied camp in dense jungle. Here he carried out a successful attack, killing one CT and capturing important documents that led to further operations.

Two weeks later, commanding 2 Platoon, Bhagtasing located a further CT camp, and after rapid reinforcement a two-platoon attack was launched. This resulted in the death of twelve terrorists and the capture of another. The citation for his Military Medal (MM) commended Bhagtasing for leading his platoon with great gallantry, skilful use of rifle grenades at the critical moment and the devastating effect of the assault which this experienced NCO 'pressed home with great dash and vigour'. Sergeant Bhagtasing was presented with his MM by Her Majesty the Queen at the first Investiture of her reign, when he returned to England as part of the Gurkha Coronation Contingent.

The general pattern of military activity that I have recounted was to continue for several years, but by the early 1950s the tempo of terrorist activity had declined; amnesties and reward schemes played their part in this, as well as the successful attrition of the terrorists by the security forces. By 1959 there were only some 250 CTs still operating, chiefly in the area of the Thai border, and on 31 July 1960 the Emergency officially ended. Ninety officers and men of the Regiment had been killed, and a larger unrecorded number had been wounded. The 1st Battalion alone had accounted for 270 terrorists killed or captured. It was an exemplary record.

It seems churlish to record the fact that while recognition for this service over many years of long and arduous campaigning was the award to all ranks of the General Service Medal with the single clasp 'MALAYA', this same medal was awarded to British or Commonwealth servicemen present in Singapore or Malaya for just one day and not on operations at all.

REBELLION IN BRUNEI 1962–3

Two years on from the ending of the Emergency, by the middle of November 1962, the recruits that I had helped to enlist in Paklihawa a year earlier had completed their basic training and qualified as Gurkha riflemen. I now knew them well. If they were not yet fully adult, they were certainly very fit and had matured in mind and physique after a challenging year as recruits. They seemed to me, at that early stage in their careers, to be an impressive band. In November 1962 Major General Walter Walker, the experienced Commander of 17th Gurkha Division, took the salute at a grand Passing Out Parade at the Gurkha Training Depot in Sungei Patani in northern Malaya. We marched with our recruits and instructors on to the airstrip that served as a parade ground for a final inspection; 1,600 men were on parade.

Walter Walker was, for young officers (and more senior ones), a rather fearsome and forthright General, with a sharp moustache. He had earned a marked reputation first as a Gurkha battalion commander in the Burma campaign and then as a battalion and brigade commander during the Malayan Emergency. A steely soldier, he was, remarkably, the holder of three Distinguished Service Orders and will figure further in my story as the architect of victory in the Borneo campaign. Apparently, when he was commanding a battalion of the 6th Gurkhas during the Malayan Emergency, the soldiers called him 'Mosquito', because he stung any soldier who he thought to be idle or inefficient. More prosaically, he had recently caused much amusement among the bachelors in the mess by issuing an order forbidding officers in uniform to carry or use umbrellas. Perhaps, we said, he had wished to emulate Wellington, who had issued a similar order but had confined his disapproval to their use only while under fire! Suitably in the midst of a last-minute torrential rainstorm, we marched off the parade ground dripping wet but minus umbrellas. We then prepared to travel to our respective battalions. I was to deliver 150 newly trained young riflemen to my 1st Battalion housed in Singapore's Slim Barracks.

I had been away from my Battalion for over a year, and during my absence there had been some changes in the British officers' mess. Monty Ormsby had sadly finished his tour as Commandant. His extravagant talents as a raconteur and a wonderfully irreverent brio were among many other sterling qualities that I would much miss. Command of the Battalion had passed to another 2nd Goorkha veteran from North Africa and Italy, Gordon Shakespear. Gordon had been badly wounded commanding A Company in one of the Battalion's assaults on the Gothic line in the Italian campaign and had won a Military Cross in demanding circumstances in the aftermath of the battle for Monte Cassino. His father and grandfather had both served in the 2nd Goorkhas, and his son was to join us later.

John Chapple, too, had left the Adjutant's office for the Army Staff College. We would not see him for another three years, and Digby Willoughby, now installed in that important office, was always prepared to command the bachelor officers on the Parade Ground or wherever else he chose. My old chum David Stephens was still exploring some of the shadier night spots of Singapore and exhorting me – still unsuccessfully – to accompany him. The tall and genial 'Boots' Burlison – he took a large size in shoes – had also arrived to join us from the 60th Rifles. Captain Bhagtasing Pun was still Second-in-Command of A Company but sadly, I heard, had been earmarked for pension. I would miss his wise counsel and gentle nature. Major Pirthilal Pun, the Gurkha Major, continued to rule the Battalion with an iron rod. Tony Lloyd-Williams, an absolute stickler for everything regimental and brave to the point of foolhardiness, was the Second-in-Command. The younger officers tended to steer well clear of him lest a youthful sartorial or military indiscretion catch his eye. Welcoming me back, Colonel Gordon told me to resume my job as Battalion Intelligence Officer.

In my absence the Battalion had moved from its camp at Ulu Tiram and returned to Singapore and the fine Lines at Slim Barracks. After the ending of the Malayan Emergency the Battalion was still, somewhat reluctantly, adjusting to peacetime soldiering. It was honing up on internal security duties for possible deployment on the streets of politically volatile Singapore. Military pamphlets entitled 'Keeping the Peace Parts 1 and 2' were our bibles.

Keener souls, including myself, were reading *Street without Joy*, Bernard Fall's graphic account of the French in Vietnam and their defeat at Dien Bien Phu. We had begun casting our minds north to the tunnel tactics of the Viet Cong in Indo-China and to potentially new styles of revolutionary warfare. We were not looking south to the island of Borneo. With the arrival of the fresh recruits, the Battalion was well manned, over 750-strong and possessed of operationally experienced British and Gurkha officers and NCOs. Most of them were familiar with the jungle from the Battalion's campaigning in the Malayan Emergency. Others, like myself and the new young riflemen I had recently brought with me, were at best military ingénus.

Some ten days after my return, on 8 December, the call came – as it always tended to – at around three o'clock in the morning as we were drifting into Saturday. The previous day had been the Battalion's annual administrative inspection, carried out by nosy staff officers from our Brigade Headquarters. With its successful conclusion we had all gone to the cinema in central Singapore – the 'bioscope' as Digby called it – to see the film of the moment, *The Longest Day*, with John Wayne leading his men to victory across the Normandy beachhead. It was to prove prescient. In the frighteningly early morning I was roused by Digby. A telephone order had been received from Brigade Headquarters ordering the implementation of Operation Ale, about which we knew nothing. Two Rifle Companies and a Tactical Headquarters were to prepare for an immediate move to Brunei. Initial ideas that it might be a testing extension of the administrative inspection quickly proved groundless!

Apparently, the designated battalion for this operation was the Queen's Own Highlanders, but they were largely deployed on anti-piracy duties elsewhere and were not immediately available. It was not clear exactly what had occurred, but some sort of insurrection was taking place in Brunei, and order needed to be restored. Our own more modest 'longest day' was about to begin. I regret to say that, having returned to the Battalion some ten days previously and been in the role of Intelligence Officer for less than a week, I had little idea where Brunei was, let alone the background to any local problems. Nor did many others. I dressed and, in the darkness, hurried to my office, passing as I went a frantic humming bustle in the soldiers' barrack rooms as the men made their preparations for an operational move. I started to make my own preparations, not least to find out what Operation Ale was all about.

I quickly established the broad details of the Sultanate of Brunei's geography as a small British Protectorate some 700 miles from Singapore in the South China Sea. It was oil-rich and somewhat akin to Norfolk in size; its population was 85,000, of whom some 59,000 were Malays and the rest a mix of Chinese and indigenous people. Its coastline was on the South China Sea, and it ran into the middle of Sarawak, with the separate state of Sabah to its east; all these shared the island of Borneo with Indonesian Kalimantan to the south. Ruling over Brunei was, I learned, His Highness Sir Muda Omar Ali Saifuddin Sa'adul Khairi Waddin DK, PSPNB, PSNB, PSLJ, SPMB, PANB, KCMG. The Sultan's dynasty had ruled Brunei for over 600 years. As far as the medals were concerned, I vaguely recognized KCMG as being British in origin, but the remaining decorative cluster held mysteries I could not fathom. We quickly abbreviated his name to 'Sir Omar', and two days later I was to meet him in his *Istana* – the Sultan's palace. He had called for British assistance under the terms of a 1959 Treaty of Protection.

At the time, and certainly at battalion level, background intelligence on the supposed insurrection was sparse, and Colonel Gordon giving his orders at seven o'clock that morning had been forced to put together a plan with no reconnaissance or even acquaintance with the country, and no worthwhile information on the actual situation in Brunei. Was it to be dispersal of crowds with our banners and bugles to the fore, or something much more demanding? Certainly, no intelligence on Brunei or the

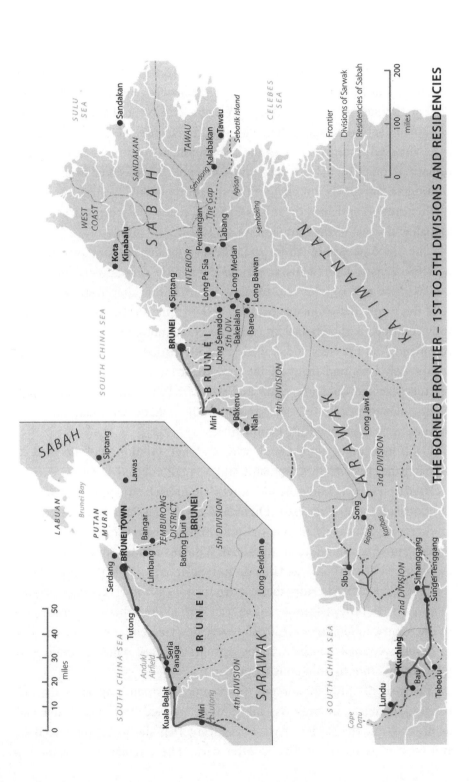

THE BORNEO FRONTIER – 1ST TO 5TH DIVISIONS AND RESIDENCIES

developing threat had been passed to the Battalion – a general fog seemed to be lying thick on the ground. As Intelligence Officer, beyond the Sultan's plentiful supply of decorations my knowledge was decidedly shaky.

The Colonel ordered Tony Lloyd-Williams to command a force consisting of a small Tactical Headquarters with C and D Companies, with the aim 'to assist the civil administration in the restoration and maintenance of law and order in Brunei and to be ready to move by 4pm'. This seemed to cover most contingencies, but the urgency of the situation quickly became apparent as further orders confirmed the initial force was to leave as soon as aircraft were available; the rest of the Battalion was to follow.

The outcome said much for the efficiency of our preparations. In spite of some logistical problems at various Singapore depots, perhaps due to the lassitude and languor of a tropical Saturday morning, from a standing start the whole Battalion was paraded at 9.00 a.m. on the square. We were fully equipped with personal kit, weapons and ammunition and rations, and command Land Rovers and trailers were all loaded with their radios and equipment. I spotted many of the new fresh-faced young riflemen – my recruits – in the Company ranks and wondered how they would perform. At first glance they looked eager and up to the task, but they had done little training with their new Rifle Companies.

I did not quite understand why Colonel Gordon had decided to despatch his Second-in-Command and a small cobbled-together Tactical Headquarters in the lead echelon rather than himself and his main Battalion Headquarters team. Not least, Digby and I were desperately concerned we might miss out on a new regimental adventure. Perhaps those were his initial orders from Headquarters. Tony Lloyd-Williams and his force reached the mounting RAF airfields at Changi and Seletar by mid-morning. But it was not until 2.45 p.m. that the first troops took off in a Hastings aircraft, followed by Beverleys – those British transport aircraft that were precursors to the American Hercules C130s and were described by some pilots as akin to flying a council house from the upstairs lavatory window. They were followed by more commodious Britannias.

The use of different aircraft from separate mounting airfields, and frustrating delays in their assembly, were coupled with a seeming lack of urgency on the RAF's part. This meant that the force got mixed up and most of it arrived in Brunei after dark. There remained a paucity of intelligence, but while in the air Tony had learned that the main Brunei police station in the capital had been attacked during the night by 100 armed rebels. This assault had been successfully repulsed by the police. More importantly, Brunei airfield was still in Government hands.

Tony and his companies had a difficult and somewhat chaotic arrival – in the dark and with no knowledge of the ground and little intelligence. The Britannias were too large to land in Brunei, and the element of the force in those aircraft had to be ferried from the larger airfield on Labuan Island off the coast by other planes. By 11.00 p.m. that night Tony's Tactical HQ and major elements of C Company plus a platoon of D Company had arrived at Police Headquarters on the edge of a large grassed *padang* (playing field), the size of two football fields, in the centre of Brunei Town. Two further platoons of D Company and its Headquarters had yet to reach the capital.

In Police Headquarters Tony was briefed by Police Commissioner Outram. It was clear that an attempted rebellion against the State was taking place. The airfield, Police Headquarters and the *Istana* were thinly guarded. Police stations at Penaga and Kuala Belait, to the west in the area of the Shell oilfields and some sixty miles from the capital, were thought to be still tenuously in police hands. Many other stations had fallen and lost their weapons to the rebels in the process. The Seria oilfields appeared to be in rebel hands, and some European and Malay employees of Shell had been taken hostage.

There were other hazy reports of a large rebel force on its way to Limbang in East Sarawak on the Brunei border. The Police Commissioner gave Tony Lloyd-Williams the immediate task of securing Brunei Town and recapturing the Seria oilfields, relieving Penaga and Kuala Belait police stations in the process. This was a formidable set of objectives for his moderate force. It was clear that banners and bugles encouraging crowds to disperse would not be required at this stage!

Because the sixty miles of road to Seria twisted through patches of dense jungle, Tony Lloyd-Williams decided to wait for first light before sending the relief force of C Company commanded by Captain Tony Lea. But shortly after midnight a telephone message reached Police Headquarters to say that rebels were preparing to attack Panaga police station outside Seria, using European hostages as a screen. A depleted

C Company therefore left immediately in commandeered Public Works tipper trucks and the Company Land Rover. Their orders were to move through the two small intermediate towns of Sengkurong and Tutong, seize and secure Anduki airfield on the oil camp just outside Seria and relieve Panaga police station. This was no small task for one depleted Rifle Company.

Accompanied by a small section of police, C Company set off for Seria and the oilfields. They brushed aside a rebel roadblock, the rebel-held Senkurong police station and two further parties of rebels, and drove fast to Tutong, some thirty miles from Brunei Town. Just short of this modest township on the banks of the Tutong River, the rebels opened fire on the convoy. Fire was returned, but as the vehicles entered the small town a heavy fusillade of fire crashed out from the upper stories of two blocks of houses and shops. The Company Land Rover containing Tony Lea and his signaller, Corporal Sombahadur Thapa, who was wounded, crashed into a monsoon drain. The Company also took some further casualties, and in darkness it required some time for it to consolidate, deal with its casualties and set about clearing Tutong and its police station of rebels.

At first light Tony Lea requested assistance for his casualties – seven wounded Gurkhas, including one of the young riflemen, Chandrabahadur Gurung, who I had helped recruit and train. I particularly remembered him because he had two elder brothers in the Battalion. With operations developing elsewhere, Tony Lea was now told to bring his Company and their prisoners back to Brunei Town and assist in consolidating the Battalion's hold on the capital. Later that morning, he returned with his own Gurkha casualties and 108 captured rebels, including some wounded. It had been an eventful night.

While C Company was driving to Tutong, Tony Lloyd-Williams was attempting to consolidate his position in Brunei Town from his temporary base in Police Headquarters. Since his initial arrival everything in the town had been relatively quiet, but at about 2.00 a.m. movement was spotted in the deep and broad concrete monsoon drains in front of the Government offices that lined the *padang*, to the left of the police station. Tony instructed David Stephens and a half platoon of Gurkhas to investigate. As David and his patrol moved forward in tactical formation, heavy fire broke out from the upper floors and rooftops of the buildings, and David and four Gurkhas fell wounded. The remainder of the platoon returned fire. In addition

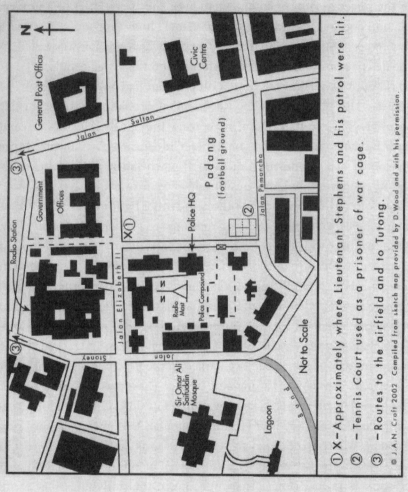

BRUNEI TOWN CENTRE IN DECEMBER 1962

N

General Post Office

Jalan

Sultan

Civic
Centre

Jalan Pemancha

Padang
(football ground)

Radio Station

Jalan

Stoney

Government
Offices

③

③

Jalan Elizabeth II

X①

Police HQ

Radio
Mast

N

Police Compound

②

Sir Omar Ali
Saifuddin
Mosque

Jalan

Lagoon

Not to Scale

① X – Approximately where Lieutenant Stephens and his patrol were hit.

② – Tennis Court used as a prisoner of war cage.

③ – Routes to the airfield and to Tutong.

© J.A.N. Croft 2002   Compiled from sketch map provided by D. Wood and with his permission.

to David, the wounded included a regimental hero from the Malayan Emergency, Captain Manbahadur Pun, possessor of a fine Distinguished Conduct Medal (DCM).

At the same time that David's patrol was engaged, the rebels had opened rapid fire on the police station, and while moving to the north side of the police perimeter in anticipation of the attack, part of a D Company platoon was raked with fire. Lieutenant Thote Gurung and some of his men were wounded, and Lance Corporal Dalbahadur was killed, before the defence position could be reinforced and the attack repulsed.

Thote was a fearless Gurkha officer who had won the MM in Malaya and had also been part of the Regiment's Coronation Contingent that had so impressed me in London nine years previously. He was to campaign with me later as a platoon commander in Borneo. As morning broke, the remainder of D Company on its way from the airfield had debussed on the sound of gunfire and was pushing its way forward on foot. At first light they cleared the Government offices and other buildings around the *padang*, and sentries were posted on the rooftops overlooking the *padang*. By 9.00 a.m., together with the police, Tony Lloyd-Williams' scattered force was in control of the centre of the town, a curfew had been established and mobile foot patrols were on the move. The tennis court in the corner of the *padang* became a temporary holding area for prisoners, before the local cinema was commandeered for this purpose. A good deal of blood was found by D Company on the veranda of the Government offices, and it was later assessed that a number of rebels had been killed in the previous night's firefights.

All this activity in Tutong and Brunei Town was unknown to me until the Beverley aircraft containing Colonel Gordon, Digby and me, together with the men of Battalion Headquarters, landed on the offshore island of Labuan, where we needed to refuel. Anxious for news, Colonel Gordon and I made for the airport control tower in the hope of speaking to the police station in Brunei. Amazingly, given the difficulties that seemed to persist with communications, we eventually established contact with Tony Lloyd-Williams. Through him we learnt what had happened to his force during the night and early morning. He promised some sort of transport to meet us at the airport and asked us to fix with the Beverley pilot the carriage of the Battalion's wounded back to Singapore. Without more ado we hurried back to the aircraft.

Half an hour later, we landed at Brunei airport. It had been a huge tactical error on the part of the rebels not to block the runway to prevent the arrival of British troops. This airfield was now firmly in the hands of a troop of Gurkha Engineers. They, fortuitously, had been on exercise in Sabah and were flown into Brunei immediately trouble was suspected. Under Digby's lead, and not knowing quite what to expect, we bailed out of the aircraft's back doors as fast as we could, weapons loaded and at the ready, and took up defensive positions around the terminal building.

On its veranda and in the small terminal building itself was the sombre sight of the Battalion's wounded on stretchers and awaiting evacuation. I was shocked to see the casualties our Gurkhas had incurred in the course of the night. This was all more serious than we had imagined when we set off from Singapore. Digby and I saw the wounded quickly and safely loaded into the Beverley and then prepared for our move to Brunei Town and Police Headquarters. David Stephens was too ill to be moved and was in a Brunei hospital. There was a certain tension in the air.

Three vehicles, two tipper trucks and a somewhat dilapidated coach, had arrived to move us. Generously, Digby decided that I and a proportion of the Gurkhas should travel in the bus, while he and the Colonel each took a tipper truck. I soon realized the advantages of rank. The tipper trucks offered a certain protection and good fields of fire, as well as the possibility of a quick debus in the event of ambush. The bus trapped its passengers inside with little opportunity to respond effectively in any brush with rebels. We poked a few rifles out of our narrow windows as best we could and, with fingers crossed, set off for the town. Apprehensively I tried to remember the anti-ambush drills that I had learnt on forest tracks in the Brecon Beacons as an officer cadet.

All went well, and half an hour later we arrived safely at the Police Head-quarters compound. While Colonel Gordon talked to the Commissioner and Tony Lloyd-Williams, 'Boots', who had arrived the night before with Tony, filled me in on the dramas of the previous night in his usual bluff, relaxed way, constantly mopping his brow as he did so. He'd had a long night.

Colonel Gordon's first task was to assess the situation with his Second-in-Command and the Police Commissioner. He needed to decide priorities for the Battalion and then deploy his Rifle Companies and other assets accordingly. It was soon clear that the widespread nature of the rebellion, the critical situation at the Shell oilfields and other outlying areas and the need to protect a number of key points meant that we had insufficient troops. Colonel Gordon made all this clear in his first signal reporting on the situation to Far East Headquarters back in Singapore.

A Company arrived later that morning. It was immediately ferried by Borneo Airways and Shell aircraft to secure the airfield at Lutong and the oilfield at Miri along the coast in Sarawak on Brunei's western border, where a threat was apparently developing. B Company was still in transit and did not arrive until the following morning. Intelligence was poor, and it was difficult at that early stage to know what sort of enemy we were facing, beyond their title – the TNKU – Tentara National Kalimantan Utara, the National Army of North Kalimantan. Colonel Gordon quickly appreciated that with his two companies his first priority was to ensure the security of Brunei Town, the seat of Government, and then work forward to the outer areas of the country. Rumours of enemy movement were of course flying in every direction at this stage.

At the request of the acting British High Commissioner there was also a need to organize the evacuation of British expatriates, who were increasingly jittery. The Sultan, as Head of State, had to be looked after, and although he was temporarily guarded by a few of our Gurkhas, there were insufficient troops for a long-term commitment at the rambling *Istana*. It was decided to bring Sir Omar and his immediate family into the police station. Colonel Gordon ordered Digby and me, together with two strong sections of Gurkhas, to make a rapid move to the *Istana* in our stripped-down Land Rovers and bring the royal party in.

Arriving safely at the *Istana*, we found a sad but dignified 48-year-old Sir Omar with his wife and a small accompanying party equipped with some modest possessions waiting for us in the front hall of his palace. He seemed pleased to see us. We shepherded his party into the backs of our Land Rovers and drove at full pelt rather uncomfortably and nervously the eight miles back to Police Headquarters, scanning the roadsides for possible ambushes. Gurkha bodyguards were at high alert either side of Sir Omar. On arrival, and rather unceremoniously, he and his retinue were provided with two police cells in which to make themselves temporarily but regally comfortable!

On the third day we were there I heard that David Stephens had died from his wounds. 'Boots', who had originally got him to the Brunei hospital, gave me the news. Tony Lloyd-Williams had rescued the Battalion float money that David had been carrying in his breast pocket when he went on patrol and asked me to take care of it until we got better organized. I saw that there was a neat bloodstained hole drilled straight through the middle of the thick wad of red ten-dollar notes. David had looked after me when I first came to the Regiment, and I ruefully reminded myself that there would be no more trips to those Singapore drinking dens of which he was so fond. David's father, a prisoner of war of the Japanese and a Brigadier in the Malayan Emergency campaign, had commanded the Regiment. It would be a bitter loss for him, as it was for all of us.

The next few days were full of activity as we developed our knowledge of Brunei Town, and we dominated it with our patrols. We bade farewell to the Sultan and moved out of an increasingly overcrowded police station and into the Civic Centre, a large hall on the other side of the *padang*. An ad hoc Force Headquarters had arrived from Singapore to take command of the operation, and additional British troops had started arriving: the Queen's Own Highlanders landed by air and sea and 42 Marine Commando had debouched from its aircraft carrier, HMS *Albion*.

L Company, 42 Commando, was commanded by Captain Jeremy Moore, later to figure prominently in the Falklands campaign. Mounting his marines in commandeered Ramp Cargo Lighters discovered in Brunei Bay, he carried out a dawn assault from the river on the town of Limbang. The town had been heavily invested by the TNKU, who had occupied the police station and taken the British Resident hostage together with a number of other Europeans. The Commandos dealt effectively with this large group of rebels and rescued the hostages unharmed. This was a further significant blow to the rebellion, albeit at the cost of several marines killed and wounded.

At the same time the Queen's Own Highlanders undertook two successful air coup de main operations. Elements of the Highlanders were transported in small RAF Twin Pioneer aircraft, each carrying some twelve soldiers. They landed precariously on some clear ground close to the Shell golf course at Seria. Beverley aircraft carried others on to the nearby Anduki airstrip belonging to the oil company. Here they quickly seized the control tower from the rebels and retook the airfield. After a series of brisk firefights, the Highlanders were able to recapture the police stations, release the Shell hostages and eventually retake the oil town of Seria. Order was quickly re-established on the oilfields. Our own B Company, the last company to arrive from Singapore, was flown into Anduki, and the Gurkhas, advancing through the Queen's Own Highlanders, cleared Kuala Belait, the final coastal town still in rebel hands.

With these two major operations under way, and with Brunei Town reasonably secure, the Battalion was able to extend its authority outside the capital. In addition, A Company had returned from Lutong, where their responsibilities had been taken over by a Battalion of the Royal Green Jackets which had also arrived from their base in Malaya. This gave Colonel Gordon the additional flexibility that he needed to maintain security in the capital but also to extend the Battalion's area of influence and move against the remaining rebels in Tutong. This was the town that had inflicted early damage on C Company on that first chaotic night. Since then we had not had the capacity to revisit the scene.

'Boots' had done sterling work in the Brunei Public Works Department (PWD) yards. Together with a team of Gurkhas from the Mechanical Transport platoon they had worked night and day welding steel sheets on to the sides of the PWD tipper trucks that were still our only means of moving men about and gave a degree of protection from possible ambushes. He had also welded 4ft steel pickets on to the front of each of our stripped-down Land Rovers. These were designed to prevent taut guillotine wires strung across the road by the rebels from decapitating the vehicle's drivers and passengers. A further welcome reinforcement had also arrived by sea – a once much-derided mobile bath unit had set up shop alongside the Civic Centre and provided a much-needed hot shower for us all.

With C and D Companies mounted in 'Boot's' 'armoured personnel carriers' and commanded by a small Tactical Headquarters that included Colonel Gordon and myself in open Land Rovers, we set off for Tutong. It was a modest form of advance to contact and, aware of what had befallen C Company four days earlier, we travelled cautiously. We allowed the lead company to clear through individual villages on foot as we progressed. But we soon reached Tutong without incident, debussed and patrolled through the town. Not surprisingly, the local Brunei Malays and the Chinese shopkeepers appeared frightened and sullen. We moved through the town smiling at people and attempting to reassure them. The Gurkhas with their knowledge of Malay were adept at this. We established ourselves on the high ground above the town. Then, acting on police information, an ambush was laid along the river line, and that night a large group of rebels, seemingly unaware of our arrival, attempted to re-enter the town by boat. They were quickly despatched.

Together with news reaching us of the activities of the Marines and Highlanders, it was soon apparent that the rebellion had faltered and that we had the upper hand. By the end of December the revolt was to all intents and purposes over – only elements of TNKU leadership remained at large. 'Boots' in his usual laconic style had disappeared deep into the jungle with a platoon of A Company to operate close to Brunei's southern border with Sarawak. He was liaising with local indigenous Ibans in their longhouses and checking for signs of fleeing rebels seeking sanctuary outside the State. The rest of the Battalion were carrying out what might be called framework operations throughout the State, seeking out the remaining rebels and providing a hopefully reassuring presence to a population that had largely rejected the aspirations of Azahari.

After I arrived in Brunei I had established close liaison with Police Special Branch, and together with other sources I had pieced together a picture of what had occurred in Brunei over the previous weeks. As Intelligence Officer I was also responsible for building up an order of battle of the TNKU, the so-called rebel army. If most of the rebels had by now been accounted for, a few names that featured at the top of my organization chart remained elusive.

The background and a major catalyst for the rebellion had been the growing tension between Indonesian President Sukarno's expansionist ambitions for the region and the plans for 'Malaysia' just proposed and announced by Malaya's Premier, Tunku Abdul Rahman. These plans envisaged a federation of Malay States that, in addition to Malaya itself, included Singapore, Sabah, Sarawak and Brunei. The Sultan had not yet committed his State to this proposal. But the plan was anathema to Sukarno as well as to a local political activist in Brunei, Azahari, who generated a challenge to the concept. He proposed, instead, a Brunei-controlled crescent, with the Sultan as its titular head, which would span Brunei, Sarawak and Sabah. This found little resonance with a large majority of the people involved. However, from early 1961 a secret rebel militia – the TNKU – had been building under Azahari's Chief of Staff, Yassin Affendi, designed to press the issue by armed means. By December 1962 Azahari's ragged army had reached an active strength of some 4,000. About 1,000 of these men were armed, mainly with shotguns and *parangs*, but their military plans included the early seizure of more lethal weapons from coordinated attacks on local police stations, followed by the capture of the oilfields and the seizure of the Sultan. A strong nucleus had received some training in Indonesian Kalimantan. This threat to the State of Brunei had been grossly underestimated if not unrecognized by Brunei Special Branch and other State apparatus. Azahari himself had deserted his TNKU and pushed off to the Philippines the day before the rebellion was launched. He was soon reported to be in Jakarta pursuing wider aims.

Some of the rebel leadership still at large included Azahari's field commander, Yassin Affendi, together with Salleh bin Sambas who had initially captured Limbang but escaped when the Marines landed, and Sheik Osman, a brother of Azahari. These leaders were thought to be holed up in the jungle, but as coastal dwellers they would not be at ease in that uncomfortable environment. The TNKU had been quite unprepared for the fast build-up of British forces and they were not surprisingly beaten in all major actions. With no outside support materializing from Indonesia, the rebels had little option but to surrender or be captured or killed. Disorganized, demoralized and with poor leadership, it was only a matter of time before they were all accounted for.

After two months in Brunei we were almost at the end of our tour. Operations had quietened down, but we were still searching hard for the final remnants of the TNKU's leadership. In the jungle we had been sealing off escape routes into Sarawak. It was then that I had an interesting experience that I well remember.

On the final list of wanted men on my order of battle was Sheik Osman, Azahari's brother. Azahari himself was still thought to be in Jakarta, but Osman had been responsible for a large area of TNKU operations within Brunei. As far as we knew, he was lying up in the jungle with little food and few friends, experiencing all the agonies of a hunted man.

January 1963 had brought extremely heavy rains to Brunei with much flooding, and some of our military effort had turned towards flood relief.

In these monsoon conditions the desire of men on the run to return to their homes for food and shelter must have been compelling, for the jungles of Brunei are inhospitable at the best of times. Sensing this, I organized a night visit to Osman's house in the hope that he might have crept home. The chances were remote, but there had been little military activity in the area of his isolated village and he might have thought the risk worth taking. At 1.00 a.m. I set off with two Brunei Special Branch constables and some six Gurkhas under command of my Intelligence Corporal, Kushiman Gurung, on a drive and approach march to Osman's village. It was raining hard and very dark, conditions providing ideal cover for our move. After about two hours we reached Osman's small, square, wooden house standing on stilts, slightly apart from the rest of the village at the edge of the jungle.

The Gurkhas melted away to form a loose cordon around the house, while the policemen, Kushiman and I silently crept up the wooden steps leading to the front door. As gently as I could, and certain that the beating of my heart would arouse the whole village, I pushed open the door and, with pistol in hand, listened hard. The creak of the door and the rain spattering on the tin roof were the only sounds.

We quickly entered the house and with powerful torches searched it. The interior was a simple open living area, and it did not take long to see that there was no one there. The small outhouse which served as a kitchen had, however, been in use, and the remains of a meal not more than two days old lay on a plate. Carefully leaving everything just as we found it, I swept my torch round the interior one more time to see if we had missed anything and spotted a trapdoor in the ceiling.

Silently we lifted a table into position below the trapdoor and placed a chair on top of it. On to this I climbed and paused, listening intently. I could hear nothing to indicate the loft was occupied and very carefully I pushed the trap door up and slid it to one side. Once more I listened and again I could hear nothing. Finally, I raised my head just above the level of the hatch and swinging my torch around the loft quickly inspected it. Osman was not there, and the loft was empty.

The remnants of food in the house seemed to indicate Osman had visited, however, so in the hope of capturing anyone who came to the house I decided to leave Kushiman and three of his men inside it for a few days. There was just a chance that, providing we had not been spotted, Osman might return later. The ensuing days were difficult for Kushiman and his men, concealed in the house, talking only in whispers and moving as little as possible as they waited for a possible arrival. On the evening of their fourth and last day their patience was rewarded. Someone was heard approaching the house and coming up the steps. Kushiman watched it all through a crack in the wall and was ready when the door swung open. It was Osman's wife.

Subsequent interrogation revealed that the distraught woman had some food and a note for her husband. But there was no opportunity to follow this up, for we had started our operational handover to a battalion of the 7th Gurkha Rifles. In the flurry of that activity the pursuit of Osman was left to the police and the new battalion.

Sometime later, and with additional information, a follow-up operation was planned by the 7th Gurkhas and Intelligence Officers. I heard later what had happened. Once more, a night-time visit was paid to the house. It appeared to be as empty as before, but once more, a final sweep revealed the trapdoor in the ceiling. A British Military Intelligence officer, Captain Keith Burnett, placed a table and chair below the trap door and listened intently. Hearing nothing, he pushed his hand upwards and slid the hatch to one side, poked his head upwards and swung his torch round the loft. Thereupon an automatic weapon seized by Osman's men on a police station raid the previous December opened up, and Keith was killed.

Retribution was swift. The Gurkha cordon opened fire into the roof, Sheik Osman, mortally wounded, died shortly afterwards, and the search for one more rebel leader was over. While much saddened by the death of Keith Burnett, I reflected with Corporal Kushiman that we had been lucky not to find Sheik Osman at home when we called.

Following our departure, the 7th Gurkhas who had relieved us put paid to the final senior TNKU group, including the field commander, Yasssin Affendi, together with Salleh bin Sambas who had commanded the TNKU at Limbang, and relatives of Azahari. They carried out a difficult but highly successful operation in the swamps of Brunei Bay, where the remnants of Azahari's ragged army had finally holed up.

Returning home to Slim Barracks and Singapore, we were able to reflect on our experiences in Brunei, sort ourselves out and digest what we had experienced over three short months. We briefed other units on lessons learnt and told elaborate and embroidered war stories to anyone who would listen. Our experience had improved our confidence, and we had sorted out our battle procedures and drills. At all levels we knew each other much better. In the end, the rebellion was contained and then defeated by the loyalty of the Brunei police and the majority of the Brunei people, as well as by the swift and bold action of the British forces. The Sultan of Brunei was ever grateful to the Gurkhas for the rescue of his throne. To this day a battalion of Gurkhas remains stationed in Brunei.

A few weeks after we returned to Singapore, on 12 April 1963, the police station at the border town of Tebedu in the First Division of Sarawak was attacked by a large party of Indonesian Army soldiers disguised as irregulars. Having crossed the border, they killed a corporal and wounded two other policemen before looting the bazaar and then recrossing the border back into Indonesia. Confrontation had begun, and we would soon return to the jungles of Borneo.

Chapter 9

Confrontation

One of the most efficient uses of military force in the history of the world.
—Denis Healey, Secretary of State for Defence 1964–70

SOME BACKGROUND

In the wake of the Brunei Rebellion, President Sukarno's Indonesia posed a threat to the formation of Malaysia, due to take place in the autumn of 1963. The initial Indonesian raid at Tebedu, although in itself a relatively small affair, gave a hint of what was to come. Over the next six months, thirty border incursions and raids involving 'volunteers', but with an increasing stiffening of Indonesian Army regulars, took place along the border with Sarawak. Upping the temperature, the Indonesian President brought both political rhetoric and military pressure to bear in an attempt to prevent the formation of Malaysia. His immediate objective was to destabilize Sabah and Sarawak, in spite of a UN survey determining that the people of Sabah and Sarawak, if not Brunei, generally supported the concept of joining Malaysia. Sukarno was to title his campaign

'Konfrontasi' – confrontation. Amidst increasing political tension on the day after Malaysia Day, 16 September 1963, 10,000 Indonesians attempted to sack the British Embassy in Jakarta, rampaging around its compound as they did so, while elsewhere in the country a number of British commercial interests were seized.

Over the next three years an increasing tempo of operations would, at its peak, see the deployment of some fourteen British and Commonwealth battalions along Malaysia's eastern border with Indonesia, together with artillery and the Army's other supporting arms and services. Crucial to these operations were Royal Navy and RAF helicopters, for without their lift capability it would have been impossible to deny vast areas to the guerrillas. Additionally, Royal Navy ships and RAF and Commonwealth forces would guard sea and air approaches to Malaysia. In an escalation of Sukarno's campaign in June and August, raiding parties landed on the west coast of Malaya. They were followed by an audacious but ill-prepared and scattered drop of ninety-six Indonesian paratroops into the area of Labis – a hotbed of Communist activity, as we had learnt during the Malayan Emergency. This airborne assault was effectively dealt with, not least by the 1st Battalion of 10th Gurkha Rifles who, deep in the jungle, killed twenty-four and captured a further twenty-seven paratroopers. Sadly, the operation cost the life of one of the Battalion's most popular and experienced officers, Richard Haddow, a good friend of mine, when he and Lance Corporal Tejbahadur Rai were killed. The operational temperature was rising.

In command of Borneo operations would be Britain's most experienced jungle warfare expert, General Walter Walker, and he, and his Gurkha battalions in particular, would play a decisive role in this eventually successful campaign. He succeeded because he had excellent intelligence at all levels, he waged a successful 'hearts and minds' campaign and his battalions dominated the jungle. Briefly describing some of the many incidents in my Battalion's campaigning over the next two years, I am conscious that similar engagements were occurring all along the border, with many different British, Commonwealth and Gurkha battalions involved. My story is no more than an illustrative snapshot.

After the exertions of the Brunei Rebellion my Battalion was to remain in Singapore for some six months, but as operations gathered pace it was clear that we would soon be back in Borneo. As the Battalion's Intelligence

Officer, I was closely following the operational reports and attempted to keep abreast of developments. All the while, we were ensuring that our jungle skills and procedures were kept up to the mark.

Gordon Shakespear had by now completed his tour in command, and Johnny Clements had been appointed in his place. Our new Commandant had a formidable record in jungle soldiering, having twice been awarded the Military Cross during the Burma campaign with the 8th Gurkhas. In addition, he had considerable operational experience in the Malayan Emergency with the 7th Gurkhas. For most of us he was an unknown quantity, but we were impressed by his record, and he seemed to be the right man for the challenges ahead. Operationally, Colonel Johnny would be a hard and unflinching taskmaster, and I knew we would need to be on our mettle. An aggressive soldier, forever keen to engage with the enemy, he had a direct and uncompromising style and cared little for parades and flummery. However, one of his first and very few non-operational decisions was to persuade both 2nd Goorkha battalions that long trousers for formal parades was the intelligent way to dress. To the horror of some of the older generation, who regarded it as sartorial blasphemy, our famous Gurkha shorts, with their associated hose-tops and puttees, were binned forever. I for one welcomed this sensible move to a more contemporary and utilitarian style. Eventually the other Gurkha regiments followed suit. But all this was a minor matter compared to the campaigning that was to come.

Brunei had introduced us to the massive island of Borneo, but recent operations had confined us to the Sultanate. Now we needed to study its wider geography. Following the formation of Malaysia, which Brunei had declined to join, Eastern Malaysia embraced Sabah, formerly known as North Borneo and about the size of Scotland, and Sarawak, about the size of England; both lie on the northern side of Borneo, the third largest island in the world. Together these two states share a 1,000-mile land frontier with the vast area of Indonesian Kalimantan to the south, accounting for some eighty percent of the whole island. Sarawak from west to east was divided into five Divisions, while Sabah's Interior Residency formed the major part of its border with Indonesia, adjacent to Sarawak's Fifth Division.

The country as a whole was then largely undeveloped beyond the coastal areas – it was a huge expanse of mountainous tropical rainforest with few roads, and the main means of travel in the interior was along a number of major rivers. The largest of these was the Rejang, navigable by seagoing craft including Royal Navy minesweepers for about 160 miles, and by traditional local longboats for very much further. From the west, Sarawak's southern border with Kalimantan rose rapidly to about 3,000ft and culminated in mountains of around 8,000ft. This range continued into Sabah, gradually falling away until the coast was reached. The whole frontier was a natural watershed, with many saddles and passes forming passable if difficult crossing points between Malaysia and Indonesia. Chinese and Malay people tended to congregate in the major towns, but in the interior a variety of indigenous people – Ibans, Muruts, Dayaks and many others – lived by hunting and subsistence farming, many in isolated communal longhouses built along the rivers. Many of the indigenous people had close relatives living on the Indonesian side of the border, and they had had a reputation as head-hunters in earlier times. At the outset of Confrontation, on both sides of the border, these peoples' lives were largely untouched by modern civilisation, but most of them, encouraged by a strong hearts and minds campaign, quickly became our friends and were generally to prove staunch supporters of our operations. Some were enlisted into a local lightly armed force named the Border Scouts to act as eyes and ears in the interior.

Initially, the Indonesian guerrillas consisted for the most part of a mixed bunch of volunteers led and trained by Indonesian Special Forces, Marine Commandos (KKO) and Army paratroopers (RPKAD). But as the campaign developed, Sukarno realized that if he was to succeed he would need to deploy more of his Special Forces, and well-armed Indonesian regulars became more involved. Regimental historians can sometimes exaggerate the competence of their enemies, but the Indonesians were mostly effective opponents, certainly ruthless and dangerous at times, even if their planning could occasionally be wayward. Some of their commanders had been trained at the British Jungle Warfare School at Ulu Tiram.

Borneo had all the features of the Malayan jungle, but on a larger scale. It was similarly hot and humid with heavy rainfall and offered much the same medical hazards and general discomforts associated with such environments. The leeches were certainly bigger and thirstier. The vast size and rugged and underdeveloped nature of the interior made for difficult communications and often left Battalion sub-units in isolated positions

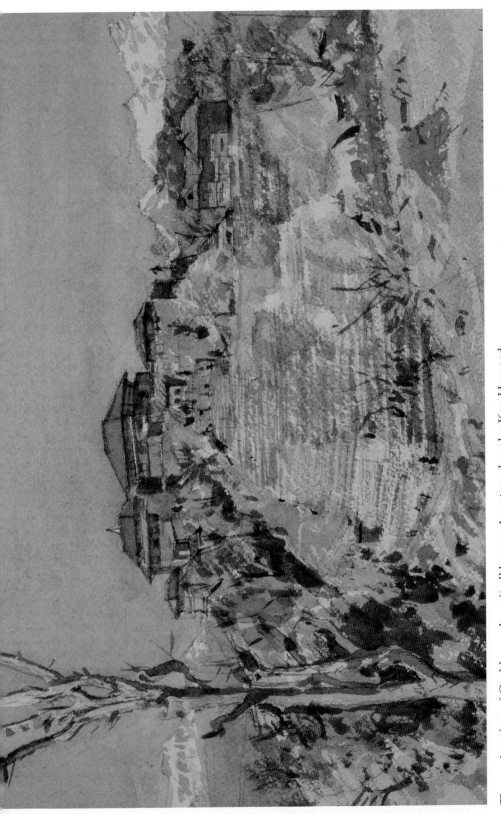

The ancient fort of Gorkha – where it all began. A watercolour by Ken Howard.

Eight soldiers of the Gorkha Army of Nepal, c. 1814, from the Fraser Album. (*Gurkha Museum*)

Preparing to face the Taliban – eight soldiers of the Royal Gurkha Rifles in Afghanistan, 2011. (*Crown copyright*)

(*Above*) Machapuchare – the 'fishtail' buttress of Annapurna in Nepal's western Himalaya.

(*Below*) HRH the Prince of Wales hosts an Afghanistan medal parade at Buckingham Palace with his Regiment, the Royal Gurkha Rifles, 2017. (*Crown copyright*)

A panorama of Old Delhi before the siege. (*By kind permission of W. J. C. Meath-Baker, 2nd Goorkhas*) The Key for the picture is as follows:

1. The Ridge and British Lines
2. Hindoo Rao's House
3. Sabji Mundee
4. Jumna Canal
5. Grand Trunk Road
6. Kissen Gunj
7. Bridge of boats
8. Jumna River
9. King's Palace (The Red Fort)
10. Cashmere Gate
11. Kabul Gate
12. Chandee Chowk

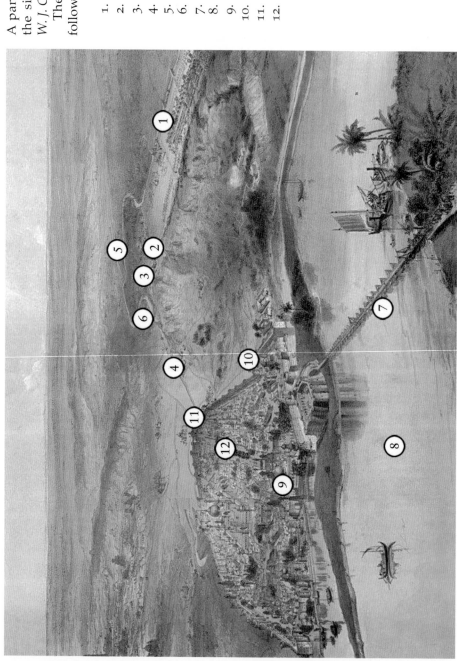

The author shares a drink with five holders of the Victoria Cross during the 50th anniversary celebrations of VJ Day, 1995. L to R: Honorary Captain Agansing Rai, Honorary Captain Gaje Ghale, Subedar Major Ganju Lama, Havildar Lachiman Pun and Havildar Bhanbhagta Gurung. Photograph taken by Field Marshal Lord Bramall.

A portrait of Kulbir Thapa VC in the sand at Lyme Regis as part of Danny Boyle's *Pages of the Sea*, commissioned by 14–18NOW. (*By kind permission of 14–18NOW*)

(*Above left*) General Frederick Young, first Commandant of the Sirmoor battalion, later the 2nd Goorkhas. Portrait by J. P. Beadle. (*Gurkha Museum*)

(*Above right*) General Sir David Ochterlony, victor in the Anglo-Nepal Wars, 1814–16. Portrait by A. W. Davis. (*Gurkha Museum*)

(*Below left*) Amar Singh, Commander of the Gorkha Army in the Anglo-Nepal Wars. (*Buddhiman Gurung/Gurkha Museum*)

(*Below right*) Prithi Narayan Shah, Prince of Gorkha. (*Gurkha Museum*)

Lord Palmerston's 'barren rock with hardly a house on it'. The Hong Kong waterfront in 2019. (*Rachel Duffell*)

Durbar Square, Kathmandu. Watercolour by Ken Howard.

(*Above left*) A 2nd Goorkha signaller, 1979. Watercolour by Ken Howard.

(*Above right*) A potential recruit is tested in the demanding Doko race. (*Crown copyright*)

Public duties – the Queen's Truncheon and the Queen's Colour on parade together at Buckingham Palace. (*By kind permission of Richard Pohle*)

very much dependent on their own resources. Helicopters proved the lifeblood of the campaign, and there were never enough. A series of landing points (LPs) for them had to be developed almost from scratch and, with weather, distance and unforgiving terrain, there was some hazardous flying involved. Logistics, too, were a constant challenge, and in the vast interior could be particularly difficult, with re-supply often possible only by airdrop or helicopter. Additionally, mapping of the interior and of Kalimantan was poor if non-existent, although air photographs could be a useful aid to navigation. Radio communications, with difficult atmospherics and extended ranges, were often challenging.

BATTALION OPERATIONS

We had little notice of our return to Borneo. After a couple of orders to move were cancelled, an Indonesian incursion into the Third Division that killed another of my contemporaries, Hugh Wallace of 6th Gurkhas Rifles, left that Battalion overextended in a huge area of responsibility. General Walker called for reinforcements, and we were ordered to move rapidly to Sarawak. Under the command of 3 Commando Brigade, with their headquarters in the capital, Kuching, we were to assume operational responsibility for the Third Division of Sarawak and, not least, 382 miles of the Indonesian border! The sheer size of this massive jungle estate was daunting, particularly in a fighting environment that just swallows up men.

In the middle of August 1963 the Battalion flew into Sibu, the administrative capital of the Third Division, and some of us began to move up country. Until now incursions had largely been confined to the First and Second Divisions of Sarawak, closest to major conurbations and with more robust communications, but it was already clear that larger groups of guerrillas, increasingly bolstered by Indonesian regulars, were now being used. They had begun to focus on the Third Division and further east. It was one such group that Hugh Wallace had encountered, and intelligence suggested that remnants of it were still in Sarawak.

The first task given to us was to deal with this group, while deploying part of the Battalion to other potentially sensitive areas of the Third Division. We quickly extended our reach into the heart of the Third Division, with two Rifle Companies deployed into the area of Song and Kapit. These were small administrative centres and settlements on the River Rejang, relatively close to the 6th Gurkhas' contact. I was based at Song with the Battalion's small forward Tactical Headquarters, and almost immediately we had a lucky break. A group of about thirty guerrillas, clearly disorientated and on the run, had arrived at a longhouse on one of the Rejang's tributaries seeking assistance back to the border and Indonesia. The headman had directed them on their way and then set off for Song in his narrow longboat, a familiar craft on all the rivers of Sarawak, to report to the local authorities.

C and D Companies were immediately deployed into the area of the longhouse, and between it and the border, using shingle river banks to land in helicopters, and the hunt was on. Aggressive ambushing and patrolling on these rivers flowing down from the border watershed – entry and exit lines for the guerrillas – then began. Within two days, some signs of enemy movement were detected, and in an initial fleeting engagement on the edge of a river line C Company killed one Indonesian, while a rapid pursuit accounted for five more, with weapons, packs and documents recovered. One of our riflemen was wounded in the engagement but was brilliantly evacuated in rain and gathering darkness by a Royal Navy Wessex helicopter. Next morning, D Company surprised the enemy commander and one of his men and killed them both. A day later, the Company managed to capture a lone Indonesian who was to provide valuable intelligence on the makeup of the group and its objective of attacking Song. It was clear that the enemy group was in disarray, and those not accounted for by the Battalion had either disappeared across the border or died in lonely places in the savage jungle. Patrolling continued for another two weeks, but beyond a single terrorist surrender there was no more contact. All the enemy dead were recovered and lifted out to Song by helicopter in somewhat macabre fashion, gathered in a net slung under the aircraft – but there was little alternative.

We had started our tour with some success and felt we had begun to make our mark. But a more testing operation was to come. Evidence from interrogation and elsewhere suggested that the Third Division was now clearly an area of Indonesian interest. We had recognized that the potential enemy entry points into Sarawak's Third Division from across the border lay through the watershed's many saddles and passes; and that in an attempt to reach objectives such as police posts and administrative centres, enemy groups would tend to follow the river lines where they could, since movement there was easier and a sense of direction could be maintained. Indonesian garrison towns well south of the border might also be places from which incursions were mounted. While continuing to focus much of our military attention on the lower reaches of the Rejang, there was an operational need to push at least some eyes and ears further into the interior and the headwaters of the Rejang, without overstretching our forces within the vast Division. For this we were to be assisted by elements of the newly raised Border Scouts.

In late September, one such listening post was established at Long Jawi, where a longhouse 100 yards in length, together with a number of huts, formed the last settlement before the border, some thirty miles away. It sat in a very isolated position on the banks of one of the main tributaries that fed the mighty Rejang, and here we were to have an initial setback – the result of forces being too thinly spread, with poor communications and, perhaps, in those early days, weak intelligence and a failure to appreciate the full threat posed by the Indonesians.

The small post established at Long Jawi consisted of twenty-one armed but very inexperienced Border Scouts stiffened by six of our Gurkhas, including a signaller, one of my old recruits, Rifleman Chandrabahadur Gurung. He had been wounded in Brunei, but having recovered and being a sharp and intelligent young soldier, had been transferred out of his Rifle Company to the Battalion Signal Platoon. Two police radio operators made up the group, all commanded by Corporal Tejbahadur Gurung. As we quickly discovered, radio communications were frustratingly intermittent and tenuous, and this was to hamper our response to what became a major incident. Tejbahadur's first task had been to prepare a small protective defensive position on a hill above the longhouse and to clear a helicopter LP. Many of the villagers were from a tribe of Kenyahs that had roots on the other side of the border, where there was a similar settlement named Long Nawang. There was a good deal of cross-border movement between the two, and initially the villagers had not proved too helpful.

Boots Burlison, sent to check out the post, together with Corporal Tejbahadur, worked hard on a hearts and minds campaign to win the villagers over, and soon they were helping to clear an LP and assisting with the supply of materials for the defensive position. After two days, on the morning of 27 September, Boots left Long Jawi, with the new position ready and occupied. His departure by boat was reported to us on a thin Battalion radio link. The radio sets had been tested on the hilltop position, but there had been problems with the aerials, and new high masts needed to be cut and erected before the signallers could be moved from a small hut near the longhouse and up to the defensive position. Unknown to Boots, the Border Scouts or Corporal Tejbahadur, a disguised enemy reconnaissance party from Long Nawang was already hidden in the longhouse.

That night, this recce party had led a force in longboats of some 100 mixed volunteers and regular soldiers, commanded by one Major Surjowardojo Muljano, an experienced Javanese guerrilla fighter and irregular soldier, into Long Jawi. They had come from an intermediate jungle camp established a few miles upstream, where they had based themselves after crossing the border from Long Nawang. Muljano himself was one of the Indonesians who had attended a course at the British Jungle Warfare School.

At about 0530 hours a Border Scout returning to the defensive position from the longhouse reported to the Gurkha sentry, Rifleman Amarbahadur Thapa, that a large enemy force was preparing to attack them, and Tejbahadur immediately ordered his group to man their position. Armed with medium and light machine guns, rifles and 60mm mortars, Muljano's force launched their attack on Tejbahadur's small defensive position. Rifleman Chandrabahadur and a fellow police operator in the signal hut were killed at their sets immediately, although a second wounded police operator managed to escape to the main position. All hope of communicating with the outside world had now gone. Accurate machine gun and mortar fire on to the hilltop position killed a second rifleman, Dhanbahadur Gurung, and a Border Scout, and wounded two others. Corporal Tejbahadur, together with Riflemen Amarbahadur and Karkabahadur, who was shortly also wounded in the chest and thigh by mortar bomb splinters, and the remaining Border Scouts, held out in their position for some three hours. At 0800 hours the inexperienced Border Scouts, having expended their ammunition, slipped away from the position and most were promptly captured by the Indonesians. Many of them were later murdered.

At 0845 hours, having beaten off one determined attack and with only three effective men left, vastly outnumbered and with a wounded Gurkha and policeman, Corporal Tejbahadur decided to withdraw from his untenable position and managed to move across a small stream into the jungle to the rear. He realized that he must get to the next listening post at Long Linau, at least a day's jungle march away, and given the state of communications it would be some time before it was realized that an attack had taken place and the alarm raised.

At this stage the Battalion was deployed across the Third Division, with C Company held as Colonel Johnny's reserve at Kapit, some 75 miles from Long Jawi on the River Rejang, ready to respond to any emergency. Our Battalion Headquarters was double that distance away, at Sibu. Here we had organized a joint Headquarters with the police in their main Third Division station at the Third Division's administrative centre. As Intelligence Officer, I was manning our Operations Room. Two days after the Jawi attack, an excited Police Inspector came dashing in with alarming news. The police radio operator at the listening post at Long Linau was reporting that Long Jawi was lost and that the remnants of Corporal Tejbahadur's group had reached them. I listened to his agitated and excited voice coming over the police net, then with a pounding heart immediately reported the details to Colonel Johnny, and we swung into action.

C Company was immediately warned to move and the ever-responsive Naval Wessex air squadron called up. Three helicopters with a platoon of C Company and with Colonel Johnny in the lead helicopter flew immediately and bravely into the LP at Long Jawi. The village had been ransacked and was deserted. The villagers had fled, and a terrible stench of death pervaded the longhouse. Further platoons followed, roped down from helicopters into makeshift LPs on river lines well above where it was thought Muljono had set up base camp prior to the assault. The aim was to attempt to cut off the Indonesians before they reached the border.

Our operations against Muljono's force lasted a month, in an area of greatest operational difficulty with big, fast flowing rivers almost impossible to cross and the most rugged jungle terrain that we had yet come across. By the end of it, when they were eventually extracted by helicopter, many of our officers and riflemen were totally exhausted, their clothing in rags. Early on, one of C Company's platoons, under command of Lieutenant Pasbahadur Gurung, had set up an ambush position on the banks of a tributary that was thought to be Muljono's most likely escape route. He had an early success. Two large powered longboats taken from Long Jawi and packed with Indonesian soldiers entered his carefully prepared ambush position.

They were killed, and although many of the bodies were swept away by the river, it was conservatively estimated that twenty-six of Muljono's force had been eliminated. Some machine guns and mortars and our own radio sets from Jawi were recovered from one of the boats caught on rocks. Eventually, a further platoon under Digby Willoughby's command, in a hazardous river crossing that drowned Rifleman Bhimbahadur Thapa, managed to reach Muljono's deserted base camp. Here Digby found the bodies of seven murdered Border Scouts, the graves of some Indonesian soldiers and three boats that had clearly been used to ferry Muljono's force to and from Long Jawi. He estimated that the makeshift base had held at least a hundred men.

The search for the rest of the enemy group continued with a few fleeting contacts and the recovery of some more weapons, but by the end of October it was clear that the remainder had either escaped across the border or died somewhere in that grim and challenging jungle. Our rapid follow-up to the attack at Long Jawi had brought some reward, but Muljono himself escaped, only to be executed in 1967 for his part in a Communist uprising in Indonesia. Retribution of a sort, I suppose.

It had been an exhausting and costly operation for us and had underlined the challenges of operating in that most difficult country in an entirely defensive posture and with our forces so thinly spread. Following the operation, we built a strong Company base at Long Jawi to be occupied by A Company, now commanded by Digby Willoughby, and the Battalion did all it could to dominate the upper reaches of the Third Division. We buried our dead, including Rifleman Chandrabahadur, and reflected on the lessons learnt from the incursion: not least, that the Border Scouts had been over-extended as uniformed auxiliaries and that SAS patrols arriving to assist us needed to be ever-watchful in the areas of potential cross-border entry points.

For the rest of our tour we remained ever-vigilant in patrolling close to the most likely crossing points along the border, but for us there were no further incursions. By the end of January 1964, after six months in that most inhospitable of jungles, we once more left Borneo.

CLARET

In the early summer of 1964, after a period of inter-tour rest and retraining in our new base in Hong Kong, the Battalion returned for the third time for another gruelling six-month tour in Borneo. This time we were to occupy four fortified company base camps close the border. These bases were split between the Interior Residency of North Borneo and the Fifth Division of Sarawak. Again, it was big country. Indonesian aggression into Sarawak and Sabah, such as the incident at Long Jawi, had continued to force British and Commonwealth forces on to the back foot, but General Walker had recognized the need to gain the initiative and he obtained permission from the British and Malaysian governments to take the fight to the Indonesians. Secret and deniable covert operations would be conducted across the border into Indonesia. Strong reconnaissance and fighting patrols, mostly at rifle company strength, would interdict the enemy's lines of communication and directly assault his bases. These operations would be largely carried out only by experienced Gurkha battalions and specially selected British units on their second Borneo tour. Special Forces would assist with cross-border reconnaissance. Hedged with numerous restrictions, each individual operation required high-level clearance. They were to be collectively codenamed 'Claret'. For some time, these operations were to remain a closely guarded secret known only to those who directed or participated in them. Even citations for gallantry awards in Claret operations, including that of the Victoria Cross won by Lance Corporal Rambahadur Limbu of the 10th Gurkha Rifles, were written to suggest that the engagements had taken place in East Malaysia. Remarkably, I never saw a press report or heard loose talk that even hinted at such clandestine activity until many years later.

While some SAS recce patrols had been operating across the border for months, the first of these major and hazardous Claret operations was carried out by the Battalion's A Company, still commanded by my old friend Digby Willoughby. His Company was based at Pensiangan, a small, isolated hilltop hamlet on the oxbow bend of a river some ten miles north of the border. Intelligence from local Muruts indicated that the Indonesian Army had established a new and well defended patrol base only 2,000 yards south of the border at Nantakor, an abandoned Murut village. As a result, longhouses and settlements nearest the border in Sabah felt particularly insecure. Given the base's threatening position, General Walker ordered that it should be destroyed. Crossing the border, Digby carried out a successful flanking attack that caught the Indonesians by surprise. Four of his

Gurkhas were wounded in the engagement, but the enemy suffered severe losses; they were forced to retreat with their casualties to their main base across the River Sembakung to the south, and they were not to occupy the forward position again. Building on this initial success, Claret operations were to assume an increasing importance, and later, towards the end of our tour, Bruce Jackman commanding C Company launched another successful cross-border operation from his base at Ba Kelalan at the Sarawak end of the Battalion's area of operations.

While these initial successful Claret operations were carried out, I had been on my first long leave in England after three and a half years in the Far East. For six months I forgot about the jungle, enjoyed holidays in Europe and the pleasures of London in the Swinging Sixties. But in the autumn of 1964, with the Battalion halfway through its tour, I returned to the jungle. Colonel Johnny told me that I was to take over command of A Company from Digby, and as old friends we had a very agreeable handover. I was impressed with the success of his Claret operation and with the defences his company had constructed around a hilltop base within a small Sabah administrative centre. Strongly constructed trenches with overhead cover, together with 3-inch mortar pits, surrounded the base close to the soldiers' hutted sleeping quarters. Across the river was a dropping zone (DZ) for receiving rations and other supplies, which came by airdrop about once a week. On a prominent position on the hilltop the Battalion Assault Pioneers had built for Digby his personal 'thunderbox', the truly regal proportions of which much impressed me. This enabled Digby to watch a Beverley aircraft execute an early morning drop of supplies by parachute on to the DZ across the river, while carrying out his daily rituals. Digby, forever an enthusiastic horticulturalist, had planted climbing Morning Glory around this structure, now in full flower. Below the position was the village football field, which served as a landing and refuelling ground for helicopters. In many ways it was a typical Borneo operational company base. We were about seven miles from the border.

My company responsibilities stretched along a hundred miles of border. While incursions could take place at any point, the immediate enemy threat lay in a series of Indonesian Army bases of platoon or company size within local indigenous settlements several miles south of the border. Since Digby's Claret operation, these bases were all now to the south of the Sembakung

River, a wide and certainly unfordable waterway that ran parallel with much of the border at some six miles from it. Logistic re-supply and the rotation of Indonesian garrison troops took place from time to time and were carried out either by helicopter or by boat.

Coupled with an active hearts and minds campaign ensuring that settlements near the border were helped with medical and other resources, a useful intelligence operation tracking Indonesian troop movement and behaviour had been established. Most of the villagers from the Murut tribe had friends and relatives across the border, and some of these local people were enlisted into an intelligence network. As far as could be judged, the Indonesian soldiers had not endeared themselves to the civilians around their bases, and this helped our cause.

Coordinating this work was a Field Intelligence Officer attached to the company, Staff Sergeant Eric Steinitz from the Intelligence Corps. Eric Steinitz was an interesting man, and I took to him immediately. A Jewish refugee from Germany, he had fled to England as a young man before the war. On the outbreak of the war he had been interned and sent to Canada, but he had later been allowed to enlist in the British Army. As an artilleryman he had crossed into Normandy with his Battery on D-Day. Later, in the advance across Europe, his fluent German had gained him a transfer into the Intelligence Corps to assist in the takeover of enemy guns and the interrogation of prisoners. Subsequently, he had been based in Berlin for fourteen years, working on the Russian and East German Armies' order of battle during the Cold War. Wanting a change, he had learnt Indonesian Malay and was now putting his Intelligence background and language skill to good use.

Staff Steinitz had established a network of informers drawn from our border settlements, and these men, to whom he gave bird codenames – Robin, Thrush, Sparrow, and so on – constantly crossed the border to see relatives, bringing back information on the Indonesian forces. They were paid modest sums, and Steinitz had given them all very general training in the recognition of weapons and badges of rank, as well as in basic security, and told them what to look out for and what to discreetly ask their relatives. The information they were bringing back was proving invaluable, all cross-checked by another 'bird' sent out separately from a different location. As far as we could tell, none of his 'spies' were compromised. I was soon confident that any move by Indonesian forces north across the Sembakung

River would quickly be reported to the headmen in our villages. In each of our border villages we placed a Border Scout with a hidden radio who could immediately relay important information to my company base.

Digby left, to great farewells from the soldiers, and I was on my own. I was fortunate that I had inherited a well organized, clearly efficient and happy Company flushed with success. There was an experienced and likeable group of Gurkha officers commanding the rifle platoons who I much respected, but I was less happy with my Gurkha Second-in-Command, Captain Narbahadur Rana, who had a long-term leg injury that confined him to base and with whom I had some difficulty in striking up a warm relationship. In the close confines of a company base such relationships are very important. In addition, and unlike some Company Commanders who were happy for their Second-in-Command to run the company base while they were out on operations, I wanted mine with me when the Company was on the move, particularly across the border. I already knew how difficult it was to command large numbers of men in the jungle, and it would be helpful to have a senior Gurkha officer around to assist me and act as a confidant. Quietly, and without any loss of face, I had Narbahadur replaced, and the inestimable Captain Bhojbahdur Gurung came to join the Company from the Signals Platoon. He was to prove a brilliant success, and we became very good friends.

For the remaining three months of the tour I lived in the fortified base of Pensiangan, surrounded by a hundred-plus Gurkhas and Staff Steinitz, ready to respond to any Indonesian incursion wherever it might occur and attempting to keep an eye everywhere. Bill Smart, a somewhat laid back and laconic Etonian, was my company officer; his father, a 4th Gurkha, had been killed in Burma, and he was to be a valuable addition and completed the complement of A Company. Digby was going to be a hard act to follow, but I started patrolling with each of the rifle platoons in turn, visiting the Murut settlements and their village headmen near the border, so that I could get to know both them and my area of responsibility. I also made the first of several modest reconnaissance sorties across the border to familiarize myself with the location of the enemy bases. I visited the site of Digby's first Claret operation at Nantakor to ensure that the settlement had not been reoccupied. I recognized that although the terrain was no different on the Indonesian side of the border, crossing into enemy territory certainly produced, at first, a palpable apprehension, a feeling that I don't think I ever lost. One certainly moved with even greater care and alertness.

Then, almost in no time, we were on our way home back to Hong Kong and, in spite of endless patrolling and some near-misses, I had nothing tangible in terms of enemy engagements to show for it. I did, however, know my rifle platoons and their individual strengths and weaknesses. While we were in Hong Kong letting our hair down, doing border duty of a different kind and preparing for our next six-month tour, Colonel Johnny arrived back from a recce in Borneo with news from our Brigade Headquarters. We were to return to our old stamping grounds in the Interior Residency of Sabah and the Fifth Division of Sarawak. My A Company would go back to our old base at Pensiangan, where I had first experienced life as an operational Company Commander, an area that I now knew relatively well. He had further information, too.

For some weeks, apparently, there had been uncertain reports of enemy activity around the headwaters of the Sungei Agisan, a river that rises just inside Sabah before cutting its way across the border through a narrow valley. It then meanders south-east in twists and turns, gathering pace and volume for a hundred miles or so, before entering the Sulawesi Sea. This was an almost untouched part of the Interior Residency right on the eastern boundary of my company area. It was a vast, previously uninhabited area of primary jungle – a primeval forest the size of Yorkshire that spread across both sides of the border. It was known as 'The Gap' and was without fixed human habitation. The 7th Gurkhas, from whom we were to take over, had, however, picked up some signs of possible enemy patrolling by small enemy recce parties on the Sabah side of the border, a few footprints and an overnight resting place; but there had been no sighting of any Indonesians. SAS patrols in the area had apparently also picked up similar signs. Additionally, there were reports of occasional mortar and small arms fire from deep across the border in this huge area of forest. For whatever reason, there had been no follow-up operations by the 7th Gurkhas across the border. Colonel Johnny made it clear to me that my Company was to focus on this possible threat to Sabah as our first priority and to be prepared to carry out a possible Claret operation in due course.

In early July 1965 we returned to Borneo and I took back our operational hilltop base of Pensiangan, originally built by the Company more than a year previously. Shortly after our arrival I arranged for 3 Platoon to be lifted by helicopters into the area well to the north of the headwaters of the Sungei Agisan. My orders to Lieutenant Manbahadur Ale, a Gurkha officer in whom I had the greatest confidence, were to see what signs his platoon could pick up of fresh enemy activity and to explore the lie of the land up to the Indonesian border.

After a week's patrolling Manbahadur and his Platoon returned and gave me a clear picture of the tough jungle approach along the river line that led to the border. The going was swampy, with heavy growth along the river banks, and it was only when one broke into the high ground and primary jungle on the flanks of the river valley that it got a bit easier. It was big country, rising from the river on either side to ridgelines up at 4,000ft, and 3 Platoon had found no fresh indication of enemy patrolling but had noticed one sign of their earlier presence, a regimental symbol carved into tree bark – KKO, or Korps Komando Operasi. This was useful in confirming the identity of the unit we were up against, but I was slightly bemused as to why they wanted to advertise their presence in this arrogant way. Perhaps, singularly unsuccessfully, they wanted to frighten us.

Within two weeks of my arrival, and on Colonel Johnny's instructions, I was flown by chopper into a small jungle clearing in northern Sabah. There I received a threadbare briefing from a shadowy group of British and Malaysian intelligence operatives – E Force – working with an informer, a Kalimantan local who had been involved in the construction of an Indonesian Marine camp on the Sungei Agisan. I was given a rough layout of the base and learned that it was occupied by a mix of Indonesian marines, the KKO and some irregulars. Their approximate strength was thought to be sixty to eighty well-armed men, and their aim was to infiltrate Sabah and attack security force bases. Colonel Johnny told me that my Company's clandestine mission was to cross into Indonesia and find and destroy this camp, sited some ten miles south of the border.

Beyond what I had learnt from 'E' Force I knew little of the exact location and I had no detailed layout of the base that I had been ordered to attack. There was no mapping of any usable scale. Some hazy aerial photographs of the Agisan from Canberra photo reconnaissance aircraft taken at 10,000ft showed two possible huts protruding from beneath the jungle canopy on to a shingle beach. I assumed that there were more huts further into the jungle. Another camp had been identified a few hundred yards upstream, but that was all the ground intelligence that I had to go on. Sergeant David Brown of the Intelligence Corps spent three days at Pensiangan poring over the spread of photographs with his stereoscope, throwing up the 3D images that he carefully transferred on to tracing paper, thus allowing the contours of the land – the hills and valleys that covered our possible approach route and the objective itself – to be identified, to assist with navigation.

Initially, Colonel Johnny, always fearlessly aggressive and drawing on his experience in Burma, suggested that I move directly down the banks of the River Agisan itself and attack the base straight off the line of march. But this seemed to me to invite early detection of our approach by any defensive screen or forward sentries, with much potential for casualties; these I would have to carry out of the jungle myself, for evacuation by helicopter across the border was strictly forbidden.

I put it to Colonel Johnny that I favoured an indirect approach – moving to the objective with 'muffled oars' and coming at it as silently as possible from the flank and the high ground – the ridge well to the west of the objective – so that the marines would hopefully remain unaware of our impending arrival. This would avoid the obvious frontal approach that, more than any other, the marines were likely to have covered. It would take far longer, and I appreciated that I was going to have to apply some nifty military footwork to finally locate and direct my company on to our objective. The absolute key to success would be the degree to which we could keep our approach undetected until we were ready to launch the assault. I did not want an inconclusive enemy contact short of the objective that would put the whole marine group on the highest alert and make the destruction of their base a costly affair. I felt this approach had a better chance of success. In addition, the Battalion's Recce Platoon – thirty Gurkhas now led by a promoted Bill Smart – had been given to me for the operation. They would infiltrate across the border via the ridgeline well to the east of the Agisan to establish ambush positions some 2,000 yards south of the camp. Their role would be to thwart any possible escape following our assault and to detect any major movement up river towards the base, while allowing small parties to pass unhindered. Colonel Johnny accepted my plan.

For two weeks we busied ourselves with intensive preparation and training around our company base. We practised our movement and immediate action drills on contact with the enemy, and our battle procedures for a company move across the border. I had already learned that control of large numbers in the jungle, where visual contact is limited, is challenging, and that well-rehearsed drills are essential. Additionally, we practised snap shooting on the short range that we had built at the base, and the firing and carriage of our support weapons. I discussed all the options with my Gurkha officers and Bill and then gave a detailed briefing on our plans to the whole company.

On 5 August we set off for the Sungei Agisan. With me went three strong rifle platoons and a small support group with two general purpose machine guns (GPMGs), two 3.5-inch rocket launchers and two light mortars, plus my command group. We were nearly ninety strong. Two days earlier, I had despatched Bill Smart's Recce Platoon of thirty men on their approach march to their ambush positions. The Company was flown by Royal Navy heavy-lift Wessex helicopters into a secure LP fifteen miles north of the border. I hoped that in this way the distinctive clatter of the helicopter rotors would be shielded from the enemy, denying him any sense of our intentions.

After a two-day approach march we had silently crossed the border on foot. Our progress was slow and laboured in difficult country, and we paused, gratefully but briefly, every hour. We had entered the dark, gloomy, fetid forest that was the somewhat threatening environment of the Gap. Up on the ridgelines it was primary jungle, largely untouched by man and almost cathedral-like in aspect. In spite of the high jungle canopy at least 100ft above shielding us from the heat of the sun, we sweated profusely in the humid conditions – olive green shirts stained black by the steady stream of water dripping off us, trousers brown with mud. We began to smell of stale cabbage. My stoic Gurkhas, weighed down by their weapons, ammunition, radios, equipment and rations, all designed to keep us going for a week or more, were still prepared to engage the enemy at any moment. In particular, the machine gunners and the men of the Support Group, with their heavier weapons and ammunition, were uncomplainingly carrying more than their body weight. Intent on achieving surprise, we moved cautiously and as quietly as possible, ever watchful, ears straining to catch any unnatural sound and looking intently for signs of enemy movement or activity.

Disorientation in a jungle environment away from river lines and with no natural landmarks is an occupational hazard. Secured by a lanyard around my neck and close at hand in its pouch on my belt was my loyal and faithful Service Prismatic Compass – a close companion that I used constantly to check our direction of march.

I was quietly confident of the jungle skills and resolution of my Gurkhas and reassured by their presence all around me. We had crossed the border several times together on our previous tour. We had trained hard for this particular operation and honed the drills we were to use. My only concern was that at the last moment I had been forced to replace my 3 Platoon with a platoon from B Company. I did not know them or their standards, and their commander was an unknown quantity. They had not operated with us before – they were untested as far as I was concerned – but there had been little time to ensure they conformed to our particular jungle tactics, doctrines and idiosyncrasies. While 3 Platoon were carrying out reconnaissance in the Gap, they had succumbed to a new strain of malaria that had not been experienced before in Borneo and many had been hospitalized. The medical diagnosis was that this virulent strain had been carried into the virgin country of the Gap by the Agisan marines. As a result, the medics had told us to stop taking the normal prophylactic, paludrine, and supplied us with a new tablet that would hopefully ensure we were not similarly stricken. This was a blow to me and the whole company, for we were without our most experienced, astute and brave Platoon Commander, Manbahadur Ale, on whom I much relied. Such were the hazards of this place.

As I tramped along, my soldiers seemed to move with relative ease, avoiding the many pitfalls, the sudden hollows, fallen trees and ever-present obstacles of a jungle march. Collectively they seemed to exude a quiet strength. They had been on several operations together and many of them had taken part with Digby in the first major cross-border operation of the campaign, destroying an enemy base in the western part of the area. I sensed that company esprit de corps was good and, importantly, confidence was high. Much of this had been achieved under the command of my experienced predecessor, Digby, and to the men, the quality of their new, younger and slightly green Company Commander, I realized deep down, was still unknown. In spite of some cross-border patrols, ambushes and skirmishes already behind me, I was untested in a larger-scale assault of this sort. Nobody was more conscious than I of the responsibilities resting on me, not only to gain success for the Company and my Regiment, but also to bring all my Gurkhas safely home.

Our approach march had taken us on an exhausting climb up and along the long western ridge running north to south some 4,000ft above and some 4,000 yards distant from the Sungei Agisan. At some point, having estimated as best we could the distance covered, I would turn the company east and begin a careful descent towards the enemy base in an encircling approach that I hoped would avoid the enemy's local defence patrols.

We were comfortable in the jungle yet ever alert to a variety of natural threats, as well as the enemy. Aside from the ever-present leeches and scorpions, and centipedes that could give you an extremely painful bite out of all proportion to their size, snakes, although rarely sighted, could be fatal. We would check for these hazards whenever we stopped. Falling branches were a real danger, too, at night; prior to pitching their beds, the soldiers would always scan the treetops to identify any dead wood that might, without warning, come crashing down, particularly when it was raining.

Thus, as we began our descent to the river, was the scene set for the final stages of this modest military drama to be played out far from anywhere, known only to a few and certainly well out of range of any support. We were on our own, entirely dependent on the resources we carried and with no help if we got into trouble. A link to Battalion Headquarters 100 miles away to the north was possible only by messages laboriously translated into the complex one-pad cyphers that ensured security. Then, before the light faded and night-time radio interference took over, my rear-link signaller, sitting hunched under a tree with his HF radio, its aerial dangling from a branch above him, would rapidly key in the message in Morse code. There was never any peace for the signallers.

Their packs nobly carried by men in the rear platoons of the company, a lightly clad group of leading scouts led the way in front of us. These were drawn from 1 Platoon under the redoubtable Lieutenant Thote Gurung, a seasoned jungle campaigner. A wounded veteran from the Brunei Rebellion, he was the possessor of a Military Medal for gallantry won in the Malayan campaign, as well as being my old friend from the Coronation Contingent, and together with his platoon he was charting our way forward.

Close to the rear of 1 Platoon, I moved with my Orders group, the platoon commanders and their runners, together with my command net signaller and my estimable orderly and runner, the cheerful and immensely strong Rifleman Emansing Gurung from a high hill village close to Annapurna. He was utterly reliable and the provider of many necessities that allowed me to concentrate on the tactical matters at hand. Together, all of us were acting as a small forward Tactical Headquarters. My ever-dependable Second-in-Command, the quietly patrician Captain Bhojbahadur, much admired and respected by all, moved with the remainder of the company in the midst of the other two rifle platoons and the Support Group. He kept a wary eye on anything and everything, not least the recently arrived B Company platoon on their first Claret operation.

Surprise was going to depend on our indirect approach and the stealth we applied to our individual movement and personal discipline. We needed to use the jungle with all its light and shade to our advantage and we were determined to leave no trace of our approach. There was to be no noisy cutting with machetes or *kukris* by day or night; everyone would sleep on hammocks strung between two trees or on the lightweight Australian jungle lilos which, inflated by strenuous blowing, made a relatively comfortable bed. Lightweight mosquito nets would be strung on cords above these makeshift beds. Sentries would check coughing or loud snoring. On halts we would scrape small pits to contain the standard hexamine cookers that were used to heat the evening meal, thus hiding their distinctive blue flames. This meal would be accompanied by mugs of highly sweetened tea laced with rum. Closer to the target we would dispense with cooking altogether and depend on tinned fish and oatmeal biscuits for energy and sustenance. Prior to leaving our base we had already lightened our loads by cutting down the one-day standard Gurkha ration packs so that five packs could last eight days if necessary.

We must have been slowly descending from the ridge on a due east compass bearing through the jungle for about four hours and had traversed about 2,000 yards towards our objective when suddenly, to my immediate front, a single shot rang out. The men froze, weapons poised and packs quickly dumped, while I gesticulated to the company to spread out in a defensive arc, inwardly cursing the possible loss of surprise. Remembering the age-old military aphorism that few plans survive contact with the enemy, I moved forward as quickly and quietly as I could and with some trepidation reached Thote. Had his platoon been engaged? What had his scouts – Corporal Lalbahadur and four riflemen – seen? Thote twisted his hand round to the right in that familiar Gurkha way that signals he doesn't know what's up, grinned at me reassuringly and thrust his jaw out towards our right as if to point to the direction of the shot. With a mixture of sign language and whispers he indicated that the shot seemed to have come from three or four hundred yards away to the right. He thought it was a rifle. The platoon had not been engaged. There was no indication what it meant. Had our approach been detected and was this some form of signal from an outlying sentry to his company back on the river? Was it a hunter? It was impossible to tell, and Thote could offer no more.

I moved back to Captain Bhoj, who had joined the platoon commanders, and gave some brief orders. We would remain in a defensive posture while Thote's leading scouts gently probed forward to see what, if anything, they could discover. If nothing untoward was detected, we would continue our approach march, ever alert and slightly altering our line of descent away from the area of the shot. Shortly, Thote reported that the leading scouts could find no immediate signs of enemy movement, and with a hand signal I gave the order to continue our advance. We would learn soon enough the probable reason for the shot that had briefly interrupted our march. Perhaps the next day would reveal all. Once more we gathered up our equipment and, with weapons at the ready, regained the rhythm of the march and pressed forward.

Four days in, we heard some machine gun and mortar fire emanating, I assumed, from the marine camp. Bearings from my compass indicated that we were on the correct line of approach. Bill Smart's Recce Platoon had also heard the firing, and we confirmed to each other that it had not been directed at either of us. He was in position with his ambush parties. At about 1500 hours I estimated that we were some 1,000 yards west of the Sungei Agisan and the marine base. We had dumped our packs and camouflaged them in a rough hide the previous night, leaving a section to guard them, and then moved forward in light order, dependent entirely on what we carried on our belts. Recce patrols located the bank of the Sungei Agisan and, checking tributaries shown on Sergeant Brown's mapping, I established that we had reached a position about midway between the two possible enemy objectives. We now split into two groups; Bhojbahadur would take one platoon and the

Support Group towards the lower camp, while I would take the other two platoons to clear the upper site and then link up with him. We would lie up for the night reasonably close to our objectives. On our way, my group passed two tree platforms obviously built for sentries, but luckily they were unoccupied. By late evening we halted for an uneasy rest with only the night-time cries of the crickets, the birds and the gibbons as company.

After a fitful night, at 5.30 a.m. the following morning I led my group through the final approach towards the Agisan bank and the upper camp. It was immediately apparent that the huts were empty and, cursing that we had been misled by the aerial photographs, we turned immediately south, parallel with the river, to join up with the other assault group. As we did so, Bhoj came up on the company radio net whispering that he must open fire now on what was clearly the main enemy camp or he would be compromised.

Almost immediately came the sound of explosions and heavy firing to the south, and we doubled our pace towards him. As we did so, a number of lightly clad enemy came fleeing towards us and were brought down by the leading sections of 1 Platoon. I could hear the sound of firing above my head – 'phee, phee, phee', the bullets seemed to cry as they cracked through the trees. In this close country it was difficult to know who was firing at what, and I was reliant on some yelled exchanges with my platoon commanders to gain a sense of events. Very quickly we reached Bhojbahadur and his assault group. Beyond the occasional shot, the firing had largely stopped. The Support Group had caught the enemy completely by surprise, and a number of enemy bodies lay scattered on the shingle bank in front of a shattered hut. A large group had been roasting a boar on a spit – presumably killed by the shot we had heard on our approach march. The Support Group had edged their way very slowly through very thick undergrowth to reach the river bank opposite the camp, guided by the smell of cooking. The excellent Corporal Karnabahadur Thapa, who had carried his 3.5in rocket launcher, and Rifleman Dhakabahadur, who had carried two 3.5in rockets in socks throughout our approach march, had loaded their launcher forty yards from the enemy and fired it straight into the unsuspecting group. This opening salvo killed a number of them and clearly caught the whole camp totally by surprise. Fieldcraft of a very high order had resulted in this telling opening volley. Shortly afterwards, as the marines recovered, machine gun fire opened up from a flank but was quickly dealt with by Lance Corporal Manbahadur Thapa, who had been wounded during Digby's earlier raid at Nantakor. He moved bravely on to the open shingle bank to launch his 2in light mortar bombs in the machine gun's direction and effectively silenced it.

With Bhojbahadur's group providing covering fire from our bank, I pushed two platoons across the easily fordable river to clear the camp and secure the high ground above it, while we ensured that we were in all-round defence on the home bank. After about twenty minutes, just as I thought the enemy were done for, they bravely launched a counter-attack from the high ground to the east that took us, and certainly me, somewhat by surprise. I heard shouting – it seemed like 'Come on, come on!' but was probably something in Malay. Later, I was told by 2 Platoon that the attack had been led by a man clad only in shorts and wearing what appeared to be a field dressing around his head. By now we were in strong fire positions above the enemy camp, and the attack quickly petered out with more casualties to the enemy. We had been lucky; two riflemen had gunshot wounds – Dalbahadur Pun was hit in the cheek and Manbahadur Thapa had a bullet through his left ear. A further rifleman had had a bullet through his trouser leg without touching the flesh. An entry one inch further left in all three cases, and these men would have been very serious casualties.

While pushing out from the perimeter to check for any further signs of enemy, we also searched the camp. It had been occupied for some time, but beyond some stone *sangars* for the heavy weapons, there were few defensive trenches. We found large stocks of food and ammunition and retrieved fourteen rifles, a light mortar, a medium machine gun and documents. These were distributed to the platoons to carry back to our base, together with samples of rations and clothing. I sent a quick message in guarded Gurkhali to Bill and his Recce Platoon saying that all was well and that remnants of the enemy might be coming his way. I drafted a short contact report for the rear link signaller to send to Battalion Headquarters. We covered the enemy dead with ponchos. We estimated by body count that sixteen at least had been killed.

At midday I concentrated the company; we had a thorough check of all our weapons and equipment – only one rifle magazine was lost, which I thought was pretty good, but we had fired a good deal of ammunition; we accounted for everyone and began the march back to the hide where we had dumped our packs. Here we would sort ourselves out and have a meal, and from there I sent a more formal contact report back to Colonel Johnny. We maintained alertness, but it is fair to say that we moved a good deal more rapidly than we had on the approach march. After five fairly stressful days we were in high spirits, and I reflected sombrely that nothing improves soldiers' morale more than successfully killing the enemy.

On reaching the hide where we had stowed our packs, I had a contact report from Bill. A group of four enemy in a small boat had approached their ambush position; they had been killed and their bodies recovered from the river. Then, just before we moved off again, at about 3.00 p.m., I had another report from him. A further group of five enemy in a boat had approached his ambush position led by two scouts on foot, both wounded and armed. On reaching the edge of the ambush killing area the scouts had motioned the boat forward, before they were engaged by the Recce Platoon. A short firefight ensued, five of the enemy were killed and some more equipment and documents were recovered. Bill then moved his ambush position and remained on the Agisan for a further 24 hours, but that was the end of it. We all moved back to the border to await helicopters to lift us out, and after ten days the final elements of the Company reached Pensiangan. Colonel Johnny sent an approving message. We all felt we had done all right, and we got on with dealing with our disgusting laundry. Eventually, E Force reported enemy losses in the Agisan as thirty-nine.

For three days after our return to Pensiangan we could speak of nothing else, and for some time I continued to talk only in whispers, until Bhojbahadur asked me if I could possibly speak up! In the Company we felt the enormous sense of unity and camaraderie that springs from the shared hazards of combat, probably incomprehensible to those that have not experienced it. Everyone had a tale to tell about the assault, and a rich tapestry of individual stories emerged. Some were no doubt exaggerated, but no one had seen everything so there was much to tell. As Commander I had only snapshots of the early engagements: fleeting figures in the jungle, a tremendous amount of deafening noise, much shouting. Sometimes, unable to see what was happening, local firefights were beyond my immediate influence, but Bhojbahadur and my stout platoon commanders did not let me down and kept tight control of their men. Perhaps some of my Gurkhas were braver than others, but no one let me down – all were resolute.

Our successful assault had been an interesting, somewhat stressful, but by no means unique experience. Claret operations were now beginning to dominate the campaign but they still needed high-level clearance and very careful planning if they were not to come unstuck. Certainly, Bruce Jackman and LB, with their rifle companies and from their bases well to the east of my location, were to undertake equally valuable operations in various stages of our tour. Similarly, across East Malaysia's long border with Indonesia there were other successes, although most resulted from ambushes rather than direct assaults on enemy bases.

Staff Sergeant Eric Steinitz, my excellent Field Intelligence Officer, excitedly fell upon the documents we had brought back, and for two days, before we sent them back to Battalion Headquarters, he patiently translated some. They included a high-level Operation Order for ambitious Indonesian plans in Sabah, a campaign that the Agisan group was designated to spearhead. The information the Operation Order contained more than justified our pre-emptive strike, and Staff Steinitz mused that his Intelligence bosses in Singapore Headquarters would be turning up the air-conditioning a few notches as they read them. Other documents included a Marine commander's diary, in which he had written of the sighting by one of his patrols operating in the Agisan headwaters of a 7th Gurkhas Rifles patrol, including a description of one tall red-haired British officer, who I quickly identified from a meeting at the handover of the Pensiangan base when we had first arrived. We kept that information to ourselves rather than embarrass our friends, but they had been careless – and fortunate not to be shot! There was also an entry with a noted presumption that the practice firing of their heavy weapons in camp would, apart from training, keep the Gurkhas away! Such naivety and their failure to maintain strict alertness, conduct dawn clearing patrols or occupy their external sentry posts well before first light – all standard procedures for us – had cost them dear. We had been lucky, but perhaps our detailed preparations and our indirect approach had earned us our luck.

I was proud of my Company. I wrote some citations for gallantry awards but sadly, as always, the final results were less than I thought the men deserved. That is often the case; there is always strict rationing, and some men who had done particularly well were disappointed. I supposed the powers that be were keen not to devalue the currency. The recommendation that

I made for the Military Cross, which I certainly thought Captain Bhojbahadur deserved for bravely leading his group to the bank of the Agisan and opening the assault, was not accepted, although later it deservedly earned him promotion to Gurkha Major.

We spent the rest of our tour in Pensiangan covering our wide front with frequent patrolling, keeping in touch with all the local settlements and maintaining a successful hearts and minds campaign. Staff Steinitz continued to run his network of 'birds', who built up a rich storybook about the elements of the Indonesian Army operating opposite us.

In the course of what was to be our last tour we carried out four more Claret operations focussing on the bases that lay to our front. None of them produced quite the rewards of the Agisan, and my hope of crossing the deep and fast-flowing River Sembakung was, as I secretly realized it would be, thought too risky by higher command. Instead, we stuck to ambushing and possible interdiction on the Indonesian lines of communication along the river, with some bad luck and narrow escapes. One of our ambush positions was compromised by a local hunter, and the position was attacked with heavy fire by the Indonesians minutes after I had reluctantly decided to move it. On another occasion, a Mitchell bomber and a Mustang fighter of the Indonesian Air Force bombed and strafed one of our cross-border OP positions shortly after we had vacated it.

Based on intelligence, we also carried on soldiers' backs a heavy Browning anti-aircraft machine, broken down into its constituent parts, deep into Indonesia to engage an expected Indonesian re-supply helicopter. Waiting expectantly in an eyrie we had established well above an enemy base, I heard with mounting excitement and a certain trepidation the distant sound of an approaching aircraft. But we soon realized that it was not a helicopter but a fixed-wing plane; an aircraft that I had no permission to engage. We could only watch discontentedly from our eyrie as it carried out a re-supply by parachute drop. We also located and escorted two Special Forces patrols who had got into trouble back across the border. But although we kept the Indonesians well south of the border and behind their defensive barrier of the River Sembakung, we undertook no more major assaults.

At the end of January 1966, what turned out to the Battalion's fourth and final tour in Borneo for us was complete, and we handed our bases over to a battalion of the 6th Gurkha Rifles. By early 1966, too, Indonesian enthusiasm for Confrontation was on the wane, incursions dwindled and internal unrest, Communist insurrection and dissent within Indonesia hastened its demise. Having been soundly defeated by the British campaign, Confrontation formally ended in August of that year. The Gurkha Brigade as a whole had made an impressive contribution to the outcome of the campaign, the Gurkha rifleman proving himself once again a superlative jungle soldier. After twenty years of almost non-stop campaigning since joining the British Army, my Battalion, along with all the Gurkha regiments, would need to turn their attention to other matters.

As for my own A Company, Claret operations were now no more than short reports and statistics set down in the annals of the Regiment, mostly long forgotten, the accompanying operation reports gathering dust in some military archive. But even after fifty years, and while other events and campaigns cloud the mind, I can still recall the names and faces of all the Gurkhas that came with me to the Agisan.

Chapter 10

Brush Strokes of Empire

*Prosperous but precarious, on borrowed time in a
borrowed place, that is Hong Kong.*

—Tom Wu

THE BEGINNINGS OF A CHINESE COLONY

It being obviously necessary and desirable that British subjects should
have some port at which they may careen and refit their ships when
required, and keep stores for that purpose, His Majesty the Emperor of
China cedes to Her Majesty the Queen of Great Britain, the island of
Hong Kong, to be possessed in perpetuity by Her Britannic Majesty, Her
Heirs and Successors, and to be governed by such laws and regulations as
Her Majesty the Queen of Great Britain, shall see fit to direct.

Thus in 1842, with suitable Chinese brushstrokes, chops, seals and
signatures, did the Treaty of Nanking finally secure Hong Kong
for the British Empire, in settlement of the wars resulting from
the disreputable opium trade between the British East India Company
and China. The colony seemed at first to offer an uninviting prospect.

Its mountainous terrain had little fertile land or water, and its population was no more than a few thousand, many of them living on fishing sampans along the coast. But it had one great natural asset – a sheltered and spell-binding natural harbour strategically placed on the Far East trade routes.

About the outcome of the treaty neither side was particularly happy. The cession of part of their country aroused shame and anger among the Chinese, while Britain's Foreign Secretary, Lord Palmerston, was equally displeased, contemptuously describing Hong Kong in an oft-quoted phrase as 'a barren rock with hardly a house upon it'. But amidst the diplomatic skulduggery the beginnings of a great commercial centre and a grand hub for entrepôt trade with China had been laid.

Two further agreements lent coherence to the Hong Kong story. The settlement of intermittent hostilities with China between 1856 and 1860 led to the first Peking Convention. With this came the outright cession of a small tip of the Kowloon peninsula across the harbour on the mainland of China, with a perpetual lease up to what became known as Boundary Street. Stonecutters Island, in the middle of the harbour, was also included.

This gave the British secure control of the harbour and its approaches from the sea. Then, by a second convention signed in Peking on 9 June 1898, came an extension to Hong Kong's territory: the New Territories, comprising the rest of the Kowloon peninsula south of the Shenzen River, together with some 235 islands – a total area of some 370 square miles, and all leased for 99 years. The political impact of this lease, which expanded Hong Kong tenfold, was to figure greatly in the history of Hong Kong, and in the later years of my Gurkha journey!

Hong Kong was unlike any other British colonial possession and never central to the imperial ethos; it was not like India – the so-called jewel in the crown – with a thousand years of history, architecture and culture already in place. It was an almost empty mountainous landscape that Commodore Sir Charles Bremer and his party of marines found when they landed at what was to be known as Possession Point and first planted the British flag. The influence of China across the harbour – 'the Great Within' – was to be all-pervading.

Throughout its history, and particularly during periods of unrest in China, large numbers of immigrants – mainly Chinese but also members of the international and entrepreneurial community of Shanghai – sought sanctuary in Hong Kong. The Taiping Rebellion against the Manchus, the Boxer uprising, the Japanese occupation, civil war, famine and the chaotic eruptions of the Mao Zedong era stretching from the Communists' Long March through their Great Leap Forward to the depredations and madness of the Cultural Revolution; all these drove a mass movement of people to forsake the miseries of the mainland for the freedoms, security and general stability of Hong Kong. By the mid-1950s Hong Kong's population was estimated to be 2.2 million, and since then it has continued to rise; it was 5.7 million by the end of the 1980s and by 2018 it had reached 7.5 million, all crammed within its 412 square miles. It is one of the most densely populated places in the world.

This increasing Chinese population, loyal to Chinese traditions but not to the Communist regime, thrived under liberal British rule. Eventually, it absorbed the spirit of the Colony, its community and its settled conditions. Governance followed normal British practice for overseas territories, with a Governor nominated by Whitehall, and Executive and Legislative Councils drawing their membership from local officials and worthies. In due course I was to play my part as a member of the Executive Council at a time of great historic challenge for the Territory. In general terms, Government policy was laissez-faire in character, treating the Territory as a market place where all were free to come and go and where government held the scales impartially. The energies of this unique market place were largely unfettered, and democratic machinery was almost non-existent.

In spite of its British heritage and international outlook, Hong Kong has always been a Chinese city, albeit one overlain with many western characteristics. Today, among glittering skyscrapers and a frantic jostle for space by peoples and vehicles, the general throb, thrust and fever of its activity are ever-present. These combine successfully with Chinese geomancy or *feng shui* – the wind and water and their balance which ruled much of Chinese decision making and for many continues to do so; it can certainly be unfortunate for those unwise enough to upset its cosmic balance. Straight lines and acute angles are thought to be particularly malevolent, and it quickly became apparent that the Chinese-American architect I. M. Pei's shimmering new Bank of China building thrusting skywards had potential problems. In the middle of central Hong Kong, it had a triangulated glass and steel structure, and one piercing angle projected 'secret arrows'

MIRS BAY

Rocky
Harbour

Port Shelter

Tolo Harbour

Starling
Inlet

Shau Tau Kok

Man Kam To

Sheung Shui

Fanling

Tai Po

Sha Tin

Sai Kung

Lo Wu

KOWLOON

Kai Tak

Lye Mun

Chai
Wan

Kowloon City

Ha Kwai Chung

Kennedy
Town

CENTRAL

HONG KONG ISLAND

Shenzhen

Lok Ma Chau

Maipo Marshes

THE NEW TERRITORIES

Shek Kong

Tsuen Wan

Tai Mo Shan
3,143 ft.

DEEP BAY

Lau Fau Shan

Yuen Long

Tuen Mun

LAN TAU ISLAND

0   5   10
        miles

HONG KONG

directly at the elegant northern facade of Government House. The fall of Margaret Thatcher was locally blamed on this potent force. The judicious planting of a weeping willow tree in His Excellency's garden ensured that, in due course, any ill reflections were suitably diverted!

This bustling Chinese city has grand hotels and Manhattan-style skyscrapers rising majestically along the shoreline of the Island and Kowloon. A thousand shops decorate their windows with goods of brazen luxury. There are food markets full of traditional Chinese vegetables, delicacies and cookies, seafood and ducks and chickens galore. Next to them are the incense sellers and Tao temples, stalls selling cheap 'designer' handbags, and Chinese pharmacies and acupuncture surgeries still flourishing in the age of modern medicine. More new buildings rise within the framework of traditional bamboo scaffolding. Joss sticks and chopsticks and fortune tellers abound, together with dance halls and cheongsams and Suzie Wongs. The ancient abacus assesses profit with a rapid staccato beat. Antique shops demonstrate delicate Chinese workmanship with intricate carvings of wood, or bone where once it was ivory. Porcelain, calligraphy and painting skills are on show. Distinctively shaped sampans and the occasional junk seem to hazard themselves in the harbour as they seek space alongside the plethora of commercial tugs, ferries, barges and international shipping. Everywhere gaudy neon signs in Chinese characters advertise commerce above all else.

In addition to the Chinese there were, firstly, the British, particularly in Government service. Alongside them were assorted Europeans, Americans, Japanese and others – in commerce, the finance houses and the professions. In addition, Filipinos, Indians, Pakistanis and Nepalis had arrived – forming separate communities but very much part of the mix. The westerners were, however, and still are a small largely transient group beside an overwhelming Chinese population. Some stayed, but most of the Europeans were never intent on settlement. They simply wanted to taste the East and its delights, before retiring back whence they came, returning home economically and hopefully spiritually the richer for their experience.

ENTER THE GURKHAS

Throughout its history Hong Kong had a military garrison. The first military forces were raised in India – Bengalis, Punjabis and Pathans – but

British regiments also left their mark. The Headquarters, the Garrison's Victoria Barracks and the commanding General's generously proportioned residence – Flagstaff House – occupied prime position and much valuable real estate right in the centre of Hong Kong Island – a source of some irritation to the administration and commercial interests. Close by were in modern times only the remnants of what had once been the Royal Navy's largest station in the East. It remained after the war as a more modest naval base at HMS *Tamar*, centrally placed on the harbour front.

The Gurkha soldier was a latecomer to the Hong Kong military scene. He had first been based in the New Territories in 1948, but did not really become a firm fixture until the end of the Malayan Emergency in the very late 1950s, when there was scope for his wider deployment.

Shortly after I arrived in Malaya, in late 1960, I was sent to Hong Kong on modest regimental duty to visit our 2nd Battalion. It was a short flirtation with the place lasting only three days. It was winter and there was a distinct chill in the air for which I had not been prepared; the bare hills of the New Territories were very different to the tropical jungles of Malaya or the urban centres of Kowloon and Hong Kong Island. It was only later that I was to experience the searing heat and draining humidity of a Hong Kong summer, and also to enjoy the variety and vibrancy of Kowloon and the Island. I caught only a glimpse of bustling urban Kowloon as we drove to Hong Kong's airport at Kai Tak on the eastern reaches of the peninsula. From the aircraft window, as we flew out, I caught glimpses of the enticing pattern of islands that made up the whole of the Territory.

In 1964, during a four-month break from operations in Borneo, we found ourselves leaving Slim Barracks and its Singapore comforts, to become part of the largely Gurkha garrison in Hong Kong. For me this was the start of an association with the Territory that was to play an important part in my military life and that of my Gurkha soldiers. Our domestic circumstances on that first posting were not great. We were far from the bright lights of Kowloon and the Island, based in a rough hutted camp in the New Territories, close to the small town and railhead of Fanling, some three miles from the border with China. The camp was a legacy from the era of the Korean War and the security uncertainties of the early 1950s. Defensive fortifications and concrete ammunition supply roads still criss-crossed the high ground that rose above the Chinese border. The late 1940s had been a jittery time for the Colony. There was civil war in China, and a pragmatic policy of non-involvement had been the Territory's successful approach. But spies, manipulators and collaborators, both Communist and Nationalist, slipped in and out of the Territory and kept the Government and Police Special Branch very much on their toes.

On the border itself, to improve surveillance of the mainland, a line of seven observation posts had been built on high ground looking into China. They were named MacIntosh forts after the Police Commissioner who had devised them in the early 1950s. In due course, these forts would allow the garrison's patrols to monitor closely the activities of the People's Liberation Army (PLA) in their camps on the other side of the border. Additionally, they could watch for the movement of illegal immigrants or observe changes to a regular pattern of military behaviour – perhaps the arrival of reinforcements heralding a new Chinese approach towards Hong Kong.

Well south of the border area there were other broken fortifications, stemming from the earlier conflict with the Japanese, that stretched along a line of old defence emplacements. This was the so-called Gin Drinkers Line – a chain of pillboxes that zigzagged eleven miles along a rocky and precipitous hillside between Tsuen Wan and Sha Tin across the southern part of the New Territories. Tsuen Wan had apparently been the scene of some alcoholic picnics in happier times, hence the name. The whole of the New Territories then had a remote feel about it, with isolated villages inhabited by farming and fishing communities.

At that time, 48 Gurkha Brigade embraced the garrison units based in the centre of the New Territories. Its Headquarters and support troops were based in the Shek Kong bowl below the towering peak of Tai Mo Shan. All its Gurkha battalions were housed in barracks close to the Chinese border. British battalions, initially within a separate brigade command, occupied more salubrious space in Kowloon at Gun Club Barracks and on the Island at Stanley Fort. The great opening up of the New Territories, with highways and New Towns, was still far away, and the Island seemed remote. The grand Hongs, the great trading houses of Jardine Matheson, Swire and the Hong Kong Shanghai Bank ('The Bank') were well established, but many of the other great entrepreneurial endeavours that were to drive the Territory's economic success were still in embryonic state. Further to the south of the New Territories, huge colonies of refugees and migrants remained camped in terrible shanty towns in the hills above Kowloon. Landing at Hong Kong's main airport at Kai Tak still gave the arriving traveller the slightly unnerving experience of swooping past blocks of flats and being able to peer into a bathroom window.

For junior officers such as me, marooned north of Fanling in the early 1960s, a journey to the Island represented something of an expedition. It required the careful husbanding of financial resources, close attention to timings and that most sought-after of assets, a serviceable vehicle in the shape of the mess car that the bachelor officers shared. The road from Fanling to Kowloon was then single-track and dependent in Taipo on a planked Bailey bridge built by the Royal Engineers. One then climbed up and over the hills of Sha Tin and slipped down into Kowloon, before crossing on the Yau Ma Tei car ferry to Hong Kong Island. A smile from Governor Black's daughter Barbara was the coveted prize of many of these expeditions!

Barbara's father, Robert Black was one of that special breed of British proconsuls who were, not least, fierce champions for their citizens. Carrying out intelligence work in Borneo during the Second World War, he was captured by the Japanese and spent three years as a prisoner of war. A well-furnished mind helped him to survive those dire conditions. After serving as Colonial Secretary in Hong Kong in the early 1950s he had been appointed Governor of Singapore, before returning to Hong Kong as its Governor in 1958. His greatest challenge had been the famine-driven influx of refugees from China that peaked in 1961, and it was he who had directed the first massive housing programme as well as a system for returning refugees to China.

But apart from my passing interest in Barbara – unsurprisingly, if irritatingly, shared by many others – to write about the Governor in this way might suggest that I was on familiar terms with the administrative challenges of the day and Sir Robert himself. For junior officers such as me he was as remote as the *Taipan* of Jardine's, the Chairman of the Hong Kong Shanghai Bank or the portals of the Hong Kong Club. It was only in later years that this became more familiar territory. Over fifty years later, I was able to meet up briefly with Barbara, happily married for many years, still living in the Territory and as beguiling as ever!

After a Borneo tour, bachelor officers such as myself would return to Hong Kong with wallets fuller than usual. Money that was ready to be squandered on the heady delights offered by Nathan Road in Kowloon and – for some – the more dubious dens and night life of the Wanchai district on the Island – altogether a hedonist's paradise when compared to the jungle. But shortly there would be more serious matters to attend to in Hong Kong.

British officers and Gurkhas and their families serving with their battalions tended to live a life that was somewhat isolated from the Chinese or the British expatriate communities. It was confined largely to the regimental and brigade family. There would be shopping and dining expeditions to Kowloon at the weekends. A visit to Sam, well positioned just off Nathan road and, by appointment, tailor and banker to the regimental subalterns, was often a necessity. In summer, some of us might secure a prized invitation to an expatriate's junk for a day at sea, or a trip to the races.

But it was rare to persuade members of the well-heeled expatriate community to travel north to the New Territories to socialize with us, and generally, neither the Gurkha soldiers nor their officers mixed with the Chinese. There was no animosity, but the Chinese kept to themselves. British soldiers, too, had few social equivalents within the European community. A few expatriate watering holes attracted the attention of some officers, and golfers might enjoy subsidized membership of the fine course at Fanling, but clubs on the Island were largely out of the financial and motoring range of junior officers. Some modest games of polo were played in Shek Kong on Borneo ponies. These were so diminutive that their tall British riders cut somewhat ridiculous figures as they galloped across a sequestered football field. Many of the unmarried subalterns lived a largely introverted existence in a Gurkha battalion. The officers tended to socialize with their soldiers on the games field in the early evening, dine with the married officers in their quarters or enjoy life in their messes. Tours on the border would also eat into opportunities for any socializing down town.

RIOTS AND COMMOTION

By the mid-1960s Hong Kong was again facing a vast influx of illegal immigration as a result of Chairman Mao's Cultural Revolution. The Gurkha battalions were heavily involved in patrolling the border day and night, 'demonstrating sovereignty' and continuing to monitor the PLA in their camps and on patrol on the Chinese mainland.

Looking across the border at that time, we saw a terrain of timeless pastoral quality. Duck farms and rice fields rolled back as far as the eye could see towards the distant hills that hid the mysteries of Mao Zedong's China. The country seemed inscrutable and unreachable, and oppressed by years of ideological excess. It was closed to tourists, and restrictions denied us any form of contact, despite the presence of PLA patrols 20 yards away on the other side of the border. It all represented an east-west relationship based on ignorance and suspicion, an atmosphere that only began to change years later, with the death of Mao and the period of reform and economic growth initiated by Deng Xiaoping's open-door policy. It was this border, defined by that Second Peking Convention leasing the New Territories to us in 1898 for 99 years, that we got to know so well. It dominated the working lives of successive Gurkha battalions throughout much of the last thirty years of the British administration in Hong Kong.

The Territory's land frontier with China extended for some twenty-two miles from Deep Bay in the west to the small fishing township of Sha Tau Kok on the coast of Starling Inlet in the east. For much of its distance the border followed the course of the west-flowing Sham Chun River, navigable as far as Lo Wu. This was roughly its mid-point. Here was a single rail crossing into China with customs posts and immigration offices, and it was here that the Kowloon–Canton railway used to carry permitted travellers from Hong Kong to the mainland. Passengers, mostly travelling to family reunions, would disembark from their Hong Kong train and cross the border on foot. They would then board a Chinese train on the far side. International statesmen and political celebrities would be photographed setting off for a probably unique visit to China, possibly to meet the Chairman and hopefully manoeuvre a significant démarche.

Further east was a second significant crossing point where a small Bailey bridge spanned the River at Man Kam To – used by the Chinese from Guandong Province that abutted the border to export livestock and vegetables to the Territory. It was at this crossing point where, every day at four o'clock, captured illegal immigrants would be handed back to China.

Lastly there was Sha Tau Kok – a fishing settlement that spilled across both sides of the border; a small township with a series of boundary stones dividing its central thoroughfare, Chung Ying (Chinese-British) Street. Sha Tau Kok presented some unique security problems; local residents were permitted to come and go within the township as they pleased, and no barriers separated Chinese and Hong Kong territory.

There were further significant crossings over the Shum Chun River – the water conduits. In 1960 Hong Kong had reached agreement with China for the supply of 5,000 million gallons of water a year. This was delivered through a pipeline and gravity feed from the Shum Chun Reservoir, some three miles inside Chinese territory. Additional pipelines were added as Hong Kong's population grew, and by 1976 24,000 million gallons, about 25 per cent of the Territory's needs, came from China. The political and security implications of this arrangement were obvious to all.

Along the length of the border ran a sophisticated double-tier fence erected by the Hong Kong authorities. This fence, topped with razor-sharp barbed wire, was within a restricted zone that stretched back into Hong Kong to a depth of about one mile and was designated the 'Closed Border Area'. In due course, a single-track vehicle road was also laid alongside the fence to allow rapid deployment of garrison troops and police by truck or bicycle to assist in the capture of illegal immigrants.

Technically the border lay on the high water mark on the north bank of the Sham Chun River, but the fence ran along the south bank where maintenance and patrolling were easier. Within this closed area there were a few scattered farming settlements, but the security forces were able to move freely here. A night curfew was enforced, and the general public was not permitted inside at any time. Tourists could not travel to China but they could go by road to Lok Ma Chau police station, one of ten stations strategically placed within the border area. Standing on a hillside close to the station they could gaze across the river to the flatlands of Guangdong and consider, as we did, the remoteness of it all. The landscape represented something of a time warp when compared with the noise, development and general hubbub of Kowloon, Hong Kong Island and, increasingly, the New Territories.

Within China the mid-1960s heralded the start of the Cultural Revolution, an attempt by Mao to reassert his power and authority and accompanied by a ruthless purge of many of his top lieutenants. These included Deng Xiaoping and others who were considered to have deviated from the party line. Remnants of other capitalist and traditional elements within Chinese society were also targeted, and the Revolution came with an appeal to the young to organize themselves into cadres of thuggish Red Guards. They were to launch an assault on 'capitalist roadsters' and reimpose Maoist thought as the dominant ideology. Violent struggles across the country resulted in a wide range of abuses, including imprisonment, torture, harassment and humiliation. Millions were forcibly displaced, and there was widespread destruction of anything that was interesting and old in China. State anarchy reigned. The Thoughts of Mao were to become the staple of life, and the mounting chaos not unsurprisingly produced growing tensions in Hong Kong. The Territory was vulnerable to Communist confrontation, and the garrison needed to be increasingly alert.

Johnny Clements, who had commanded my Battalion with great operational success throughout the Borneo campaign, moved on. He had given his young company commanders – the four rifle company commanders were all under twenty-five – every encouragement to engage with the enemy and had been very much a man of his time. He was an excellent fighting soldier but he had little regard for any other form of regimental activity, leaving such matters to his Second-in-Command. In Johnny's place, again at the right time as operations began to scale down, we inherited another former 7th Gurkha officer. Birdie Smith could not have been more different from the laconic but aggressive Clements. The sobriquet 'Birdie' was due to his diminutive size, a marked beaky nose and a rather high-pitched voice.

But the outward appearance belied the man. He was a Second World War veteran with a reputation for singular courage and service. As a twenty-year-old Gurkha Company Commander with his 7th Gurkhas in the Italian campaign he fought at the battles of Tavoleto and Monte Cassino. His courage had won him a Distinguished Service Order. He knew at first hand the strengths – and the occasional weaknesses – of Gurkhas in the toughest of battle conditions, and was to write movingly about his experiences. He had been wounded several times in the war. More recently, he had lost his right arm in one of the many jungle helicopter crashes in the Borneo campaign – one of which I had survived.

Birdie, together with six Gurkhas and his Battalion medical officer, Patrick Crawford, was on his way to visit a 7th Gurkha rifle company on operations near the Indonesian border. Descending from about 100ft into a tight jungle clearing, the Navy helicopter in which he was flying lost power. The engine gave a cough and cut out, the helicopter dropped like a stone and there was a splintering crash as it slammed stern-first into the ground, before toppling over into a ravine and landing on its back. A tree stump punched a hole into the cabin, crushing Birdie's right arm and breaking his hip. The six Gurkhas scrambled clear, but Birdie was trapped. Bruised and shaken, Patrick Crawford climbed through the wreckage to Birdie, who was hanging by his shattered arm. In hazardous conditions Patrick worked for an hour on Birdie's injuries in the semi-darkness of the fume-filled cabin. He had no morphia or surgical instruments. With a Gurkha supporting Birdie, he applied a tourniquet, then, using a clasp knife sharpened on a stone and without any form of anaesthetic, carried out an amputation of the arm. This enabled him to extract Birdie from the helicopter, and in so doing he undoubtedly saved his life. Eventually, Birdie was airlifted out of the jungle for further surgery. Throughout the operation, and perhaps conscious of the presence of his six Gurkhas, Birdie made no sound. Patrick was awarded a George Medal for his brave action. Having heard all this, I thought Birdie also deserved a medal.

In spite of his impressive military record, Birdie was a sympathetic and gentle man who enjoyed enormous rapport with the Gurkhas; their welfare was always close to his heart. Command of the 1st Battalion was his first appointment since recovering from the loss of his arm. He appointed me as his Adjutant and we began to get to know each other as he worked out how to manage all the manifold tasks of life as a commanding officer with only one arm, and that his unnatural left one.

We had our first taste of impending troubles in Hong Kong caused by the Cultural Revolution during the Easter holiday of 1966. On 6 April in the late afternoon we had returned to Queen's Hill from a Battalion command post exercise testing all our vehicle-mounted radio systems and were looking forward to the Easter break. On reaching the Lines we picked up some news of rioting in Kowloon. Birdie sensibly decided that we would leave all the radios mounted in their vehicles in case a call came.

At one o'clock in the morning that call did indeed come. Without warning we were rudely awakened by the Brigade duty officer and told to move the Battalion immediately to Kowloon in support of the police, to help contain serious and widespread rioting. I harried the Company Commanders and

Gurkha officers to rouse their men and load our internal security equipment, weapons and ammunition. I thought back to 1962 and the Brunei Rebellion, when the Battalion had been similarly alerted without notice at an unearthly hour in the morning and told to move with best possible speed. I was glad to reflect later that the Battalion was once again able to react with commendable sharpness. We reached the Kowloon police compound in Nathan Road from way up in the New Territories before the British Battalion had debouched from Gun Club Barracks 500 yards away.

Aside from echoes of the Cultural Revolution to the north, the immediate catalyst for the severe Kowloon disturbances was a protest at the raising by 5 cents of the first-class fare on the Star Ferries operating between Kowloon and Hong Kong Island. But the three nights of disturbances were symptomatic of wider social discontents – the gap between rich and poor and the frustrated ambitions of the young. The density of population in the urban area of Kowloon allowed rioting to spread rapidly. What was clear when we arrived was that the disturbances – rioting and looting, the long lines of burnt-out buses – had by the early hours exhausted the police. Additional assistance was urgently required. The centre of the disturbances was the broad Kowloon thoroughfare of Nathan Road and its immediate byways.

For young officers such as me it was a very different feeling from earlier social expeditions as we marched down Nathan Road. We were in full internal security order and were pelted with flower pots and other bric-a-brac from the balconies above those very dives that in earlier times had been part of my course of liberal studies as a Gurkha subaltern. The riflemen were wearing their Gurkha hats, both as protective headgear and to signal militarily who was about. I quickly noted that the reputation of the Gurkha soldier was such that the hostile crowds melted away as we moved forward. We fired not a shot, nor was tear gas used. Banners and bugles, the somewhat archaic internal security appurtenances of the time designed to encourage crowds to disperse before the use of more lethal weaponry, remained unused.

For the following three days we enforced a curfew. We cordoned off the worst affected areas and guarded sensitive places such as Kai Tak airport, as well as acting in support of the police in crowd control. Our presence seemed to be both effective and welcomed, and by the end of the Easter holiday we were back in our barracks. If we had lost our holiday, then at least to the delight of those with motor cars, half of Kowloon's parking meters – a modest symbol of Government authority – had been destroyed by the rioters and were not replaced for several months.

These disturbances in Kowloon were but a prelude to events in the hot and steamy summer a year later, when the tremors of the Cultural Revolution surfaced strongly in Hong Kong, inspired by Communist cadres to the north urging on their radical supporters across the border. There was mounting industrial unrest, rioting and a bombing campaign, with many hundreds of incidents recorded. A fever of violence overtook the Territory. Hotels and shops were boarded up, and Mao's little red books seemed to be waved everywhere, not least in front of Government House. Some fifty police and civilians were killed and several hundred injured during a campaign designed to severely test, if not engineer the collapse of, the colonial government.

Events took a dangerous turn on the border. I kept a close track of what occurred and locked away the lessons learned at that time about border integrity, readiness and restraint. A few years later, as a more senior commander with direct responsibility for security on the border, I remembered them. On the border the Chinese militia were actively involved in creating pressure and mayhem. One incident impressed me with not only its potential seriousness but also the style of its successful resolution. At that stage the Hong Kong Police had primary responsibility for the security of the border. The Army were in a secondary supporting role, and 1st Battalion, 10th Gurkhas were the designated Frontier Battalion on stand-by to be deployed to the border if required. A firm but non-provocative response to intimidation was very much the policy.

Police Special Branch had learned that a demonstration coupled with an attempt to remove and burn the Union Jack would take place on 24 June at the small border police station at Sha Tau Kok. The police had therefore ensured that road blocks and a cordon were in place to thwart such an attack. As predicted, two hundred rioting coolies, many of them disguised Chinese militiamen unrestrained by any border barricade, had stormed the cordon. They had been dispersed by the police use of baton rounds and tear gas, albeit with some casualties on both sides. Sha Tau Kok was then reinforced with an additional platoon of Pakistani riot police. By Saturday, 8 July there were eighty-six Hong Kong Chinese and Pakistani police based at the border police post, with a further Police Tactical Unit company of four anti-riot platoons – some hundred more men – about 250 yards behind it. On the Chinese side of the border and to the rear of Sha Tau Kok were elements of 7085 Border Regiment from the People's Liberation Army.

During the morning a large crowd built up on the Chinese side of the border. Around 1100 hours, a crowd of several hundred surged across the border assaulting the police with bottles, stones and fish bombs – dynamite used illegally by the locals to stun fish. With the police under some pressure, the Tactical Unit to their rear formed up eight abreast in anti-riot formation and began to march forward to reinforce their colleagues. Immediately and cruelly, a Chinese medium machine gun (MMG) opened fire on the advancing unit, killing one policeman and wounding others. The unit scattered and dived for cover. Police in the Sha Tau Kok post and buildings close by were also engaged by Chinese sniper fire, and more police were killed and wounded. The police were neither equipped nor trained to respond to this kind of attack. They had only a few carbines and shotguns, and they were not allowed to fire across the border. Their position was critical and as totally unexpected as it was shocking; they fought back and wounded some Chinese militia but were hopelessly outmatched. By this stage five policemen had been killed and eleven wounded.

The Commanding Officer of the 10th Gurkhas, Ronnie McAlister, had now been given orders to deploy his Battalion to the border. Lead elements reached the main Sha Tau Kok police station about a mile back from the border at around 1300 hours, just as firing died down. Information was sparse, and the implications of committing the British Army into the border area were serious indeed. But by 1430 hours Colonel Ronnie had been given orders by his 48 Brigade Commander, Brigadier Peter Martin, to clear British territory of armed infiltrators. The Colonel saw that his first task was to secure Sha Tau Kok village up to the line of the border and clear the aggressors from it. He would then evacuate the police from the village. He was told to use minimum force, opening fire only in self-defence and only if enemy fire was effective.

In this critical situation the Battalion advanced forward in tactical bounds, with D Company on the left of the road that led to the border. A Company, supported by the Life Guards' Saladin armoured cars, was on the right and commanded by my good friend and contemporary, Jonathan Edwardes. Firing again broke out, and Colonel Ronnie recalled:

> Brigadier Martin landed on the road by helicopter right beside my Tac HQ and told me to press forward at best speed. We walked up the road together and had just come level with the troop leader's armoured car when the MMG opened up. The armoured cars 'closed down'; the leading one was hit by a few rounds which ricocheted off into the distance. The Brigadier and I took cover behind the troop leader's vehicle and we were joined by Captain (QGO) Bhaktabahadur Limbu DCM (Second-in-Command A Company). I found his presence comforting. As the MMG continued to fire in short bursts we periodically looked round our cover trying to pinpoint the origin of the fire. None of us could tell and this improved morale no end to find that Bhakte's pin-pointing of the enemy was no better than mine.

Jonathan Edwardes remembers rounds striking the ground and water all round his Company Headquarters, but fortunately there was only one casualty, when a round hit a soldier's rifle and damaged his hand. Fire was not returned – it was deemed not to be effective! What was effective was the sight of armed and well-disciplined Gurkha soldiers together with Saladin armoured cars advancing deliberately but tactically towards Sha Tau Kok. It was sufficient to make those Chinese who had been on British territory quickly melt away, taking their wounded comrades with them. The leading company of the Gurkha Battalion reached the police post at about 1630 hours, and by 1700 hours the British ground of Sha Tau Kok had been secured. Defensive positions were erected on top of commanding buildings, and the difficult evacuation of police dead and wounded got underway. Colonel Ronnie wrote:

> It was an unmilitary, uncanny, unreal feeling for commanders at all levels, standing in the open directing soldiers to the best fire positions while perhaps 200 Chinese soldiers and militia trained their weapons at us at ranges of fifty yards or less, across an unwired, scarcely discernible border in a scruffy village of minimal value to either side.

Inconclusive diplomatic protests and counter-protests were to follow. But the disciplined restraint and skilful handling of a dangerous situation by the Gurkha Battalion had prevented escalation into a serious international incident.

As a result of the Sha Tau Kok incident and consequent considerable damage to police morale, the British Army assumed prime responsibility from the police for border security. Weeks of political demonstrations, provocation, insults and intimidation directed against the Gurkhas manning the border followed. Occasionally, machine gun fire would be directed over the heads of soldiers in their defensive positions. Further potentially serious incidents took place at the Lo Wu and Man Kam To crossings. The Chinese were forever attempting to engineer a dramatic confrontation with the British security forces.

On one particularly tense occasion Colonel Ronnie McAlister, the District Officer and assorted police officers were abducted while engaged in delicate negotiations with mainland Chinese. They were held for several hours by armed militia before being released immediately prior to a rescue operation being mounted. In situations such as this the Gurkhas proved their worth, refusing with great restraint to respond to endless incitement to engage with fire. No shots, apart from the use of gas and smoke grenades, were ever fired across the border by our troops in that long hot summer.

Together with the Gurkhas, the British and Hong Kong Governments had stood firm and refused to kowtow to pressure as a result of these disturbances; or, in August, to the torching of the British Embassy in Peking by Mao's Red Guards. Some Hong Kong Chinese millionaires departed the Territory for the safety of Vancouver or elsewhere, but the British continued to play cricket on their ground in Central and the Governor could occasionally be seen on the golf course at Fanling! By the end of the summer the disturbances began to decline in the face of the sturdy resilience of the Hong Kong people, the tenacity of its Government and the restraint and sensitive handling of provocation on the border by the Gurkha battalions. Fundamental, too, was the issuing of orders by the Chinese authorities to cool the ardour of their supporters. Mao's intention had been to provoke a kowtow from the British, not to take back Hong Kong 'ahead of time'. It was economically too valuable as it was.

In the mid-1970s I returned to the Territory after a gap of some six years, having left in 1967 with my Battalion for a tour in Brunei and, two years later, a year at the Army Staff College in Camberley. This was followed by two years as Brigade Major – the Chief of as Staff – in a British Brigade Headquarters on yet another border, this time in Northern Ireland in 1972, a year of rampant difficulty for the Province. That was followed by further service in England experimenting with air mobile operations. All of this was a valuable introduction to the rest of the British Army and the wider world of soldiering outside the Far East.

After this absence I came happily back to serve with my old Gurkha friends in the 1ˢᵗ Battalion and for the third and last time to command a rifle company. In my absence the Gurkha battalions' barracks in the New Territories had been considerably modernized with funding from the Hong Kong Government; in the wake of the Cultural Revolution disturbances they had perhaps recognized the importance of attending more closely to the needs and comforts of the Gurkha garrison.

If the Border was still a sensitive area, the excesses of the Cultural Revolution within Hong Kong had largely disappeared, although China itself remained as distant and enigmatic as ever. One issue, however, remained. Dealing with the Communist-inspired disturbances in Kowloon and on the Island had enhanced the reputation of the Hong Kong Police Force, and they were given a royal title. This hard-earned reputation had, by the early 1970s, been badly damaged by the gradual exposure of deep-seated corruption within the force. Superintendent Peter Godber, the Deputy Commissioner of Kowloon, an effective but unattractive policeman whom I remembered meeting in Kowloon Police Headquarters at the time of the Star Ferry riots, was graft's unacceptable public face, and it was discovered that he had amassed a fortune of several million dollars. He beat a hasty retreat to Sussex before he could be arrested but, eventually extradited back to Hong Kong, he spent four years in prison before joining his criminal cohorts in southern Spain.

The widespread and endemic corruption at many levels within the force led to the formation of the Independent Commission against Corruption – the ICAC as it became known. But the myriad arrests, including those of some 200 police officers, led to a difficult and dangerous confrontation between the police and the Government over the perceived witch hunts that ensued. There was unrest, a loss of morale and accompanying protests. The possibility of police strikes raised the unhappy spectre of the garrison and its Gurkhas being forced on to the streets to police Hong Kong – an unacceptable and unattractive prospect both for us in the garrison and for the Territory.

At this difficult and volatile time, the Governor was Sir Murray Maclehose, an enlightened and energetic, if to some an autocratic, public servant. He was, controversially, to be the first official to discuss the future of the Territory with Beijing, as well as persuading the people of Hong Kong to think about their environment. He felt it was necessary to offer some concessions and amnesties to the police, and a dangerous situation was gradually defused. But it was a bad moment for Hong Kong and caused much reputational damage. Conformity with the law eventually followed, and evidence of corruption within the force – and elsewhere – steadily declined. The garrison let out a collective sigh of relief that it had not been called upon to police the Territory.

REDUCTIONS AND REDUNDANCIES

Ever since I had joined my Regiment, the life expectancy of the Gurkha regiments had been regarded by many as limited. Most of us had recognized in the aftermath of the Malayan Emergency that we might be vulnerable to cuts. Without some new campaigns or military responsibilities, amalgamations and redundancies might come. The Brunei Rebellion and the protracted Borneo campaign had saved the day. Now in the wake of the successful culmination of those operations the profoundly pessimistic – particularly those in British Regiments – were happy to suggest that the whole Brigade might be abandoned in one fell swoop. 'You will all be gone in five years, Peter', hinted the cynical sages.

But others, including myself, were more optimistic about military opportunities. To the south, events in the killing fields of Indochina – Vietnam, Laos, Cambodia – seemed to suggest that so long as the British Government had interests, alliances and defence commitments 'East of Suez', there would be employment for the Brigade of Gurkhas. Their proven experience in the Asian environment seemed a valuable military commodity. The so-called dominoes could collapse to communism at any moment, threatening the security of Thailand and Malaysia. In the final event, the dominoes did indeed fall, but not in the expected direction. Nonetheless, it soon became apparent that as the Borneo campaign wound down the

British Government's policy was to begin a withdrawal from the Far East. Security responsibilities would remain in Hong Kong and Brunei, but the major British garrisons in Singapore and Malaysia would certainly leave. Plans in hibernation since 1962 were soon revived to reduce the Brigade from 14,500 to 10,000 men.

The staff in the Gurkha Brigade Headquarters were quickly at work assembling the necessary data to plan both the rundown itself and the compensation terms required. There was a need to persuade the Ministry of Defence and Her Majesty's Treasury what compensation was fair and adequate for a Gurkha soldier being despatched prematurely back to the hills of Nepal after years of testing operations. At the start of negotiations there was a wide gulf between the thinking of the civil servants in London and the Gurkha staff. In the end, this gulf was adequately, if not generously, bridged. Eventually, the plans were announced: between August 1967 and December 1969 5,000 men would go on redundancy from all units across the Brigade. The 2nd Battalions of the 6th and 10th Gurkha Rifles would be disbanded.

Worse was to come. Even before the first phase had been completed it was announced that there would be further cuts to the Brigade. Another 4,000 men would go, reducing the Brigade to a strength of 6,000. The two remaining 2nd Battalions – those of my own Regiment and the 7th Gurkha Rifles – would be lost, and there would a number of other ancillary cutbacks. In the space of four years, and after twenty years of almost non-stop stressful campaigning, over half the Gurkhas of the British Army would be gone.

Soon after these announcements were made there was to be some curtailment of the plans; not least, our own 2nd Battalion would eventually be spared for some years. But there were now serious concerns among many that the Gurkhas might not survive at all. Across the Brigade, and in addition to the painful business of selecting and interviewing men to be sent on redundancy, a number of British officers were invited to leave the service or transfer to British regiments. Some decided that it was in their own best interests to go; to cut their ties with the Gurkhas and opt for service with British regiments or become civilians. A number of high-quality officers, seeing no future in the Brigade, were lost.

The challenge for those of us who chose to keep faith and stick with our soldiers was how to remain operationally effective through an extended rundown process. Detailed planning of the selection process, and the way it was handled and communicated, with sympathy, transparency and honesty, ensured that this was achieved. A major programme of resettlement was launched. The Major General of the time, Pat Patterson, instituted a Gurkha Welfare Scheme, which found huge support not least among the British public. It was designed to alleviate distress particularly among those Gurkhas whose past service had not provided them with a pension, particularly the pensionless veterans of the Second World War. All told, it was a painful and unhappy time for everyone.

It was especially unhappy down at battalion and rifle company level. Here the selection process had to balance the need to maintain a sensible age and rank structure for the future with ensuring that those who had to return to the Hills had, by virtue of their length of service, earned a pension or at least worthwhile lump sums. Given the numbers involved, this was not always easy or possible.

Within the Battalion I had to say farewell to some of the men I helped to enlist in Nepal in 1961. These were the men I had brought by train across India and then by ship to Malaya, had trained for a year at the Gurkha Depot and then campaigned with throughout operations in Brunei and Borneo. Perhaps there is no room for sentiment in matters of this kind, but these men were my friends. Not least, some had risked their lives with me on the successful adventures in the Sungei Agisan and elsewhere. It was not something I found easy, looking a man in the eye and telling him he had to go, with expectations lost and ambitions gone. Much later, at a different level of command, I was to face the same process all over again, and more senior rank did not make it any easier.

BACK TO THE BORDER

In the mid-1970s, as in the past, hundreds of refugees tried to cross the border fence every night, threatening to overwhelm Hong Kong's ability to cope. In the face of this problem and the need both to deter and to apprehend them, a garrison battalion was continually deployed for several weeks at a time along the border. For this duty we would base ourselves either in the border police stations or in the MacIntosh Observation Forts. On the eastern and western coastlines we occupied cottages in long abandoned fishing villages; many of their former occupants were now running Chinese restaurants in England or other entrepreneurial ventures elsewhere.

The double-tier chain-link and barbed-wire fence was now equipped with sophisticated monitoring devices. These set off fence tamper alarms in the patrol bases, indicating crossing points. The obstacle itself still proved only a modest hindrance to illegal immigrants, or 'IIs' as we called them. A hastily thrown protective blanket or coat over the barbed wire and a would-be young migrant could be over the fence well inside a minute. Rapid reaction and excellent fieldcraft were required to ensure the IIs did not penetrate our defensive lines and quickly disappear into the concrete jungle of urban Hong Kong.

Almost without exception, these potential immigrants would be the same sort of people I had seen ten years previously, typically young, illiterate, Cantonese peasants, ill clad and penniless and seeking, like a latter-day Dick Whittington, the gold of Hong Kong's pavements. None of them spoke English. The only difference from earlier times was that in place of the blue Mao pyjamas worn by their predecessors, they now sported designer jeans and Los Angeles-style T-shirts in an attempt to merge into the urban environment.

Captured, these IIs would be handed over to the immigration authorities for processing, before being returned every day at 4.00 p.m. across the Man Kam To bridge to China. An agreement had been reached with China that immigrants, on both sides of the border, would be humanely treated. Smuggling cartels, the so-called snakeheads, charged heavily to lead would-be immigrants to the border, avoiding the local militia and border guards. They would then leave their clients well short of the fence to fend for themselves. Many, but not all, would be apprehended on one side of the border or the other, for the Chinese authorities were keen to prevent illegal emigration.

In early 1976, as Mao's life was moving to its close, I was on a border tour with my Rifle Company stationed not on the land border but on the shoreline of Starling Inlet and Mirs Bay to the east of Sha Tau Kok. It was here that I had my most memorable engagement with an illegal immigrant. I had set up my very small company headquarters in an old fisherman's cottage close to the beach. Each night I despatched small-sized patrols along the coastline itself and across the hills to our rear to seek out and apprehend any II who attempted an overnight sea crossing; and we had achieved some success. Early dawn was the key time to watch for overnight swimmers risking all by pitting themselves against the currents and the sharks that infested the dangerous waters of the bay. Depending on where he or she launched themselves, a swimmer had about a mile to cover from the Chinese shoreline to the possible sanctuary of a Hong Kong beach.

About six in the morning, as dawn broke, Corporal Nandalal Ghale reported to me by radio that he and his patrol had picked up a swimmer. Apparently, he seemed rather different from the typical II, and Nandalal was bringing him in to my headquarters straight away. I immediately tasked the company signaller to contact the Marine Police post at Sha Tau Kok and summon a launch to pick him up. This was the only means of returning people to the land border area and the immigration authorities; otherwise there was a long trek across the hills to the nearest roadhead.

I left my hut and with my field glasses could pick out Nandalal and a couple of men from his patrol walking towards me. They were with an older man, a little stooped and clad only in a pair of blue shorts. His hands were held behind him in the plastic handcuffs with which IIs were always secured when captured. Nandalal seemed to be deeply engaged in conversation with him. I was somewhat mystified at this, for I knew that, like most Gurkhas, his knowledge of Cantonese was at best rudimentary and certainly not up to prolonged debate. As Nandalal brought him in, I could see that the II was indeed older, a little bent but clearly a cultured individual. He had an almost noble quality, in spite of being clad only in shorts and showing signs of exhaustion from his night-time swim. I learned later he had crossed clinging to a child's rubber ring. As he came into the hut, he said to me in excellent English:

'Have you read Thackeray's *Vanity Fair*? What a wonderful character is Becky Sharp.'

I told him I was familiar with the book, but this seemed an unusual conversational gambit on the Sino-Hong Kong border at the time of the Cultural Revolution! I told Nandalal to remove the plastic handcuffs, and we gave this interesting man a mug of tea and a blanket. I asked him if he knew who we were, and he immediately replied:

'Oh yes, you are Gurkhas; everyone in Canton knows there are Gurkhas on the border.'

It turned out that he was Professor Wang, a university professor of English Literature, and he recounted to me, and to Nandalal's patrol and the rest of Company Headquarters who were now huddled around him, the story of his life. He had spent two long periods in detention during the Cultural Revolution on what he called 'national farms'.

'I found farming uncongenial, Major', he said.

He had twice tried to escape to Hong Kong but each time had been caught by the local militia. For an hour he described life in Mao's China, about which we then knew little.

He complained, 'We're sick of all this damned revolution.'

The Professor then wept as he recounted watching trains arriving in Beijing carrying hundreds of casualties from a huge earthquake east of the capital that had recently destroyed the city of Tangshan, with the loss of half a million people. About this we had heard only rumours.

Finally, he stated, 'My brother is a merchant on the Queen's Road, and I am off to join him. When I reach him, you must come and dine with us.'

I said that I didn't think this would be possible. During our talk, and along with my Gurkhas gathered around us, I had warmed to this interesting and seemingly kindly and intelligent man. Secretly, part of me wanted to tell him to move off quickly up the hills to our rear, while we looked for more IIs coming in off the sea. That was clearly not possible, however, and I could already see the police launch that I had summoned arriving at our small jetty to take him off the peninsula.

Nandalal had told me that he had found the Professor hiding behind some scrub close to where he had landed from the sea. When spotted, he had raised his hands in some kind of threatening gesture – 'Kung Fu', Nandalal called it – as if to attack him. This aggressive approach had forced my Gurkha Corporal to bring the bamboo baton, which all the soldiers carried as their only weapon, down on his hand, and I noticed that the Professor's right hand was swollen as result.

The police came into our fisherman's hut, snapped metal handcuffs on the Professor and led him away. I can still see the look of pained surprise and resignation on his face. After our friendly exchange, it was clear that he felt I had in some way betrayed him. I was sad to see him go, and so were the Gurkhas, although normally, I fear, all of us were generally unmoved by the plight of the IIs. I wanted to think that some enlightened immigration officer might recognize what this cultivated and entertaining man had to offer. He could provide information about the political situation in China as well as other intelligence, and this might have stayed his return. I also knew that if a would-be immigrant was injured and required more than three days treatment he would not be returned to China but could be granted asylum. I thought the Professor's hand might have been broken by Nandalal's baton and that, paradoxically, this blow might save him. I made some inquiries over the next couple of days, having warned the authorities to look out for him and asked that his hand be medically examined. But I heard later that Nandalal had only bruised the hand, and that three days later the likeable Professor had been returned across the Man Kam To bridge to China. I hoped it would not be to another national farm.

A few years later, when I was in a more senior position in Hong Kong, I got to know more about the immigration system and enquired further about my Professor Wang. I drew a blank on him but I did realize that the immigration business was then a shadowy world where things were not always as they seemed, and that valuable people did occasionally find sanctuary in Hong Kong or elsewhere. But there was always the fear of possible Chinese stool pigeons being infiltrated into Hong Kong for nefarious purposes.

Long after I had left the Army, I told this story to a friend of mine, an author of spy novels, Charles Cumming, who turned the incident into a successful thriller called *Typhoon*. In the book the Professor is allowed to stay by the authorities. He is indeed discovered to be a Chinese placeman, but is turned by the joint efforts of the CIA and MI6 and returns in their service to China, where he has many adventures. But I always assumed that this did not happen to my professor!

Shortly after my meeting with Professor Wang I again left the Territory, this time to work for two years as Military Assistant to the United Kingdom Commander-in-Chief, General Sir Edwin Bramall, and also the Regimental Colonel of the 2nd Goorkhas. Then in early 1979 I heard news of the appointment that is the ambition of all Army officers – I was selected to command my own Regiment and would soon return to Hong Kong.

THE COMMANDANT

Commandant of the 1st Battalion of the 2nd Goorkhas was an esteemed appointment, but it was also daunting to follow in the wake of men such as Frederick Young, Charles Reid, Francis Tuker and James Showers, all with superlative and distinctive records in command. It seemed highly unlikely that my Battalion would face the stern challenges that they had experienced at Bhurtpore, on the Ridge at Delhi, at Wadi Akarit or at Monte Cassino. Border duties in Hong Kong certainly lacked some of the military drama and hazard faced by my predecessors. But the intention was always to be ready for anything. Exactly one hundred years earlier, the Battalion had unexpectedly marched 300 miles with General Roberts from Kabul to Kandahar, where they had taken part in a victorious battle and had captured an Afghan gun to prove it!

After a last tour on Hong Kong's border with China, and after nine months in command, the Battalion moved on a two-year posting to England – a new experience for most of the riflemen. This would present the Battalion with some fresh challenges and a welcome change of environment. On an earlier similar tour by the 7th Gurkhas, in 1982, they had joined the Marines, the Parachute Regiment and Guards Battalions to form the Task Force that was to retake the Falkland Islands. In so doing they had overcome Foreign Office concern about deploying Gurkhas in this way. Such objections had been quickly dismissed by Mrs Thatcher, who gave her support for their inclusion, and a useful precedent was set.

Before we left Hong Kong, we had an important engagement – the first visit from our newly appointed Colonel in Chief, the Prince of Wales. Both battalions of the Regiment were based in Hong Kong at that time, so it was a chance for him to meet all of us, and during a two-day stay we introduced him to something of the 2nd Goorkhas' style and ethos. Together with my friend Bruce Jackman, commanding the 2nd Battalion, we paraded the whole Regiment formally in front of our Colonel. The Queen's Truncheon, our unique colour from Delhi, was positioned in front of the saluting dais, where it was held by Bhanbhagta Gurung VC. We had flown him down from Nepal especially for the occasion, and his sons were on parade with their Battalion. The Colonel in Chief inspected us all. Then, after a splendid breakfast, we conducted a series of demonstrations designed to show off our military skills. We flew up to the Chinese border so that he could meet soldiers manning Observation Posts and patrolling for illegal immigrants and, like the rest of us, gaze into the People's Republic. The Regimental Band sounded Retreat one evening on a floodlit football pitch, and this was followed by a party with all the soldiers. Everyone sat around a very large log fire on a balmy evening, and we were entertained *Kalratri*-style by the Battalion dancers. Even the Prince was persuaded to dance. At the regimental Dashera celebrations later in the year, this allowed a Mess member to announce that he had 'danced with a man who had danced with the Prince of Wales'! This whole programme seemed to go off with a swing and without a hitch; it was clear at the end of two days that the Gurkha soldier and his Colonel in Chief seemed to have taken a strong liking to one another.

Proof that we had forged a close relationship with our Colonel in Chief was to come during our stay in England. His Royal Highness paid us three visits during the course of our tour, including dining with us all one evening in our mess. Later in that tour, I was lucky enough to be invited to accompany him on a trek in Nepal most beautifully organized by Jimmy Roberts and his trekking agency, Mountain Travel. The week-long trek produced marvellous views of the Himalayas, glorious weather, most enjoyable walking and engaging conviviality; Prince Charles was able to visit some of the hill villages where our soldiers came from and meet many of our pensioners. The level of outdoor comfort on that sublime trek, as we progressed royally through the Hills, was far removed from that early sortie of mine twenty years earlier, staying in Thakali *batties* and travelling with a single porter. Of the varied personalities who accompanied us on that walk, I particularly remember the Prince of Wales's personal porter, Pertemba, a very fine Sherpa climber who had reached the summit of Everest three times, then a unique achievement. He was a most impressive man.

During our stay in England we were deployed for six months on an operational tour in hot, tropical Belize. Mexico was to our north, the Caribbean Sea enticed us to the east and an unhappy Guatemala pressed on our borders to the south and west. Our task as part of a British garrison was to deter possible aggression by a Guatemalan regime that laid claim to much of Belize. There was a good deal of rhetoric, but the threat of aggression or incursion seemed to have been contained. In the south of the country we patrolled hard in unattractive jungle that lacked the moisture of Malaya but had more than its fair share of virulent mosquitoes. We familiarized ourselves with the border, but of the Guatemalans and their aggressive intent there appeared to be no sign. Then out of the blue we had an interesting engagement.

A small patrol from B Company that included the Company Commander, David Scotson, came across a platoon of Guatemalan soldiers who had crossed the border and were making themselves at home in Belize. Quickly surrounded, they were escorted back across the border. Guatemalan Army engineers had been constructing a road up to the border, and there was a clear intent to push it into Belize. The Guatemalans that David had encountered maintained that they were in Guatemalan territory, but this was clearly not the case given the position of the border stones marking the international boundary. Having reported matters to the British Force Commander and agreed a plan of action, I visited David's patrol. We made contact with the Guatemalan Lieutenant who had transgressed into Belize and was now encamped on the other side of the border. I asked him to arrange a meeting with his superior commander so that we could discuss the incident. I intended to leave the Guatemalans in no doubt as to the location of the border and the dangers of any transgression by armed Guatemalan soldiers.

Over the course of the next few weeks we held several meetings with the Guatemalans. My Gurkhas built a splendid negotiating table, with suitable awnings and log benches around it and with two legs in Guatemalan jungle and two in Belize. The Adjutant designated it 'Lancaster House', and here the two military delegations met! My opposite number was a very large Guatemalan Colonel with smart pearl-handled revolvers at his hips; my perceptive Gurkha signaller suggested the Colonel was so large he must be a General. I had a Police Special Branch interpreter to translate the Colonel's Spanish, and we served very hot Gurkha curry to our potential aggressors. We took care to match the strength of the Colonel's escort with exactly the same number of Gurkhas. We had been provided with detailed mapping identifying the agreed international border. Needless to say, our negotiations got nowhere, the Guatemalans never accepting our designation of the international boundary. But we certainly left them in no doubt of the dangers of any further transgression. In due course the talks escalated to diplomatic level between the respective capitals. But we all enjoyed these meetings and learning something about Guatemalan intransigence. Our patrols kept close surveillance along the border until we handed responsibility to a new incoming battalion and went back to England. It was particularly fortunate that we had had a patrol in the right place at the right time and had forestalled an incursion. But that was the limit of our operational excitement.

For the remainder of our tour we took part in a series of testing exercises with the UK Field Army, and ceremonial commitments also took up a good deal of time. We lined the route for the State Visit of the President of Kenya, from Victoria Station down Victoria Street to 'the second bollard outside Sainsbury's', according to our parade instructions. We had our first taste of public duties at Buckingham Palace where, as always, the relative heights of the Gurkha and the Guardsman, parading together, produced much public interest and occasional amusement. This was an important occasion for us as the duty covered the State Visit of King Birendra of Nepal, who also visited one of our Rifle Companies, a visit which gave much pride and pleasure to the riflemen he met; and for two or three days the press took a great deal of interest in the Gurkha soldier. While these public duties were enjoyed by the Battalion, they were not something you could just turn up for. They took a good deal of preparation and training on the drill square, with much assistance from Guards sergeant majors, there to ensure that we mastered all the varied and intimate intricacies and procedures of 'Changing the Guard at Buckingham Palace'. Companies took it in turn to provide the Guard so that all had a chance to experience the duty. It was also customary, apparently, for the first and last Guard of a tour to be commanded by the Battalion's Commanding Officer, so I was equally required to be on my mettle. These duties certainly put the Gurkha soldier in the public eye, and this was to prove helpful in the coming years.

One of our saddest duties was to provide a company-strong marching contingent for the funeral of Lord Mountbatten, killed by the IRA.

The soldiers also took leave. Scotland was always popular, and some parties of Gurkha riflemen headed off on well organized trips that promised five European capitals in seven days; others set off for the slopes of Austria, where British officers taught them to ski. Then it seemed almost time to prepare for an older and wiser Battalion to return to Hong Kong; it was certainly time for me to move to much less attractive pastures in the corridors of the Ministry of Defence. My time in command was, all too quickly and sadly, over.

Chapter 11

Higher Command

'And Hong Kong belongs to us, doesn't it?
'Definitely, Lord Copper.'

—Evelyn Waugh, *Scoop.*

I was to hold two senior appointments in Hong Kong and on both occasions I was fortunate to have Gurkhas under command. These were periods of critical interest and historic importance, both for Hong Kong and for the Gurkha Brigade. They centred round the transfer of sovereignty from the United Kingdom to the People's Republic of China. In addition, I was to attend the elaborate handover ceremonies in July 1997. Since then, over the course of the next twenty years, I have returned to the Territory on several occasions.

COMMANDER GURKHA FIELD FORCE

I had been away from the Territory for five years commanding my Regiment and heading a branch in Military Operations in the Ministry of Defence.

Then, in January 1984, I was fortunate enough to be promoted to Brigadier and to return to command 48 Gurkha Infantry Brigade. It had been rather curiously re-titled 'The Gurkha Field Force'. I thought at first the new name must be some sort of backward tilt towards an imperial provenance. But a number of other brigades had also been similarly renamed in one of the British Army's periodic bouts of reorganizational fervour; a change that seemed to lack any form of coherent rationale. I supposed there was one, but the title did not last very long.

The Gurkha Field Force had exactly the same role as previously. Its Headquarters remained in the Shek Kong bowl in the New Territories. It was a large formation, with some ten major units spread throughout Hong Kong. The Gurkha infantry battalions were at its heart. A British battalion on the Island, and Gurkha Engineer, Signals and Logistic units, were integral elements of the formation. We answered to the call of Commander British Forces and his Joint Headquarters on Hong Kong Island.

The underlying security concerns in Hong Kong were much as I had known them previously. In addition to supporting the police in internal security duties, the infantry battalions were still manning the Sino–Hong Kong border. They were still 'demonstrating sovereignty' and spending long periods on the border rounding up illegal immigrants and handing them back to China. Observation posts, largely manned by the Gurkha battalions, continued to monitor the activities of the People's Liberation Army. It could be a repetitive routine, with long periods of absence from Battalion lines and families. Meanwhile, a new dimension had entered the arena, one that was to dominate our affairs for the next thirteen years and become central to the political, social and security climate of Hong Kong – the ongoing negotiations between the UK and China over the future sovereignty of the Territory. The debate occupied every newspaper column and monopolized discussion over every dinner table. After ninety-nine years, the lease of the New Territories was to end in 1997, and it was causing huge uncertainty about Hong Kong's future. The business community was anxious about its long-term investments, and the real estate merchants were similarly worried about the renewal of leases and mortgages expiring immediately before 1997. Everyone was concerned about their freedoms.

Sino–British talks and exchanges had started with Governor Murray Maclehose's visit to Beijing and his bold but delicate testing of the water in 1979. This had heralded the uneasy start to a possible transition process, one that did not involve the people of Hong Kong in the dealings that would eventually determine their destiny.

Paramount leader and Vice-Premier Deng Xiaoping's response to Governor Maclehose's early démarche had been to instruct the Governor to tell investors in Hong Kong to put their minds at ease. He also left his visitors in no doubt that it was now firmly on the PRC's agenda to recover Hong Kong. China saw the return of Hong Kong as setting an example to Taiwan of rejoining the motherland, and Deng applied the idea of 'one country, two systems', originally conceived for Taiwan, to Hong Kong. The Politburo confirmed that sovereignty would be returned to China in 1997 and that the Territory would continue to serve the PRC's political and economic interests.

Flushed with her victory in the Falklands campaign earlier that year, in September 1982 Mrs Thatcher arrived in Beijing for talks with Deng Xiaoping. The two leaders met in the Great Hall of the People, and an historic photograph records the event. Seen in London, the picture seemed to epitomize the issue that was to dominate affairs in Hong Kong and my own service up to 1997 and beyond. It shows two confident national leaders each at the top of their game, both immaculately turned out and coiffed but representing a rich counterpoint between East and West. The Chinese spittoon sits at Deng's elegantly shod feet, while a black handbag stands in haughty disdain close to the Prime Minister's trim ankles.

Deng made no concessions over sovereignty, and early British proposals for leaseback arrangements proved unacceptable. He set a two-year time frame for negotiations on the future of Hong Kong. Should these prove fruitless, a unilateral solution would be imposed. Talks got underway with the British very much as supplicants – a geopolitical shift from the days when we acquired Hong Kong in 1842. Apart from the common objective of maintaining stability and prosperity in Hong Kong, great differences separated the two parties, and in the Territory a mood of anxious anticipation prevailed. Looking back, there seemed to be echoes here of Brexit, albeit without a referendum to ascertain the people's wishes.

While the negotiations were proceeding, there were other developments for me to note. The first was the radical change in the Sino-Hong Kong Border. In place of the placid duck farms and paddy fields that I remembered four years earlier, there was now a city. From a distance, it appeared to possess the size and vigour of Kowloon. This was the Shenzen Special Economic Zone, and it seemed to have risen like a mushroom almost overnight to overshadow the western half of the border. Although still slightly grubby at the edges, it was evidence that decades of separation, isolation and distrust were beginning to fade. The policies of Deng Xiaoping – his four modernizations in agriculture, industry, defence and technology, all designed to rejuvenate the Chinese economy – had begun to take hold.

There was, too, a perhaps misplaced sense of improving relations with the West. Memories of the Cultural Revolution – hopefully the last of the traumatic events that swept across the vast canvas of China over the previous 50 years – were beginning to fade as the thrust of Deng's 'Open Door' policy took hold and the Republic opened up. The little red books containing Mao's thoughts were now in the curio shops of Hong Kong's Hollywood Road rather than being waved in front of us in the streets.

Next, I noted that the British military authorities had handed over their sprawling Victoria Barracks and Flagstaff House – a last reminder of colonial architecture and an imperial military presence in Central – to the Hong Kong Government. The barrack site was to become Hong Kong Park – some much-needed lungs for Central. Flagstaff House re-emerged intact as a teapot museum – no doubt some ghostly Generals still stalk its corridors today. In return, the British garrison had received a new high-rise building regarded by many as architecturally akin to an upturned gin bottle. This was the Prince of Wales Building at HMS *Tamar* – a splendidly cost-efficient and effective Military Headquarters. Later, I was to get to know the building well.

After two years of most difficult negotiations accompanied by wobbles of confidence in Hong Kong, in December 1984 came the significant Sino-British Joint Declaration on the future of the Territory. In the Great Hall of the People it was signed by Prime Minister Margaret Thatcher on behalf of the British Government, while Chinese Premier Zhao Ziyang signed for the People's Republic. In symbolic attendance, but not a signatory, was the Governor of Hong Kong, Sir Edward Youde. Geoffrey Howe, the British Foreign Secretary and a key negotiator, hurried from Beijing to Hong Kong to explain to a combined meeting of the Executive and Legislative

Councils the architecture of the agreement. In my Shek Kong office I listened to his briefing on the radio.

The Foreign Secretary laid out the bones of the agreement. Hong Kong's sovereignty would pass from the United Kingdom to the People's Republic of China on 1 July 1997. Hong Kong would then become a Special Administrative Region (SAR) of China, and a 'Basic Law' would, in due course, enshrine the agreement in detail. Deng's philosophy of 'one country, two systems' had been embraced. Hong Kong's capitalist system and way of life, its current freedoms and its social and economic systems would remain unchanged for fifty years. Crucially, Hong Kong would be invested with executive, legislative and independent judicial powers, including that of final adjudication. The SAR would enjoy a high degree of autonomy, except in defence and foreign affairs; its customs arrangements and free trade policy would remain unaltered, its currency and status as an international financial centre would be retained.

I noted that while the Hong Kong Government would be responsible for the maintenance of public order, it was worryingly clear to many that the PRC would maintain its own PLA garrison in Hong Kong. But as far as the outside world was concerned, the agreement seemed generally to be regarded as a clever piece of peaceful diplomacy and the best that could be extracted from an unpromising scenario.

The people of Hong Kong viewed the agreement with a mix of acceptance, scepticism and reservation. In the New Territories, far from the dinner tables and political chatter of Central, my sense was that young people, those born in Hong Kong who knew they were Chinese but perhaps had some difficulty with their identity, had recognized the changes wrought by Deng Xiaoping and viewed the post-1997 future with a certain wary acceptance. Older people, the first-generation refugees who had experienced and suffered in some of Mao's upheavals, did not trust China. They thought the regime was rotten and were much less sanguine about their prospects. It remained to be seen whether the Territory's confidence would hold through to 1997 and beyond without a flight of capital and talent.

The uneasy political climate produced, for me, two major challenges. Firstly, I had inherited a somewhat dated and misguided operational plan for the defence of Hong Kong in the event of intervention by the PLA. It envisaged the Brigade fighting a classic withdrawal battle down through the infamous Gin Drinkers Line to Kowloon. This contingency now seemed to me to be extremely unlikely. Beyond regarding it as simply a training exercise for Brigade officers to consider as part of their general war studies, it was no longer a plan in touch with military and political reality. If such a threat existed, we did not possess the military strength or resources to take on the massed ranks of the PLA. For the Chinese, if they felt it necessary, there were plenty of other less costly ways to exert their will. The British were certainly not going to wage general war on behalf of Hong Kong which, in any circumstances, in the built-up urban environment would be a disaster for all concerned.

In military terms the threat along the border lay far more in the potential for the Chinese Government to exert some threatening pressure on the British and Hong Kong governments. This could be designed to extract a diplomatic gain, signal displeasure or threaten intervention in response to local internal disorder. We had learnt our lessons on the vulnerability of the border to this kind of political squeeze during the Cultural Revolution. The security and integrity of the Closed Border Area were key to any plans that we had. It was there that trouble needed to be contained while diplomatic exchanges attempted to resolve any difficulties.

My staff and I sketched out some possible forms of belligerent behaviour or intimidation by the Chinese along the border, and considered how individual units might respond in a calm and non-escalatory fashion. Incidents might start with low-level verbal exchanges, particularly at border crossing points. Stone-throwing and the display of inflammatory banners encouraging incitement might follow. This could lead to mass illegal immigration or civilian incursions across the border; Chinese militia or PLA troops might close up to the border; local officials could be kidnapped, or hostages taken; small arms fire might be directed across the border. The possibilities for friction and intimidation in a deteriorating political climate were endless. I discussed our plans with the Commander British Forces, Major General Derek Boorman, for whom I had worked in London at the time of the Falklands War. He was entirely supportive of our approach. I had no doubt that once my commanding officers had been briefed, they would be alive to this kind of threat. They would need to respond with intelligence and restraint and, through imaginative exercise scenarios, train their officers and NCOs to finesse such Chinese activity accordingly. I was sure that the Gurkha riflemen would take Chinese provocation very much in their stride, with the characteristic military insouciance they had shown in 1967.

At the same time, I did have some concerns about the Gurkhas. After years on jungle operations, their standards in the changed urban environment of Hong Kong needed to be enhanced. Many procedures also needed to be modernized. In so doing we needed to recognize that we were increasingly part of the mainstream British Army, while still retaining our Gurkha identity. We had to resist any suggestion that we were simply a Hong Kong gendarmerie. Such a perception was already affecting our ability to attract the brightest new officers out of Sandhurst. We needed to maintain and demonstrate a wide range of military skills. In the face of the Joint Declaration we would also need to consider the future of the Gurkhas in tomorrow's British Army. They formed the bulk of the Hong Kong garrison and could therefore face an uncertain future. All this was still in the realm of the unknown as the Territory began to come to terms with its own future. Meanwhile, I set about running a series of what I hoped were testing exercises for each battalion. These were designed to be imaginative and different for battalions that needed to demonstrate similar abilities.

After two years I came to the end of my tour in command of the Field Force and went off to think about the Russians and the threat they posed to the security of Germany's Hanover Plain and beyond. I was joining 1st British Corps in Germany as their Chief of Staff. I only wished I could pick up and take the rest of the Gurkha Field Force with me. That would have been good for all concerned.

COMMANDER BRITISH FORCES

In early 1988 I was informed that I was to return to Hong Kong as Commander British Forces (CBF) in the middle of the following year. With my previous experience and commitment to the Territory I felt as Ronald Storrs did in 1917 when appointed to the Governorship of Jerusalem – after this there can be no conceivable promotion! Meanwhile, I was to attend a year's course in International Affairs at the Royal College of Defence Studies, followed by a secondment to the Cabinet Office in London.

Among the overseas students on that defence course, there was for the first time an officer from the PLA, Zhou Borong. At that time the PLA did not use ranks, but I soon learned that he equated to a Major General. In view of my pending appointment I was given a discreet briefing about his background, and it was suggested that I should not fraternize too closely. I immediately got to know him and his wife well and invited them home! He was an attractive, outgoing man and popular on the course. Over the next twenty-five years we were to meet several times in various guises.

On one occasion during the course I remembered Borong becoming uncharacteristically angry. A visiting lecturer had strongly criticised China's record on human rights and its lack of freedom. At question time, Borong roundly rebuked the speaker in perfect English, suggesting that he did not understand how difficult China was to govern and change; what a vast and complex polity it was; and how determined the Chinese were not to experience again the chaos resulting from the Long March, the famines, the Great Leap Forward and Chairman Mao's Cultural Revolution. This made a distinct impression on many of his fellow students and left the lecturer rather floundering for a response.

In 1997 Borong was the Deputy Commander and leader of the advance party of the PLA that arrived in Hong Kong at the time of the handover, although I did not see him at the ceremonies I attended. He later told me that he had been at the border supervising the arrival of his troops. In 2003, several years after I had left the Army, Borong invited my wife and me to dinner, somewhat incongruously, in a restaurant in the London suburb of Swiss Cottage. In a curious piece of military cross-dressing he had become an Air Marshal. We had some good but slightly guarded talk, for he was still a serving officer.

Later, in 2012, I invited Borong and his wife to dine with me in Beijing when I was on business there. He, too, had retired, and I asked him whether the PLA had treated him well as far as his pension was concerned. He told me that he had retired on full pay and been allowed to keep his staff car and driver. I suggested that British Generals would be very content with such arrangements! We talked in an open way about Hong Kong, and he told me that in his time there as the Deputy Commander there were some 4,000 personnel of the People's Liberation Army stationed in the Territory, together with six Generals.

But he added, with a twinkle in his eye, 'Peter, six Chinese Generals are much cheaper than one British General!'

I am still in touch with Borong, and every year he sends me an amusing electronic Christmas card.

Prior to my arrival as Commander British Forces I looked down the roll of Generals who had previously held the appointment. I sensed that one CBF difficult to categorize would have been Major General Black. In the tensions that followed the Sino-Japanese conflict in 1895 he, like many of his predecessors, had coveted more mainland territory to act as a buffer zone and better defend Hong Kong and its harbour. This had led to the 1898 Peking Convention that leased the New Territories to Hong Kong for 99 years and, in turn, to the Joint Declaration and the planned hand-back of the Territory to China in 1997. The Governor, Sir David Wilson, often used to remind me where the blame lay for all that followed. In return, I would occasionally remind him that it was the Foreign Office that had insisted on a lease rather than complete annexation. We then split the responsibility evenly by noting that the man who negotiated the agreement was both a diplomat and a soldier. Sir Claude MacDonald had qualifications of a sort for becoming British Minister in Peking. He had after all been a gunnery instructor in Hong Kong! Alas, *The Times* correspondent of the day described him as 'imperfectly educated, weak, flippant, garrulous, the type of officer rolled out a mile at a time and then lopped off in six-foot lengths'. Whatever I was as CBF, I hoped I would not be described in those terms.

I arrived in Hong Kong to take up my appointment as Commander British Forces at a sombre time in the summer of 1989. The disturbances in Beijing's Tiananmen Square – the brutal and bloody suppression of the student-led democracy demonstrations – had just taken place, and Hong Kong was reeling from the shock and consequent loss of confidence about the transition planned for 1997. The autocratic and repressive quality of the regime had been demonstrated. The Hong Kong young people, who several years earlier had been at least mildly optimistic about the future, were, I sensed, the most shocked by the television images from Beijing. The first-generation refugees, who had always been pessimistic about the agreement, were less surprised. No one present in Hong Kong at the time could forget the gathering of close to a million people on the streets of

Central to express their sorrow at events. It was a testing, interesting and pivotal time to arrive there. Eight years before the date of the Territory's handover, there was much to be done to assuage people's fears and attempt to rebuild confidence.

Shortly after arrival I attended the first of my nearly two hundred meetings of the Executive Council – Hong Kong's cabinet. Exco, as it was known, was presided over by the Governor, Sir David Wilson, and contained four ex-officio Government members: the Chief Secretary, Sir David Ford, a wise and convivial colleague and a brilliant administrator, the Financial Secretary, the Attorney General and myself. Ten other members appointed by the Governor were distinguished Hong Kong people who collectively spanned a wide range of constituencies and areas of interest – some were embryonic politicians, some were pro-Beijing and others, the so-called Queen's Chinese, were closely linked to British interests.

I particularly remember Lydia Dunn, born in Hong Kong and a Director of the Swire Group. She was a Dame at the start of my Council membership and a Baroness by the end of it; a beguiling mix of Chinese elegance and beauty and profound political and commercial experience. All this made her a formidable and much-admired member of the Council and one who commanded attention from us all.

Another colleague was William Purves, Chairman of the Hong Kong Shanghai Bank, who during the tenure of his Council membership adroitly engineered the takeover of the Midland Bank to produce one of the largest and most successful banking groups in the world. He was a courageous and very popular Scotsman who had won the Distinguished Service Order as a young National Service subaltern in Korea. Full of flinty integrity, he brought much common sense and business acumen to our discussions. With strong links to the Chinese leadership he was a valuable source of advice to the Council. Regrettably, the last Governor failed to appreciate his inestimable wisdom, and he was the target of some gross, unjustified and highly libellous calumnies from Chris Patten's office.

There were others who added to the Council's strengths, including a group of highly talented and influential Hong Kong women of differing viewpoints. The vitality, intelligence and representation of women in all aspects of Hong Kong life remains one of the abiding memories of my time in the Territory. Highly effective and intelligent Hong Kong Chinese civil servants also frequently appeared before the Council to brief us on current Government business.

Friday saw the arrival of the large red folders that I had to read and absorb over the weekend to ensure that I was fully prepared for the Tuesday meetings of Exco. Throughout the whole of my time on the Council I never received – or requested – any briefing or advice from London as to the line I was to take on any agenda item. 'The Emperor is far away, with many hills in between', as the provincial governors in China used to say. I was dependent on my own judgement in discussion with my fellow Councillors and in weighing up a variety of views. I worked hard, through visits and briefings, to understand as many aspects of the Territory as possible in order to be able to contribute with some insight to our discussions.

The Council advised the Governor on the major issues of the day, as well as considering all principal legislation and various appeals and petitions. Relations with China loomed large.

These were all onerous collective responsibilities, but throughout my time I was conscious that all of us seemed to recognize the aspirations of the people of Hong Kong. As a Council we attempted to advise the Governor on the principles of a sensible and successful transfer of sovereignty to a nation on whom the Territory's economic dependence was absolute, but about whom many of us felt some reservations. We were all deeply committed to doing the best we could for the often-competing communities of Hong Kong, and all of us possessed a strong social conscience. In 1997 we performed a balancing act between bold aspirations and the art of the possible – the successful delivery of the transfer of power.

The major issues of my time were the measures we took to try and restore confidence in 1997 after the drama of Tiananmen Square. These included a modest increase in democracy prior to handover, and decisions to build the new airport and enlarge the container port. We also approved incentives to encourage talented professional, technical and managerial people to come and work in Hong Kong or remain in the Territory. These measures included a British nationality scheme offering some 50,000 heads of household British passports, to encourage them to remain in the Territory.

We spent a good deal of our time weighing the issues surrounding the vast grand design that was the new airport at Chep Lap Kok, to be built on reclaimed land offshore from Lantau Island. Aside from the airport itself, a vast associated infrastructure of major roads, railways, bridges and tunnels was required. This produced lengthy debate and at times, in an echo of Lady Eden's comment about the Suez Canal, the runway seemed to be careering through my drawing room. In strategic, economic, political and engineering terms it was a bold vision that followed the remarkable success of two other grand projects of my time in Hong Kong – the development of New Towns in the New Territories and a Mass Transport Railway. Hong Kong was always good at designing new tapestries for its future, and once a decision was taken, plans were quickly translated into action.

I certainly believed the airport represented a massive statement of confidence in the future for the semi-autonomous nature of the Territory after 1997. I held to this view even when we were having great difficulty with the Chinese and some of my colleagues were becoming increasingly nervous about their objections, for the Chinese were expressing a concern that the expenditure involved would drain the Hong Kong Treasury and leave its economy in poor shape post-1997. With valuable land at the current airport site in Kowloon released, and the removal of height restrictions for construction around it, this economic argument did not run. In the end, with David Wilson's calm tenacity of purpose and intelligence, the day was won, and the extraordinary development with all associated transport links was successfully delivered. The airport opened in 1998 and is now one of the busiest in the world. The British Government, with its seemingly endless procrastination over an additional runway at Heathrow, could learn much from Hong Kong.

John Major, who had rather surprisingly succeeded Margaret Thatcher in 1990, visited Beijing in September 1991 to sign the airport agreement and afterwards came to Hong Kong to brief the Executive Council on his visit. It had been a difficult time for the Prime Minister. He was the first western head of government to visit Beijing after the disastrous violence in Tiananmen Square, and I sensed he had not enjoyed the experience. I remember being impressed with the quality of the Prime Minister's briefing about his visit to China. It was conducted extremely deftly and without a note for some forty minutes, but I detected some uneasiness during his time in Hong Kong.

John Major was accompanied by his foreign affairs advisor, the inscrutable Sinologist Sir Percy Craddock, whom he had inherited from Mrs Thatcher.

Sir Percy had been Head of Chancery in Beijing at the time the Embassy was sacked. He had been manhandled by the Red Guards and kept under house arrest for several months. As Ambassador he had witnessed the rise of Deng, he was chief negotiator of the Joint Declaration and had been a secret emissary to Beijing post-Tiananmen Square to keep alive the Joint Declaration and the airport development – the so-called Rose Garden Project. He was regarded with deep suspicion by many in Hong Kong for his supposedly pro-Beijing views. It was clear to me that he and John Major did not see eye to eye, and I sensed there would be problems ahead.

David Wilson had spent most of his life, inside the Foreign Office and out, dealing with China. He spoke fluent Mandarin and very good Cantonese. He struck me as brilliant under pressure and always resolute. Throughout my friendly association with him I never once saw him intellectually at a loss or lose his temper, although at times he had ample cause to do so. There were plenty of wiseacres in the press box and elsewhere telling him what to do. But it was he who was continually at the wicket, facing all the Chinese googlies and fast bowling and, not least, some overthrows from London. Rumours about his possible demise as Governor swirled around in the press and elsewhere.

One evening at the end of December 1991, the Executive Council members, including myself, were summoned for a drink at Government House. The drink turned out to be cold China tea, and in his study the Governor told us that he was leaving. No date had been set for his departure. David Ford, Lydia Dunn and I made some appropriate remarks, before we thankfully moved next door for stronger refreshment. There would clearly be a difficult stop-gap period before a new appointment was announced. I thought it a rather grubby and distasteful way to remove a fine public servant. David Wilson was left as a lame duck Governor until his replacement was appointed a few months later. New brooms were clearly at play.

While my Executive Council political duties were an important part of my professional life, as the Military Commander security issues were my core business. I had a tri-service garrison. The Army still provided a British battalion at Stanley Fort and three battalions of Gurkhas based in the New Territories. The Royal Navy ran the naval base at HMS *Tamar*, where I had my Headquarters, and manned three large and complex fast patrol craft, not least to demonstrate our continuing responsibilities at sea.

The Royal Air Force and the Army both provided fleets of helicopters to move people and other resources rapidly about the Territory.

Additionally, there were many support, intelligence and specialist units and personnel provided by all three services and manned by British, Gurkha and Hong Kong Chinese servicemen and women. Many of the latter had worries about their future – not only because of the transfer of sovereignty in 1997 but also as a result of large reductions in the strength of the British Army in the wake of the collapse of the Soviet Union and the ending of the Cold War. I needed to give some reassurance to the men of the Hong Kong Military Service Corps, some of whom thought they might be victimized by the PLA once the British had gone. There was also a need to start planning for the orderly rundown of the garrison prior to the handover.

Finally, and importantly, as Commander British Forces I wore a separate hat as Major General, the Brigade of Gurkhas. In this capacity I was responsible for worldwide Gurkha policy and the general welfare of all Gurkha soldiers. I wanted to deliver a promising future for the Gurkha soldier in the post-1997 military landscape. Responsibilities for our garrison in Brunei and our Gurkha organization in Nepal, as well as representational and liaison duties in South East Asia, also fell into my in-tray.

We would regularly welcome huge American Naval Carrier Groups sailing back and forth between Honolulu and the Middle East and victualling in Hong Kong, particularly at the time of the Gulf War. My Provost Marshal used to get nervous about all this, as his predecessor had done about R&R during the Vietnam War, twenty-five years earlier. However, we never had much of a problem, and their arrival was always good for at least part of the local economy.

Very much my prime military responsibility was in support of the Hong Kong Government's security responsibilities. Illegal immigration continued to be a problem. In this regard, and as I had always thought it might, China once again demonstrated the political leverage it could exert. Following one particular political disagreement, China refused to accept the return of illegal immigrants. Word quickly spread, and an immediate and dramatic upsurge threatened to swamp the system. There was a need to rapidly construct temporary holding camps in the Closed Border Area, until the political issues could be resolved. The Gurkha Engineers moved quickly to assist. It was an example, if one needed it, of the application of the political squeeze. As Henry Kissinger once remarked, 'There was a China card and China held it.'

We continued to keep a very close eye on the border, ready to respond most carefully to any Chinese pressure and underlining our continuing sovereignty by a military presence on the land border and the patrol craft at sea. On arrival I had rather irritatingly discovered that the operational orders I had drafted as the Field Force Commander for just such contingencies had, in my absence, fallen into disuse. I quickly ensured that the current Brigade Commander had them reactivated and rehearsed.

Probably now forgotten, by the end of 1991 a further 60,000 Vietnamese boat people – economic and political migrants – had made a rough sea crossing to seek refuge in Hong Kong and add to the many who had come before. This influx led to huge logistical, humanitarian and occasionally security issues for the Government. Large-scale brawls between Vietnamese factions, and fires and breakouts from the large tented holding camp on the Army airfield at Shek Kong, produced some ugly problems. I ensured that we provided whatever discreet background assistance was necessary; Gurkha riflemen maintained careful watch behind a Hong Kong Police presence. Eventually, through quiet diplomacy, repatriation and resettlement, the problem was successfully resolved.

The rampant seizure and smuggling of luxury cars out of Hong Kong into nearby Guangdong Province by armed criminal syndicates was a new phenomenon. Smuggling gangs possessed huge 600 hp speedboats, the so-called *Dai Feis*. These remarkably powerful craft came with sister boats equipped with cranes. At night these could lift a stolen Mercedes or BMW off the Hong Kong quayside inside two minutes and be travelling to Guandong in the twinkling of an eye. David Ford asked me for our help.

Gurkha night-time observation parties quickly manned the northern shore line of Mirs Bay opposite Guandong Province, reporting the movement of the *Dai Feis* into and out of Hong Kong waters. Royal Marines manning high-speed pursuit boats launched from our Royal Navy patrol craft then took part in exciting and exacting chases in the dark at 60 knots in choppy seas. This was dangerous for both sides, but the marines, with great daring, succeeded in boarding a number of these craft and apprehending the smugglers and their loot. They did not always succeed, however. My colleague William Ehrman, the Governor's Political Advisor, was despatched to Canton for discussion with Chinese officials on joint co-operation to curb this criminal activity. On return he told me he had been surprised to note that some Canton officials attending the talks had arrived in Mercedes and BMW saloons. Some bore Hong Kong number plates!

In preparation for the handover, and in conjunction with the Joint Liaison Group overseeing transition matters, we also held meetings with a number of Chinese PLA officers on the issue of Defence Lands. They were conducted over our Estate from Stanley to Shek Kong, for in a few years most of the Estate would belong to them. These early meetings were rather awkward as both sides assessed the other's position, but gradually, as 1997 loomed increasingly closer, sensible decisions were made by my successors. Early on, I sensed that some of the implications of a garrison presence in Hong Kong after 1997 had not yet been fully appreciated by the PLA.

GURKHA BATTLES

After a few months in post I received a telephone call in the early hours of the morning. It was from my old regimental friend, John Chapple, now Chief of the General Staff and head of the British Army. Until that point UK military strategy had been almost entirely focussed on defending Western Europe against potential Soviet aggression. As the Soviet Union had now collapsed and a threat from that quarter no longer seemed likely, there was to be an examination of future requirements. It was not a formal Defence Review, but a study entitled 'Options for Change'. A peace dividend was clearly the political objective. As the Gurkha Brigade's Major General I was required to prepare a paper for submission to the Army Board presenting the case for the continued presence of Gurkhas in the British Army. I knew immediately that we were going to have to fight hard for survival.

It would be wrong to say that up until this moment the Brigade had been living in a fool's paradise, but in early 1989 a Government announcement had charted a long-term future for the Gurkhas. There would be some reductions down to a strength of about 4,000, but all cap badges would be retained and a future after 1997 had seemed assured. This confidence was to prove misplaced. I was determined that after 175 years of Gurkha service to the Crown, I was not going to preside over the total disbandment of the Brigade of Gurkhas. But I did not see total disbandment in 1997 as a viable option. There had to be a sensible way forward to retain a Gurkha presence in the British Army in the aftermath of 1997. I was confident Gurkha riflemen could become a new elite force and play a valuable role in the future, and I never wavered in this belief. But there would be battles to be fought, and some sharp staff work would be required to present a compelling case for retention, but not at any price; we had to keep our essential Gurkha dimension, our character and culture as Gurkha units. This was the most effective way for us to operate, and we should not be broken up.

In this regard I was extremely fortunate to have an old regimental friend leading my modest Gurkha Headquarters, Brigadier Christopher Bullock. We had been fellow Adjutants of our respective 2nd Goorkha battalions. I knew him as a brave and determined soldier as well as the possessor of a sharp intellect. He had performed brilliantly on 'Claret' operations in Borneo. He knew the Gurkha soldier well and enjoyed his confidence and that of the British officers. Further, he was deeply versed in all aspects of the Gurkhas' terms and conditions of service. He knew the whole organization and its costs backwards and had a clear vision of what the Gurkha soldier could deliver. In the coming months he was to offer huge support to me as we prepared our strategy for the Brigade's survival.

I privately discussed the issue with Sir David Wilson, explaining the problems that we faced and how determined I was to ensure a viable future for the Gurkha soldier in the British Army. While always intellectually objective, as a mountaineer he had considerable empathy with the Gurkha soldiers and Nepal. And he recognized the benefits they had brought to Hong Kong's security. They fitted in well locally. He recognized, too, that the Government of Hong Kong paid a large proportion of the not inconsiderable costs of the British garrison. Any security scenario where the Gurkha had to be replaced by his more expensive British counterpart would prove extremely unattractive to the Hong Kong Government. I argued, too, that if the Gurkha soldier was to continue to provide the major part of the Garrison up to 1997, then he needed to be offered some reasonably attractive options for British Army service post-transition. Otherwise, without a future, the Gurkha could only become a lame duck and provide an increasingly ineffective garrison. Further, the Gurkha rifleman was very familiar with all the sensitivities and subtleties of the border and knew his way round the highways and byways of the Territory. He was a valuable security asset and not one to be tossed to the wind. The Governor certainly saw the logic of these arguments, and I was optimistic that he would reflect that view back to London. This logic, together with the need to recognize the Gurkha as an integral part of the British Army expecting to be treated on the same footing as everyone else, became the central tenets of my paper to the Army Board.

In the course of the next few months I made several trips to London to ensure that key people inside and outside the Services, senior officers, civil servants and others, were aware of the objective arguments for the retention of a Gurkha Brigade. Emotion and sentiment would certainly not win the day, and I avoided any such approach and encouraged others to do the same. I briefed my old regimental colleague, John Nott, the former Secretary of State, who very much recognized the Gurkha soldier's worth. Field Marshal Lord Bramall, my former Regimental Colonel and a respected figure in the House of Lords, needed little persuading that there was a case for the Gurkhas. I needed to ensure that these two influential figures, and others, understood the issues that were at stake. I hope I remained outwardly buoyant, but it was a worrying time.

Elsewhere, emotional steam was rising with rank. I had a very disagreeable meeting with the Colonel Commandants of the various Infantry Divisions of the British Army. Although not technically in field command, these senior Generals were responsible, regimentally, for the general organization and wellbeing of the six to eight infantry battalions in the eight infantry divisions in which they were grouped. They included Guards, Scottish, and Light Divisions, as well as County groupings or, in my case, the Gurkhas. We had been summoned by the Director of Infantry. He was under remit from the Army Board to make recommendations as to where the infantry cuts should be made. Several battalions would have to go, but it was not clear where the axe would fall. We were to give the Director our views and allow him to make some proposals.

The regimental system in the British Army represents a huge strength. For those that are part of it, the system engenders a strong cohesion; it creates loyalty and obligation, and through a regiment's historical pedigree, honours and privileges; it fosters pride in the institution and a distinct identity; it is an important component of morale and success on the battlefield. The Gurkha regiments felt this as strongly as the rest of the British infantry. At the same time, the passions that the regiment arouses can on occasion seriously jeopardize rational or objective discussion. It was clear that the Colonel Commandants were under pressure to ensure the preservation of their own battalions above all else.

I was already aware of the strength of feeling running in some quarters and the concern that there might be possible disbandment or amalgamations of British battalions, while Gurkha battalions remained in the Army's Order of Battle. The Colonel Commandant of the Scottish Division, and others, had made this clear in radio interviews as part of voluble public campaigns to preserve specific regiments. Lords Lieutenant and County worthies were being harried, and there was a good deal of press interest. The prejudicial argument ran that the removal of four Gurkha battalions from the Order of Battle would save four British regiments. In demanding that the Gurkhas should go, the Scots had, rightly or not, cast aside any sentiment about the regimental alliances and affiliations that bound certain Scottish and Gurkha regiments together. No sense of a common Highland legacy emerged. This was probably right. But all the while, the good Colonel Commandants studiously ignored the inability of some of their regiments to recruit sufficient men to man them properly.

It was a hostile meeting, and one that I did not enjoy. I was saddened, if not surprised, by the venom with which the Colonels repeated the mantra of the Scottish General – all Gurkha battalion should go before a single British battalion went to the wall. The Colonel Commandants were clearly under pressure from their regiments, each with powerful lobby groups – not least their Regimental Associations of 'old and bold'. There was no recognition of the fine standards of the Gurkha soldier; the possibility that he might have something to offer; the service that had been shared in endless campaigns; his ability to recruit manpower in a way that was unmatched by most British regiments; or his standards as an infantry soldier. The economic and security arguments on manning Hong Kong, and the idea that the Gurkha soldier expected to be treated on an equal footing as everyone else, cut no ice.

I thought that at least my fellow Rifleman, the Colonel Commandant of the Light Division, might have recognized these arguments and offered some material support. The Light Division contained the Royal Green Jackets, among whose antecedent regiments were the 60th Rifles, our close comrades in arms from the Ridge at Delhi – our fellow Riflemen. No support was forthcoming – all Gurkhas should go. I could only assume that the General was under pressure from his Regimental Associations. I understood the passions aroused, but the discussion tended to demonstrate the regimental system at its worst. Further, the cost effectiveness of the Gurkha soldier through retention rates was not recognized. Gurkhas served generally for at least fifteen years; the British infantryman for three. This expensive churn, the constant and expensive need to replace and retrain men, was avoided in Gurkha battalions. Perhaps I understood the pressures the Generals were under, but I thought it was a depressingly one-sided judgement.

Sometime later, when our battles had been won and a modest Gurkha Brigade had been preserved, I reflected that within a relatively short period several British battalions had welcomed Gurkha Reinforcement Companies to keep themselves afloat at a time of great recruiting difficulty.

Based primarily on the security and economic arguments that I had agreed with the Governor, and on the Gurkhas' expectation of parity of treatment, we presented our case to the Army Board. The Sultan of Brunei's commitment to station and maintain a Gurkha battalion in his country added weight to the Hong Kong and economic arguments that were to win the day. The Infantry Colonel Commandants' strictures on Gurkhas were ignored. Again, we faced substantial reductions to our strength, and these were far greater than those faced by the rest of the British infantry. This hurt, but no matter, we had a long-term foot on the ground in the UK to prove our worth and build on our strengths. We would have a Brigade of some 2,600 – sufficient for two battalions, representative Corps units of Engineers, Signals and Logistics, and a modest infrastructure. We had redundancies to manage, but here Christopher Bullock's negotiating skills won a handsome victory on terms for those soldiers forced to leave. Then came the need to address the vexed question of disbandment or the amalgamation of some or all of the four infantry regiments.

Having consulted with Christopher Bullock I made my recommendations to the Council of Regimental Colonels. Christopher had felt strongly that regimental titles in some form or combination should be retained, but I disagreed. I felt equally strongly there should be one large flexible regiment to embrace the current four. This would present no complications were we to expand or contract. Cross-posting between battalions, and the mixing of Eastern and Western Gurkhas, would be eased. One large regiment would match, in a contemporary way, arrangements in the rest of the British Army. There would be no complex combinations of previous titles or fractions of numerical identities. We needed a name that was clean, easily memorable and evocative; one that showed no particular favour to one cap badge or another. I thought a cumbersome combined title would be a nightmare. I recommended 'The Royal Gurkha Rifles'. It was a name that would need royal approval, but I sensed it would run. To this, aside from the sadness of losing their regiments' historic titles, the Regimental Colonels acceded. I was to face criticism of this decision, particularly from a few retired British and Gurkha officers, including some from my own Regiment, and I received some unhappy mail. Twenty-five years on, I am sure I made the right recommendation for a Regiment designed to forge a new and deeper place in the British Army. A few of the older generation have not entirely forgiven me. Certainly, I hated having to amalgamate my own Regiment with the others, and losing the name of that great fighting corps, the 2nd Goorkhas.

With the principle of amalgamation agreed, there were major decisions to be made about property, dress and accoutrements for the new Regiment. Only soldiers understand the feelings that such issues can arouse. This was a potentially acrimonious minefield into which I felt it would not be appropriate for me to tread! Committees were established to deal with these contentious matters, and in due course they were resolved. My instructions were to keep the best of everything. I was therefore personally disappointed that there was no agreement to preserve the sartorially distinctive *lali* piping on the new Regiment's Service Dress or to take the Queen's Truncheon into service. Apparently there had been objections from some regimental representatives, spurred on no doubt by their Regimental Colonels.

There seemed to be a fear of weighting matters too much in favour of the 2nd Goorkhas. But the Committee, or at least some of its members, failed to recognize that the unique Truncheon and the *lali* represented the distinguished performance of the 2nd Goorkhas which had won lasting recognition for all Gurkha regiments. It had raised them from the ruck of the Sepoy battalions and ensured a robust future for all. Given my personal pedigree, it was difficult for me to argue with these decisions, but it was another instance of the regimental system allowing a narrow-minded and somewhat prejudiced view of matters to pertain and thus deny the new Regiment an historic Colour and most distinctive flourish to their uniforms.

The Prince of Wales, our Colonel in Chief, who was to transfer his Colonelcy, allegiance and support to the new Regiment, was disappointed and asked me to do everything I could to put these matters right. Following my appointment as the Regiment's new Colonel, and with the agreement of all ranks, I was eventually able to reinstate both of these potent symbols of Gurkha history. Their arrival was widely welcomed within the new Regiment. The *lali* is now proudly worn by all ranks and the Queen's Truncheon has resumed its symbolic place in Gurkha service. Perhaps a suitable pause had served some purpose. Eventually, as I shall record later, the newly established 'Royal Gurkha Rifles' was to develop a strong professional reputation, participating boldly in several British Army campaigns of the new millennium and writing a new page in Gurkha history.

These broad decisions also paved the way for the Royal Gurkha Rifles to be fully integrated into the British Army, and for all Gurkhas to serve with the same terms and conditions of service as their British colleagues and eventually achieve the right of settlement in the UK. I saw this as essential. It was to take time to institute, with endless battling in Whitehall by successive Gurkha staff officers, but the foundations had been laid. The Brigade was to face difficult turbulence between 1994 and 2000 as it reduced its strength by 70 per cent, relocated to the United Kingdom and assumed new roles and responsibilities; and it also reorganized its responsibilities in Nepal. During this period, it would once again be committed to twenty years of almost continuous operational soldiering, as a new era for the British Army Gurkha began with deployment to the Balkans and East Timor.

In April 1992 a general election, surprisingly to many pundits, delivered victory for the Tory party, and John Major was returned to power. The election had, however, produced some Conservative casualties, and Chris Patten, the Party's Chairman, had lost his seat in Bath. John Major appointed him as the last Governor of Hong Kong. Just before his arrival I came to the end of my tour as Commander British Forces and went off to other military challenges. By 1992 a measure of confidence had returned to the Territory, and the economy was buoyant. I was sad to go but I recognized that the sentiments of one leaving were not necessarily shared by those that remained.

HANDOVER, 1997

With many others who had been involved with Hong Kong, my wife and I were invited to witness the handover ceremonies in 1997. In the special British Airways plane that flew us out, those in the front of the aircraft included the Prince of Wales, Margaret Thatcher and the now ennobled Lord Wilson. Peter and Annie Duffell were seated well towards the rear.

As the programme of transition unfolded, the rain never stopped. 'Washing away 150 years of imperialism, Peter', said Rita Fan, one of my old Exco colleagues, when we met in the Hong Kong Convention Centre for the formal ceremonies. I remembered a few years earlier looking out of the window of my office high up in the Prince of Wales Building at HMS *Tamar*. I took in the harbour and high-rise Central and recalled Lord Palmerston's words about a barren rock with hardly a house upon it. Hong Kong's had been a colonial regime and not without its faults. But its rich mix of British administration, legal system and associated law and order provisions had, together with Cantonese entrepreneurship, not done too badly. How I wished that his Lordship might have seen it today. Through all the peaks and troughs that I had witnessed I was reasonably optimistic about Hong Kong's future, and I gave Rita a suitable response.

Earlier, the British and Hong Kong farewell ceremonies had been held on a rain-washed parade ground. The Black Watch were on parade. The Prince of Wales and Governor Patten made suitable speeches. Flags were lowered. Pipers lamented and Elgar resonated from the orchestra. Given their contribution, I was sad not to see the Gurkhas on parade in any numbers. We moved indoors for the formal handover ceremonies between the British and their Chinese counterparts. It was a wooden, carefully stage-managed performance, with leading military and civilian participants. The Governor no longer had a part to play. Appropriate national flags, artificially fluttering, were lowered and raised. Everyone looked pretty glum. Sovereignty duly passed. Hong Kong was no longer a British possession.

I was not sure that much remained by way of our military legacy. When needed, the garrison had, I believed, responded with sense, sensitivity and resolution to the various emergencies that had beset the Territory. We had helped protect it from occasional excesses and chaos, and insulated it from the worst turbulence that sometimes threatened from across the border. The largely Gurkha garrison had been generally well respected and welcomed. We had good relations with the community and, unlike the PLA, we were generally feared by no one.

Now our old barracks are occupied discreetly by the PLA. Sensibly, in the wake of Tiananmen, they had recognized local worries and decided to maintain a low profile. There had been valuable meetings between the last Commander British Forces, Major General Bryan Dutton, and General Zhou Borong. The Cenotaph remains four-square in front of that other local bastion, the Hong Kong Club. Remembrance Sunday is still recognized, and local British, Hong Kong and Gurkha ex-servicemen still parade at the November service, along with an impressive range of civic dignitaries. The military cemeteries are still there and well maintained, and if the Naval Base at HMS *Tamar* is no more, the upturned gin bottle that was the Prince of Wales Building remains a feature of the harbour front, albeit with different military occupants. Eventually, further reclamation of the harbour was to remove it from the water's edge, and the Chinese now dock their ships in a new, more discreet base at Stonecutters Island.

Before I left as CBF I had moved a military statue from Osborne Barracks in Kowloon to Hong Kong Park and placed it there to mark the presence of a British garrison in the Territory for 150 years. It is still there, its surrounding gardens beautifully tended. I hope people notice it. High up on the Peak in Barker Road, sandwiched between the residences of the American Consul and the Chief Secretary, is Headquarter House. It had been home to the military commander after Flagstaff House was handed over to the Hong Kong Government. For nearly three years I lived there. Now it is occupied by the Commander of the PLA. In my time, in its elegant hall there hung a large wooden board. Inscribed on it were the names of every Garrison Commander since 1841, including the two Japanese Admirals who presided over the occupation between 1941 and 1945. Two decades on from the handover, it would be intriguing to know if the board remains and if it has been kept up to date.

TWENTY YEARS ON

Twenty years after the handover, and as a civilian tourist, I went back to China's Special Administrative Region Hong Kong. Throughout my long association, I had always occupied a somewhat privileged position – albeit as an outsider – in Hong Kong: mostly a comfortable expatriate's view as seen from a berth in the New Territories, from a window high up in HMS *Tamar*, from a veranda on the Peak or from a bedroom window in the Mandarin Oriental Hotel. Now time and distance lent a slightly different and more objective perspective.

What you thought had happened in Hong Kong since the handover depended on where you were coming from; who you talked to; what you read; what your background and viewpoint was; how old you were. The contemporary picture of Hong Kong under the auspices of the People's Republic seemed neither too bad nor too good. Outwardly, its individual identity, its way of life, its stability, its values seem to have been preserved. It is not a Communist state. Its currency and its financial institutions, the rule of law and the independent judiciary, all still seem to be in place. The Star Ferry still criss-crosses the harbour. A dynamic financial centre still throbs with energy and free-market zest, and a buoyant economy remains. The *Taipans* are still lunching at the Hong Kong Club and the horses still race at Happy Valley and Sha Tin. The soldiers of the PLA are there, but they remain out of sight.

But underneath, there are suspicions and worries about Beijing and the increasingly authoritarian and centralized control exercised by President Xi and his regime. There are some concerns about the pressure exerted on the Territory to conform to Beijing by a regime that seems ready to lean on people showing 'unfavourable tendencies'. More 'one country', less 'two systems', perhaps. Some of it may be clumsy behaviour by officials anxious to please. Some of it may be the result of antagonism between a local leadership endorsed by the People's Republic and an increasingly vocal pro-democracy movement gnawing away at the Administration's ability to govern. The subtleties of living next to China – the elephant's foot poised outside the cave – can be naively forgotten by some.

I detect little in the way of nostalgia for the British administration; no yearning for the status quo ante. But there is also a sense amongst some of disappointment at the direction of travel. The political hypochondria that was always part of Hong Kong has deepened. Perhaps alongside its giant neighbour Hong Kong is too small, yet too important a place for it to be otherwise. Several young people feel alienated by an increasingly ossified political system across the border. Proposed new ordinances that would allow extradition to China for certain offences have suggested a further tightening of the screws. Such laws would allow people in Hong Kong to be whisked off to China and its uncertain judicial system that lacks due process. Huge demonstrations within the Territory and international condemnation signalled the fear and uncertainty that such proposals caused and produced a stay in execution through the Legislative Council. But the proposals on the table represent a further worrying deterioration of Hong Kong's freedoms and another threat to the integrity of 'one country two systems' promised in the Joint Declaration. As I write, there is wide concern about how matters will develop in the Territory as a weakened local leadership, increasingly belligerent statements from China and continuing demonstrations all threaten Hong's stability and the future of one country two systems.

There is a Nepali community in Hong Kong, many thousands strong. Many are Gurkha pensioners or their descendants, including some old friends from my Battalion. Corporal Trilok Gurung, a pensioned NCO from the 1st Battalion, has built a multi-million-dollar construction and security business. He employs many Gurkha pensioners and Nepali immigrant workers. There are other similar endeavours with former British officers and Gurkhas at the helm. Every year, many of them attend the Remembrance Day Parade at the Cenotaph.

I took a walk along Barker Road to look at Headquarter House where I had lived twenty-five years before. No chance of entry, but for the first time in nearly sixty years of gazing at soldiers of the People's Liberation Army without acknowledgement, I wave at the guard and achieve a smile and an answering wave through the fence.

I drove up to the New Territories to have a look at our old military estate with my regimental friend, Christopher Lavender, who still works in Hong Kong. In Shek Kong hundreds of former British and Gurkha quarters lie empty. Neglected and largely in ruins, they belong to the PLA, but as a garrison unaccompanied by families they have no use for them. In a Territory where housing is at a premium, it seems a terrible waste.

Outside the main Shek Kong Lines, from where I had commanded the Gurkha Field Force and which is now occupied by the PLA, Ah Li's ramshackle old tailor's shop is still there. In its time it had satisfied the sartorial requirements of generations of British soldiers. Ah Li himself is long gone, but his nephew Richard is in charge. The shop is a shadow of its former self and the painted name above the doorway has faded. Richard gets no business from the PLA. He unearths dusty old business records and finds an order that I placed nearly forty years before. Richard enjoys a modicum of passing expatriate trade, but not much. Hanging in a dusty plastic cover is a British tropical mess jacket still awaiting collection some twenty years on. No doubt the owner will call by in due course, rather as I have done.

Finally, we travelled to the small border village of Sha Tau Kok. It had been the setting for that dramatic clash between the Gurkhas and the PLA during the Cultural Revolution, fifty years before. The village has seen much development, and the construction of a three-lane motorway slicing through the Closed Border Area towards the village will change it further. Looking east from Sha Tau Kok I can just make out an unchanged beach at Starling Inlet, where all those years ago the good Professor Wang staggered ashore to ask me about Thackeray's *Vanity Fair*. Gentle waves continued to lap across its shoreline.

Chapter 12

Into the Future

INTO BRITISH SERVICE

I was first involved in Gurkha recruiting in 1961, when a large number of boys – some 1,600 – were enlisted from East and West Nepal. Now it is January 2018, and fifty-seven years since my first visit, and the recruiting season is drawing to its close. I have returned to Nepal as an old veteran to watch the selection of young men intent on joining the British Army, many destined for the Royal Gurkha Rifles. In a sign of the times, instead of 1,600 recruits there are now 270. I wanted to see how the procedures and protocols might have changed over the years and to sense the style and character of the contemporary process. The recruiting depot is the British Gurkha Centre, a tranquil oasis of neat buildings amid much greenery on the northern boundary of Nepal's second city, Pokhara, in the western hills.

The city is now a bustling, overcrowded and somewhat dusty metropolis. But it still has a certain lush and noisy charm, a beautiful lake and much open space. It nestles in a great valley at 3,000ft surrounded by majestic highlands. It is home to many ex-servicemen who have left their hill villages for a more comfortable life in this ever-expanding town, where there are better medical facilities and more educational opportunities. It is a popular tourist resort and trekking base and blessed with the most stunning views of the Western Himalayas. Dhaulagiri stands on the western arc of the vista, and in central focus is the beautifully sharp-edged and serene fishtail buttress – the sacred Machapuchare – that rises majestically on Annapurna's southern face.

Commanding the Centre and its recruiting task was a young acting Major, James Devall, from the Royal Gurkha Rifles. In the short span of his service he has been with his Regiment in England and Brunei, experienced operational tours in Afghanistan and undertaken extra-regimental escapades in Jordan and Syria doing things I did not learn about. This seemed to me an already varied career. After two years in Pokhara, and as soon as this year's recruiting is finished, he will be off again, this time to Somalia for another testing adventure.

There is a team of doctors assisting James and conducting the detailed medical tests on all candidates. Gurkha NCOs have travelled out from England to assist with various selection tasks. They will then conduct the chosen recruits back to Catterick and train them all to be riflemen before they join their chosen regiment. James was assisted by his Second-in-Command, a sage Gurkha officer, Captain Mahendra Phagami (a sub-clan of Magar Pun), who brings much operational experience to his task. He had been one of the last recruits to join the 2nd Goorkhas before they were disbanded in 1994 and amalgamated with the other Gurkha regiments. Much later, on patrol in Afghanistan with the Royal Gurkha Rifles, he had caught the blast of a Taliban mortar bomb that blew shrapnel into his arms and the backs of his legs. His life had been saved by rapid evacuation in a US Army helicopter to the British base at Camp Bastion, where he was given immediate surgery. He was then flown equally rapidly to England for a further 18-hour operation in the military wing of the Queen Elizabeth

Hospital, Birmingham. A long stay followed at the Hedley Court military rehabilitation centre. Mahendra had lost all feeling in his legs but was not in pain, although he complained lightly that he hobbled a bit.

His most recent service had been as part of a British Army Gurkha contribution to a European Union contingent helping to train the Mali Army. A military mosaic of French, Spanish, German, Estonian and Latvian soldiers were his fellow instructors; a Spaniard did all the translation! Mahendra described the experience as 'linguistically challenging', or words to that effect!

I warmed to both these officers; strong and modest men, they seemed to fit together and suit each other rather well. Together they epitomized the quality of contemporary leadership that the Regiment possesses. I think they will have impressed the potential recruits as much as they did me.

James's remit from above was clear enough: to find and select in a totally free, fair and transparent manner, 270 Nepali young men to serve with the British Army's Gurkha regiments. For the candidates the stakes were high. The economic prize for enlistment is so great; the potential for prestige and status so enormous; the opportunities for travel and adventure seemingly boundless. Some families will have sold land or raised mortgages to send their boys to one of the many private training academies in Pokhara, institutions which proudly proclaim that their three-month courses represent a sure passport to successful enlistment. Other charlatans maintain that for a large fee they will put in a word with the members of the recruiting teams! Outside the camp, sharp practices abound. It is money down the drain, but the goal is so alluring that any price seems worth paying. Inside the Centre, the integrity of the recruiting system seems both convincing and absolute.

The process of annual selection takes much time. Months before, James and his team had tramped the hills advertising for recruits and preaching the clarity and transparency of the selection process. The facts of life about British Army service have been publicized and the need to register and have identities checked has been posted. All those who fit the age and the medical and physical profiles can be competitively considered, as can those of any caste or home district. High-caste Brahmin and low-caste Kami can enlist and serve as equals with the traditional young men from the hill tribes of Gurung and Magar, Rai and Limbu. The message is that caste has no place in a Gurkha regiment. But all applicants must be Nepali residents with Nepal passports. Only Kathmandu is off limits for British recruiters – that belongs to the Nepal Army and Police. Nationality and residency rules debar the sons of Gurkhas who have settled in England with their parents.

By the summer, just over 10,000 boys from all over Nepal have registered for enlistment. The hill tribes still predominate, but the net has been thrown wider. The Nepal Government has to be convinced of the non-discriminatory nature of the system. There are demanding minimum physical requirements to be met: 158cm in height and 50kg in weight. There are health and medical examinations to ensure that bodies can stand the rigours of high-end soldiering. Exams designed to test education and intelligence have to be passed; in order to prevent cheating, the questions are changed daily. Character and commitment must shine through at interview.

At the end of the enlistment journey, close to 10,000 young men will be disappointed; some have failed the tests, others have passed the tests but were judged not the best. Gradually, over the next few months, the numbers have been whittled down through registration checks and at regional selection gatherings around the hill districts. By early January a total of some 500 boys remain. They have been invited to attend final selection at Pokhara.

A true test of the candidate's character and physical stamina is the demanding and energy sapping *Doko* race. The *Doko* is a traditional Nepali funnel-shaped wicker basket carried on the back and held and supported across the forehead by the hands and a woven headband. It is used throughout the countryside and hill villages to transport all manner of goods on routes where vehicles cannot travel. It is six o'clock in the morning, and we watch the boys as they run the race against the chilly dawn backdrop of Annapurna. The sun already plays on the mountain's icy surface.

I watch the boys come by at the halfway point, each carrying a measured weight of 28kg of stone in his basket. They are straining hard, determination and effort plain to see as they run steadily on an uphill course that rises 400 metres over four kilometres. Agonisingly, in front of me a boy stumbles on the rough ground and falls, the stones perilously sliding out of his basket. Frantically, he scoops them back, and then he is off again, but with a precious minute or two lost. I learn later that he has just met the magic 46 minutes demanded of the course, with seconds to spare. For this is not a race in itself, with winners and losers, but more a test of grit, endurance and physical strength, and all must meet a testing finishing time. The funnel of successful selection constantly narrows.

I look in on the medical examination team. The terminology is alien to all but the qualified; ligamentous laxity, myositis, osteochondrosis dissecans, these difficulties slip off the physiotherapist's tongue. Eyes, ears and teeth are given ruthless scrutiny. Heartbeat and blood pressure are measured, and disqualifying murmurs detected amid mutual dismay. Under eagle eyes the boys stand on one leg and then the other.

'Do you smoke or drink?'

One hundred per cent say, 'No, Sir', so that's all right. And no tattoos either. Ten per cent will not pass these stringent medical tests.

After several days the group of potential Gurkhas that I have followed – about half the cohort of candidates – have now almost completed the tests and medicals. They have carried full jerry cans back and forth until they can do it no more. They have lifted heavy weights on to the back of a platform akin to the back of a four-ton Army truck, to simulate the loading of ammunition. They have sat exams in English and Mathematics to GCSE level. In their interviews with the recruiting officers they have attempted to convince James and Mahendra of their utter worthiness for enlistment. Notes have been compared, points have been added up and decisions about individual futures have been made. Of the 217 boys that set out in this first group, 135 have been accepted, but 82 will be given the news that their dreams are over.

Arriving in the camp to attend final interviews, at which James will give each candidate his result, I see a large crowd outside the camp – anxious parents and friends waiting for news. If their boy has not left the camp by the end of the morning the news can only be good. Sitting cross-legged on the grass, each clutching his modest bag of possessions, the candidates wait outside the interview room for their summons. The process of interview is brief; each boy in turn is called by an NCO, enters the room and stands in front of James with Mahendra and a phalanx of Gurkha officers beside him. Name and number are confirmed. The grim process begins.

'I am sorry, you will not be enlisted,' states James clearly in Gurkhali, and a chastened candidate is directed to the left-hand door on the far side of the room as another candidate enters to hear his fate

'Well done, you will be enlisted,' announces James, and a beaming candidate is directed out of the right-hand door.

Looking at the young men as they parade one at a time in front of James and before judgement is issued, I found it impossible to decide who might have passed or failed. Physical bearing seemed to give no clue, and emotions are well concealed. I was forgetting that all these men had passed stringent tests to reach this point, and that thousands have already been rejected. The difference between a pass and fail here is wafer-thin. One or two, on arrival in front of the officers, give a cheery 'Good Morning, Sir', perhaps in the hope that this might sway a final judgement. But the die has already been cast. Occasionally the successful manage a grateful smile, a delighted clench of the fists, a mumbled thank-you, but in general it is a strangely muted occasion.

I track a set of failed candidates as they walk slowly and largely in silence towards the gates of the Centre. In groups of two or three they halt at a table to collect the possessions they handed in on arrival and have their precious mobile phones returned; these were denied them so as to prevent contact with the outside world while attending selection. A look of resignation sits on most faces. Further on, the pay office distributes, against signature, a grant of 5,000 rupees (£34) travel allowance. Then it is out past the Guard Room and back into the toughest of civilian worlds. Some, if they have the stomach for it, if they are still young enough and still meet the physical criteria, will come back next year and try again. Others will head for the Indian Army Gurkha recruiting office and try their chances there. Yet others may head to the recruiting agents from the Gulf States looking for men to help build football stadiums or container ports. Or they will join the Gurkha communities elsewhere that collectively make up the vast international Nepali diaspora of overseas workers.

Outside the interview room, and separated from the failed candidates, it is applause, handshakes and smiles as NCOs move among the fortunate ones. They give directions on what to do next. The first issues from a seemingly generous Quartermaster are handed out in a large 'Bag travel black'. Among the contents are the military goods and chattels that will become part and parcel of Gurkha military lives for the year ahead. All are enumerated in the Army's curious convoluted language that has been the Quartermaster's patois for an age: shoes highland black; trousers man lightweight olive; socks general service black; towel bath olive; KFS. The list goes on in the same unchanging style. There is 50,000 rupees

(£344) in advance pay. All seemingly generous rewards from a beneficent Government.

Carrying their new-found wealth, the group assembles in a large barrack room upstairs. Each man in turn is handed an Army mobile phone. In the presence of an NCO he is allowed to make one call to tell his parents that he has been enlisted and to advise them to give no money to anyone – advice designed to discourage or prevent any parent from succumbing to a clan of potential claimants: the agents who will suggest that success was entirely due to their intervention on the boy's behalf; the academy claiming that their training had ensured enlistment. Payback time, it will be suggested by these, has arrived. This is Nepal.

Over the next few days the training team of high-grade Gurkha instructors drawn from all the regiments of the Gurkha Brigade will begin to explain and inculcate into their charges the mores and manners, the style and demands of Gurkha soldiering; the pride and loyalty they should feel in joining an elite organization with two hundred years of history behind it. Initiative, independence of thought, all that will come later; now it is the rudiments of dressing, marching, saluting and soldierly bearing that are the primary requirements. These must be hammered home, for in three weeks' time the head of the British Army – the Chief of the General Staff – is due to arrive on a Far East tour and will take the salute at an attestation parade in the camp. At this parade the new recruits will swear allegiance to the British Crown, and proud parents will briefly, and perhaps emotionally, be reunited with their sons.

I reflect that among the parents the number of ex-servicemen will be far fewer than in days of old, for many of those have now settled in Britain, with UK citizenship granted them and their families. Paradoxically, their sons can now join a British Army regiment, but not the Gurkhas, for that is confined to Nepali citizens only. In some ways I am sad about that, for it was the family bonds that stretched back often for several generations that had been one of the abiding strengths of my Regiment.

The principles of selection have not changed wildly since those early days of my service, when I first went to assist Alistair Langlands at Paklihawa. The scale of things is much reduced; the testing far more rigorous. Possibly the selection standards were less stringent then, the experienced eye alone more of a judge as to worth and character. Perhaps the physical tests were not so rigorous. Educational requirements were certainly far less demanding, for few of the boys that came to us then had much schooling. Intelligence tests had to suffice to sniff out academic potential. The majority of recruits in 1961 had sprung from a background of hill life and unremitting labour that bred hardiness and a natural feel for the earth that had stood them and the British Army well in the jungles of Malaya and Borneo.

Today, some of those qualities may have been tempered in the drift and migration down from the hills, while other skills equally in demand might be more dominant. Political correctness and the promotion of equal opportunities, the vast improvement in education within Nepal, all this has broadened the recruiting pool. But the traditional Magar and Gurung tribes of the West and the Limbus and Rais of the East still predominate. James and his Gurkha officers insist that the Gurkha DNA is as strong as ever. I detect the same enthusiasm and freshness; the same features and temper of spirit and character that I knew and admired so many years ago. But the traditional hill boys who served the Gurkha regiments so well in the jungles of Malaya and Borneo are now few and far between. In their place is a much more urban, savvy and better educated entrant, multilingual, swift with the mobile phone, sharp on the internet. The family's terraced fields in the hills may now be unkempt, the hill village house that I used to know so well, boarded up or looked after by grandparents. The new recruit is well educated with an excellent grasp of technology, and all but a few probably know as little about herding goats as I do. I sense this does not matter. This new Gurkha is much more alert to the outside world; well placed to patrol the bazaars of Basra and Kabul; understanding better than his father the rhythms of urban life; recognizing a car bomb when he sees one; and generally better prepared for the terrain of the new, counter-insurgency urban battlefield.

In two years, so the whispers run, the British Army will start taking women into the ranks of the combat arms – not least the infantry – and the Gurkha Brigade will follow suit. James seems reasonably relaxed about it, but Mahendra suggests that Nepali women will be more suited to the Gurkha Corps units – as Signallers, Engineers and Logisticians rather than the Royal Gurkha Rifles. He tells me the local Training Academies have already taken on some girl students in anticipation of this proposed emancipation! But the selection process, they say, will be gender-free, with the same demanding standards that are set for the men. The challenges of the noble *Doko* race will remain for all. I am not sure what Charles Reid of Delhi or General Francis Tuker might have made of it all – enlightened men that they were. Perhaps they would think that the Brigade of Gurkhas, together with the British Army, had collectively gone mad. Generations of pensioned Gurkhas might think that if this is what the Sahebs want, so be it. I remembered the stubborn bravery of the Gurkha women who together with their men courageously defended the fort at Kalunga in the Nepal wars. Maybe there is something in it, particularly in the environment of today's conflicts where women are just as likely as men to be the adversaries. In the urban battlefield the female soldier could be a useful addition. On the Afghanistan battlefield women already abound in a variety of roles, sharing threats and dangers with the men.

It was time for me to move on. In due course, the new recruits for the Regiment will have been successfully attested. Their allegiance to the Crown assured, they will be driven off in coaches to Kathmandu to catch an overnight flight to England. There they will start a new and hopefully rewarding life as Gurkha soldiers. For them the journey is not the same one I had experienced taking an earlier generation of young Gurkhas off to the British Army. Then we had travelled on trains that clattered across the plains of India to Calcutta to catch a British-India boat to Malaya on a journey that lasted two weeks via Chittagong and Rangoon. Hopefully, for the 2018 recruits, their new journey will prove just as exciting and rewarding as mine.

TAKING STOCK

Shorncliffe Garrison lies off the M20, just short of Folkestone, and as you leave the motorway there is a hint that you are approaching a Gurkha community. You pass retailers whose names seem eager to entice local custom and patronage – Himalayan Café, Pokhara Hill Travel Agency, the Annapurna Restaurant. It was at Shorncliffe, two centuries ago, that General Sir John Moore established a unique training regime which founded the British Army's Light Infantry regiments with their effective military style, and it was he who was to command the British Army in Portugal during the Peninsula Wars. There, at his moment of success, he fell at the battle of

Corunna in 1809, and the lines recording his burial in the place where he died were well known to me and other schoolboys of yore:

> Not a drum was heard, not a funeral note,
> As his corse to the ramparts we hurried.

Today, Sir John Moore Barracks is home to the 1st Battalion, the Royal Gurkha Rifles. The Barracks themselves are a modern, somewhat dreary and utilitarian set of buildings, but the name at least suggests a suitable provenance for Gurkha riflemen. These barracks were a replacement for the wartime hutted camp at Church Crookham in Hampshire which had housed the Gurkha battalion stationed in England for some thirty years, until the turn of the century.

Since leaving the Army I had always closely followed the fortunes of the Brigade of Gurkhas, but it was some years since I had spent a full day with a battalion of the Regiment. I had been the Regiment's first Colonel, so it was with a sense of belonging that I was visiting the barracks to take stock and to wish the Battalion well as it prepared to depart on yet another operational tour in Afghanistan. Twenty-five years had passed since I was in charge of Gurkha affairs as the Brigade's Major-General. It was then, in the face of possible disbandment, that I had fought, together with some of my successors, to put in place a new role for the Gurkha soldier in the British Army. Now, with the passage of time, it was an opportunity to take stock and see how he had fared.

The regimental history since then would record the battle for survival in the early 1990s and the formation of the Royal Gurkha Rifles. This new Regiment would consist of two battalions, and alongside them would be Gurkha Engineers, Signallers and Logisticians in a reduced Brigade of some 2,500 soldiers. The departure from Hong Kong to establish a permanent base in the United Kingdom and the emergence of the Gurkha into the mainstream of the British Army would follow. Campaigning in East Timor and the Balkans, in Bosnia and Kosovo, in Sierra Leone and Iraq, as well as the many costly tours in Afghanistan, had once again produced two rows of medal ribbons on the Gurkha soldier's chest. I had not seen ribbons of this number since I joined my Regiment, still with its wartime flavour, in 1960.

On my visit it was clear to me that a new operational confidence and reputation has been built, new technologies mastered and many high-end soldiering skills acquired. Complex weapon systems and armoured vehicles developed for contemporary campaigns, equipment that I inspected on my visit, had all been mastered. But if the soldiers were now fully integrated into the British Army and fully aware of the vagaries of British life, they still seemed to retain much of their cultural identity and individuality as Gurkhas. This is in spite of the ranks of smart cars outside the barrack blocks and a level of contemporary sophistication that would have surprised many of the 'old and bold'.

The old differential rank of Queen's Gurkha Officer has disappeared, and a single officers' mess satisfactorily embraces Gurkha and British commissioned officers together. As far as I could judge, the Battalion seemed well led at all levels, with Gurkha officers holding increasing responsibility. A young Gurkha officer in A Company seemed typical of this new breed, with five years' experience in the SAS and operations with the US Delta Force under his belt, but quietly modest and charming about his experiences. There is strong competition for places among young British officers from Sandhurst. The Battalion has earned a place, alongside the Parachute Regiment, in the Army's elite rapid reaction force, 16 Air Assault Brigade. Increasing numbers of young Gurkhas are volunteering for service with the Special Air Service (SAS) and similar organizations, and doing so successfully. The disciplinary record appears to be good. The Gurkha soldier's terms and conditions of service, his pay and pension, are now exactly in line with the rest of the British Army. Additionally, the serving Gurkha has achieved settlement and nationality rights in the UK and, following a public campaign, this right, controversial for some but morally right, had been extended to all Gurkha soldiers who had served four or more years in the British Army since the 'Opt' in 1947.

The campaign for settlement was forcefully led by the elegant, charismatic and feisty actress, Joanna Lumley, whose father had served with the 6th Gurkhas and with Wingate's Chindits in Burma. Two elderly Gurkha holders of the Victoria Cross confined to their wheelchairs appeared in support of her campaign, and it all proved a powerful combination. Joanna was an old friend of my family, and I had no difficulty with the moral rights of her case, which quickly won the support of the public and Ministers. But initially I was concerned about the impact of widespread Gurkha settlement on the position of today's Gurkha soldier. Settlement in the UK meant the loss to the Nepal exchequer of pension payments and remittances – important sources of foreign currency. Thus a strong rationale for Nepal to continue to allow recruiting might be lost. Further, while the modern Gurkha soldier with his English language, military skills and experience of the UK would have little difficulty in assimilation and employment, older men, who in many cases had not previously served in Britain and did not know the language, would have much more difficulty in finding jobs and settling into an alien environment. Those pensioners might have been better off remaining in the familiar environment of Nepal. But I readily accepted that the moral case for settlement was strong and eventually proved overriding. Overnight Joanna became something of a goddess in the eyes of the Gurkha soldier.

After early teething problems and a degree of local resentment, reports suggest that there is growing integration in the communities where the Gurkha has settled. Aldershot was a popular destination, given its proximity to Church Crookham, where a battalion of Gurkhas had been based for thirty years. But the arrival there of 6,000 Nepalis caused early problems, both for the local community and for the elderly Gurkha and his family with little English and few employable skills. Some of the old have struggled and a few have gone back to Nepal and an environment that they know and understand; but others have made a go of it, are prospering and have made new lives for themselves and their families. The private security industry is much in debt to many of these former soldiers, and now a good number of their children have professional qualifications. It is the cultural identity of those children, many with little knowledge of Nepal and unable to speak their mother tongue, that I am sad about.

With a challenging and costly recruiting environment for British soldiers, serving Gurkha numbers have steadily increased and are now approaching 5,000; the Corps units have expanded, and a third specialized battalion for the Royal Gurkha Rifles is to be raised. For the moment the recruitment of Nepali females to serve in the infantry battalions designed to match changes in British battalions remains a gleam in the eye, but it might occur if the Nepal Government agrees. Finally, a dynamic and well-funded Gurkha welfare scheme is providing pensions and medical and community assistance throughout Nepal and has assisted in the rehabilitation of former soldiers whose houses were lost in the disaster of the 2015 earthquake. The scheme, with assistance from the Gurkha Engineers, has built 1,200 new houses for ex-servicemen.

Over this same historic quarter-century of Gurkha soldiering, there have also been challenging times for Nepal. Political turmoil, with twenty-five different Prime Ministers; internecine political struggles; a ten-year Maoist insurgency that left 18,000 dead; regicide and abdication that ended 240 years of the Shah monarchy; and the terrible 2015 earthquake. These events produced a rich set of headlines and reshaped the country's political signature. Remarkably, however, these national eruptions, while severely damaging to the national economy and the general stability of Nepal, have not appeared to disturb the progressive tenor of British Army Gurkha service, and the recruitment of soldiers has been maintained throughout this period of national difficulty. Now, having successfully overcome this testing period, Nepal has emerged with a national democratic mandate, a new constitution and a stronger, more stable and resurgent coalition Government of the left that appears well established. Anglo-Nepali relationships seem in good shape and historically well founded, but they need to be kept in constant repair if the Gurkha connection is to continue to prosper.

Throughout the history of Gurkha service to the British crown there have always been periods of expansion and contraction as the demands of the Indian and British Armies in peace and war fluctuated. Service has never been taken for granted, and during my career there have been occasions when it looked as though the British Army might dispense with Gurkhas altogether. Periodically, when defence needs shifted or British manning was buoyant, there were suggestions that the Gurkha soldier might become redundant. But without sentiment, good judgement has generally prevailed and sensibly allowed him to fight another day. Perhaps, too, there was a recognition that, once dispensed with, this was not an arrangement that could be resuscitated. But keep a Gurkha infrastructure and numbers in place and there is always the capacity to expand rapidly should national needs demand it, as long as the Nepal Government is content.

With much positive operational performance and their recruitment increasingly satisfying a manning requirement, there would seem no reason for the Gurkhas' service to the British Army not to move forward with confidence. Cost effectiveness was often cited as a reason for Gurkha retention, but with pay and allowances now on a par with the British soldier, does that argument continue to run? An infrastructure to maintain in Nepal, and a longer period of basic training at Catterick to include an introduction to British culture, might suggest at first glance that there are some expensive overheads. Occasionally a drum is heard beating out the idea that the cost is too high and Gurkhas should be done away with; that only their popularity with the public keeps them going. This is surely nonsense. Leaving aside the burgeoning costs of British recruiting campaigns, the fact remains that the Gurkha rifleman generally serves for twelve years, while his British equivalent serves for three. Thus, for one Gurkha, four British soldiers must be enlisted to refresh the ranks, with multiplying costs in recruitment and training. In addition, the Sultan of Brunei makes a substantial financial contribution to the 'in-theatre' costs of maintaining a Gurkha battalion in Brunei as the British Army's Far East reserve. I don't think costs are an issue. But if for any reason the UK relationship with Brunei was to falter; if garrison costs were no longer met by the Brunei exchequer; or if it was decided that it was no longer in either party's interest to station a British Gurkha battalion in Brunei; then that might lead to a reassessment of the size of the Gurkhas' contribution to the British Army.

If there is a threat to continued Gurkha service in the British Army, where else might it spring from? Among the intellectual elite of Kathmandu there has always been a philosophical objection to citizens of Nepal serving in the ranks of the British and Indian Armies. Pragmatic considerations have largely kept such ideas in check, and the current administration and its robust Prime Minister, Mr K. P. Sharma Oli, speak warmly of the country's relationship with Britain that has lasted over 200 years, together with the honour that the reputation of the Gurkha soldier has brought to Nepal. This is encouraging, but there is an obvious need to maintain this warm relationship in continuing good order. Additionally, a vociferous group of ex-servicemen has been conducting a campaign over a number of years to encourage both the British and Nepal Governments to correct, retrospectively, perceived injustices in the terms and conditions of past Gurkha service with the British Army. The Treasury and the Ministry of Defence have made some encouraging and generous concessions to meet these demands, but the agitation and threats to disrupt recruiting sadly continue. Whatever the rights and wrongs of the case, the campaign itself is damaging to the public persona and reputation of the Gurkha soldier, and no doubt causes increasing exasperation in Whitehall. It would be ironic if the proud record of 200 years of Gurkha service, which has proved so popular with the thousands of young men and has brought widespread recognition to Nepal itself, was to be damaged by the action of their own forefathers. Throughout the course of my service and association with British Gurkhas the one lesson I learned – however strong the message of indispensability might be – was never to take the future for granted.

Finally, the Gurkha rifleman himself must continue, in the face of all the contemporary pressures of western culture, to maintain his own innate and distinctive character and culture, the traditional standards and skills on which he has built and upheld his reputation as a fighting soldier of much worth. Were these to falter, he might no longer be indispensable.

APPOINTMENT AT THE PALACE

On a bright summer morning we assembled in the ballroom of Buckingham Palace for a unique occasion. Over the years many have come to this ornate and regal room to attend investitures and receive their orders, decorations and awards from the reigning monarch, but this is something slightly different. One hundred and forty men of the Royal Gurkha Rifles are to receive their Afghanistan campaign medals from their Colonel in Chief, the Prince of Wales. They are worthy young riflemen but of limited service, having just completed their first tour of duty in that benighted country. Some of their senior NCOs and officers have experienced four or more tours and already possess this hard-won campaign medal together with many others. The young riflemen are on parade in their service dress with the red *lali* around the collar that reminds us all once again of the Regiment's service at Delhi. In case it is needed, their 'hats felt Gurkha' worn with the familiar tilt clearly identify who they are to the Household staff.

In addition to the presentation of medals, the Prince of Wales is celebrating forty years as Colonel in Chief first of the 2nd Goorkhas and then of the Royal Gurkha Rifles. He has followed in the footsteps of his grandfather, King George V, and his great-grandfather, King Edward VII in an association with the Regiment that stretches back to 1876. Prince Harry is accompanying his father and assisting with the presentation of medals. He had been embedded with the Regiment in Afghanistan as a forward Air Controller and Apache helicopter pilot, and like Prince Charles he appears to have a clear affinity with the Gurkha soldier and readily identifies with him. The talk is easy and friendly. For me it was a nostalgic occasion. I had welcomed the Prince of Wales many times on visits to both his Regiments. I had accompanied him on a royal visit to Brunei and memorably trekked with him in Nepal. I knew as well as any his commitment to and affection for the Gurkha soldier.

The Princes moved down the lines of smart riflemen positioning the medals on to the breast clips on their service dress jackets. The hierarchies of both Regiments, the retired senior officers, the serving officers and some wives and families, watched from the sidelines. In addition, all the Regiment's wounded veterans from the Afghanistan campaign were present, their prosthetic legs or arms poignant witnesses to the cost of their service. It is a splendid and moving occasion, and after the presentation everyone mingles informally and happily. From the beneficent Buckingham Palace cellars, plentiful Louis Roederer champagne is generously served to all regardless of rank or status. Suitable speeches and presentations are made.

The ceremonies over, the Princes depart and the riflemen assemble in the quadrangle of the Palace ready to march back to Wellington Barracks. The Queen's Truncheon with its Jemadar and escort is on parade leading the column. The Brigade's Band and the Regimental Pipes and Drums strike up with the Regimental Quick March. At a crisp rifle pace, the Regimental contingent wearing their hard-earned medals march proudly out through the central arch into the forecourt, then through the great gates of the Palace on to the Mall, swinging past the Queen Victoria Memorial and on to Wellington Barracks they go. The waiting crowd gives them a resounding cheer, and they head off ready for the next assignment, wherever that may be and whatever it may bring. Their memorable day is over, but the sight and sound of it all resonates with me still. The young Gurkha riflemen seem as light hearted and gallant, as good and confident as ever.

Index